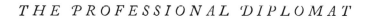

THE PROFESSIONAL DIPLOMAT

The Professional Diplomat

BY JOHN ENSOR HARR

....

PRINCETON, NEW JERSEY

PRINCETON UNIVERSITY PRESS

MCMLXIX

ACKNOWLEDGMENT

THIS study would not have been possible had it not been for the opportunity provided me by Professor Frederick C. Mosher to participate in the work of the Committee on Foreign Affairs Personnel (the Herter Committee) in Washington, D.C., throughout 1962. Since that time, I have had the exceptional opportunity of being able to study my subject at close hand. Professor Mosher has continued to provide guidance and support, and I owe him a special debt of gratitude. I am grateful also for the help and interest of Professors Eric Bellquist and Jack London, both also of the University of California at Berkeley.

Literally scores of other people have been helpful in this project over a period of years, both in Washington and abroad at field posts of the Department of State. I would like particularly to mention my colleagues on the Herter Committee staff and in the Office of Management Planning of the Department of State. Names could be mentioned almost endlessly, but two stand out above all others: former Deputy Under Secretary of State William J. Crockett and Richard W. Barrett, former Director of the Office of Management Planning. Indispensable to me was the secretarial assistance of Miss Pat Chatelaine, Mrs. Carol Meresman, and Miss Toni Meehan.

Mention must be made of the persons who helped me in the very difficult task of data-gathering and processing, both on the composition of the Foreign Service and the "Survey of the Diplomatic Profession." These include Lawrence Slaughter of the Department of State for his help in design ing and programming the survey, and Jene Lyon of the

Acknowledgment

Department of State for his help in printing, distribution, and graphics. I am grateful to the Department of State for making data available and for helping to make the survey possible; it should be made clear, however, that the survey was not an official project of the State Department.

I alone am responsible for all interpretations in this book and for any errors of fact or judgement.

Critical views expressed from time to time are never directed toward the motives of individuals; I came away from five years of immersion in the foreign affairs culture of the United States Government with the highest respect for the persons I was privileged to know there.

If the project could not have been started without Professor Mosher, it certainly could not have been completed without the support and understanding of my family, particularly the encouragement of my wife, Nancy.

Glen Ridge, New Jersey   JOHN ENSOR HARR
October 1968

CONTENTS

....

TABLES AND FIGURES

....

Table

Tables and Figures

Tables and Figures

ABBREVIATIONS

....

ACORD   Action for Organizational Development, a State
        Department program for human relations train-
        ing and organizational change
AFSA   American Foreign Service Association
AID   Agency for International Development
ARA   Bureau in the Department of State of Inter-
        American Affairs
BOB   Bureau of the Budget
CCPS   Comprehensive Country Programming System,
        the initial system set up by the State Department
CIA   Central Intelligence Agency
CISR   Center for International Systems Research, set
        up by Deputy Under Secretary Crockett in 1965
        for social science research
DCM   Deputy Chief of Mission, the second in command
        in overseas embassies
DOD   Department of Defense
ECA   Economic Cooperation Administration, the first
        major U.S. foreign aid agency, predecessor to
        AID
EROP   Executive Review of Overseas Programs, the
        special study of selected missions directed by the
        President in 1965
FAMC   Foreign Affairs Manual Circular, State Depart-
        ment method for issuing and maintaining official
        administrative pronouncements
FAS   Foreign Agricultural Service of the Department
        of Agriculture
FSI   Foreign Service Institute, training establishment
        of the Department of State

xi

Abbreviations

FSO	Foreign Service Officer—the career category
FSR	Foreign Service Reserve Officer—the temporary category
FSS	Foreign Service Staff—category for administrative and clerical personnel
IRG	Interdepartmental Regional Group, created by NSAM 341 for each of five regions of the world
MOP	Management by Objectives and Programs, slogan expressing concepts central to reorganization of the administrative area of the Department of State in 1965
MUST	Manpower Utilization System and Techniques, developed by the management group within the State Department
NASA	National Aeronautic and Space Agency
NORC	National Opinion Research Center in Chicago
NPP	National Policy Paper, prepared by W. W. Rostow's planning staff on individual countries
NSAM	National Security Action Memorandum, a directive of the President in the national security area (NSAM 341 was the directive of March 4, 1966 which provided for State Department leadership over almost all foreign affairs)
OCB	Operations Coordinating Board, an interagency group established to coordinate and assure implementation of decisions of the National Security Council, abolished by President Kennedy in 1961
PPBS	Planning-Programming-Budgeting System
SDP	Survey of the Diplomatic Profession, conducted by the author
SIG	Senior Interdepartmental Group, created by NSAM 341
USIA	United States Information Agency
USIS	United States Information Service, the overseas elements of USIA

Secretary of State
Under Sec'y of State
Under Sec'y for Political Affairs

Arms Control and Disarmament Agency*

Inspector General Foreign Assistance

Deputy Under Secretary for Political Affairs

Protocol

Executive Secretariat

Agency for International Development

Peace Corps

Deputy Under Sec'y for Administration / Director General Foreign Service

Foreign Service Institute

Foreign Service Inspection Corps

Administrative Offices and Programs

Security and Consular Affairs

Educational and Cultural Affairs

Public Affairs

International Organization Affairs

Near Eastern and South Asian Affairs

Economic Affairs

Inter-American Affairs

Policy Planning Council

Counselor

Intelligence and Research

International Scientific and Technological Affairs

East Asian and Pacific Affairs

European Affairs

Legal Adviser

Congressional Relations

African Affairs

A B C

Diplomatic Missions and Delegations to International Organizations

* A separate agency with the Director reporting directly to the Secretary and serving as principal adviser to the Secretary and the President on arms control and disarmament.

Pay scales as set by the Federal Pay Act of 1967 for the major personnel categories used in U.S. foreign affairs (the General Schedule of the Civil Service, Foreign Service Officer, Foreign Service Reserve, and Foreign Service Staff).

Category and grade or class			Salary range	
GS	FSO—FSR	FSS		
	Career Ambassador		$28,750	
	Career Minister		28,000	
18			27,055	
	1		24,944	$27,055
17			23,788	26,960
16			20,982	26,574
	2		20,280	24,336
15			18,404	23,921
	3		16,616	19,940
		1	16,616	21,602
14			15,841	20,593
	4		13,507	16,207
13		2	13,507	17,557
12			11,461	14,899
	5		11,120	13,346
		3	11,120	14,459
11			9,657	12,555
	6		9,267	11,121
		4	9,267	12,048
10			8,821	11,467
		5	8,351	10,853
9			8,054	10,475
	7		7,816	9,376
		6	7,524	9,783
8			7,384	9,598
		7	6,905	8,975
	8		6,734	8,084
7			6,734	8,759
6			6,137	7,982
		8	6,125	7,961
		9	5,575	7,249
5			5,565	7,239
4		10	4,995	6,489
3			4,466	5,807
2			4,108	5,341
1			3,776	4,910

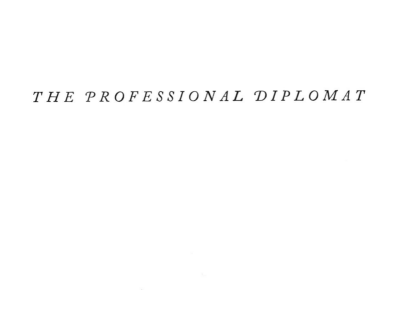

THE PROFESSIONAL DIPLOMAT

INTRODUCTION

....

THIS BOOK is a multi-purpose study of a professional group under the stress of change—the Foreign Service Officer (FSO) corps of the United States Foreign Service, the American career group of professional diplomats. For 20 years the FSO corps and its parent organization, the Department of State, have been the objects of strong outside pressure for change. In the Kennedy and early Johnson administrations, the pressure took a new direction and emerged as a serious crisis for the FSO corps and the State Department: it became a challenge to assume the role of vigorous and active management of the full multi-agency spectrum of United States foreign affairs policy *and* operations. Until that time the Department and the FSO corps had studiously avoided the operational aspect.

The challenge and response to it, as they evolved in the 1960s, constitute highly important social phenomena; they also provide an excellent opportunity to illuminate change processes in general, bureaucratic behavior, and behavior within a relatively closed professional group such as the FSO corps.

At the broadest level *The Professional Diplomat* simply tells the story of the challenge and response, hopefully in a more definitive way than has yet been done. At another level it is a case study in the sociology of the professions, intended to contribute to a more effective comparative approach than now exists to improve understanding of the pervasive force of professionalism in modern society. Finally, in the problem solving, value-oriented approach designated the "policy sciences" by Daniel Lerner and Harold Lasswell,

3

Introduction

the concluding chapter outlines for the future a managerial strategy to meet the role challenge based on a study of the challenge and response to date.[1]

As the title indicates, this book concentrates on the professional group itself. The importance of the professions in industrial and urban societies has given rise to a voluminous literature that is rich in descriptive and historical material. There are numerous articles and books on every major profession. However, there are almost no comparative studies, and few studies of professional groups are based on close-in analysis and empirical research.

Certainly much of the current attention is due to the strategic place of the professions in respect to the rapid and turbulent change that characterizes the modern world. Although normally resistant to change, the professions nevertheless are often the producers of change and at the same time are a major focal point of change, at once reflecting the needs and values of society at large and posing issues of the utmost significance.

Speaking of an "age of professionalism" in her perceptive book, Corinne Gilb views the professions on a macro-scale as growing power centers that in important respects are coming more and more to resemble the medieval guilds, especially in the close relationship with government in the renascence of guild-public regulation of work.[2] What keeps the analogy incomplete is the dynamism of modern society in contrast to the static social order of medieval times. There is thus a tension, a dialectic, between the dynamics of society, to which the professions in many respects are a contributing force, and the interests of the professionals—

[1] Daniel Lerner and Harold Lasswell, *The Policy Sciences* (Palo Alto: Stanford University Press, 1951).

[2] Gilb, *Hidden Hierarchies: The Professions and Government* (New York: Harper & Row, 1966).

4

in the status quo, in setting rules for themselves and for society, in preserving a social order in which rights adhere to functional status.

The coming together of the professions and government was characterized by T. H. Marshall a quarter of a century ago: "The professions are being socialized and the social and public services are being professionalized."[3] Increasingly members of the established professions such as medicine and the law find themselves in the employ of government.[4] There are professional groups entirely in the public service—the military, the FSO corps, the U.S. Public Health Service—and there have even been efforts to view civil service itself as a profession.[5]

It is this trend that has caused Frederick C. Mosher to engage in a comprehensive examination of the links between the professions, the public service, and higher education in the United States. Speaking of the people who administer public programs, Mosher writes: "If the bulk of them are not members of a 'profession of government,' most of them nonetheless are professionals in government—professionally trained, professionally oriented. In fact, in no country of the free world is administrative leadership in government more concentrated in professionals than in the United States."[6] Citing the conservative stance of a professional group after it has carved out and legitimized its sphere of action, Mosher comments:

[3] "Professionalism and Social Policy," in S. Nosow and W. H. Form, eds., *Man, Work, and Society* (New York: Basic Books, 1962), p. 230.

[4] For a study of considerations of identity and loyalty for professional men in government see L. Reissman, "A Study in Role Conceptions in Bureaucracy," *Social Forces*, No. 27 (1949), 305-10.

[5] Most notably by Brian Chapman, *The Profession of Government* (London: George Allen and Unwin, 1959).

[6] Mosher, *The Professions, Professional Education, and the Public Service*, in preparation, to be published by the Chandler Press, San Francisco.

5

But then, with rapid social change, the nature of the problems change; with rapid technological change, the nature of the tools and relevant knowledge changes; with rapid scientific development, the requisite knowledge both widens and deepens. Perhaps most important of all, as understandings of problems of both a physical and social nature broaden, it becomes increasingly clear that solutions depend upon no single set of methods, no narrow body of knowledge, but require contributions from a number of perspectives and with a variety of tools. They are inter-disciplinary and interprofessional.[7]

Elsewhere Mosher points out that the established career systems in the public service have been under severe pressure for change, particularly in the years since World War II: "All have changed in response to pressures from outside and within, sometimes reluctantly and bitterly; and all are in difficulties today."[8] Mosher puts the pressures for change into four classes: egalitarianism, the knowledge explosion, management, and politics.

In large measure this provides the frame of reference for this study. Another model is Morris Janowitz' excellent book, *The Professional Soldier*.[9] Janowitz deals with change in areas such as those cited by Mosher, and employs both empirical research and comparison in space as well as in time.

Following the leads provided by Janowitz and Mosher, this study deals with questions organized around the following topics:

1. *The pressures for change.* The content of change, the change agents, role expectations, new functions with a claim to professional status.

[7] *Ibid.*
[8] Mosher, *Democracy and the Public Service* (New York: Oxford University Press, 1968) , p. 155.
[9] Janowitz, *The Professional Soldier* (Glencoe: The Free Press, 1960) .

2. *The character of the professional group.* Internal composition, social origins, norms and values, the process of socialization, status and prestige, the elitist concept and the elite nucleus.

3. *Responses to change.* Attitudes on the profession and change, institutional defenses, ferment within the ranks, the role of political leadership.

This is not an outline of the study, but a crystallization of key areas of investigation, most of which are interwoven throughout the study. Using Mosher's schema, for example, the challenge of egalitarianism is dealt with directly in Chapter 5; the challenges of the knowledge explosion, management, and politics are dealt with, explicitly or implicitly, in virtually every chapter.

The management challenge is partly a product of the knowledge explosion, of the changing nature of the problems with which the professions must deal, and simply of the growth in size and complexity of many professional groups. It is especially acute for career services located entirely within bureaucratic settings. Mosher points out that few career systems and professions give "much if any attention to management," and yet "the bulk of activity at the upper levels of any given organization is managerial, not technical or professional."[10]

Mosher's concept of the challenge of politics is as a summation of the other challenges, in the sense that "politics has provided one of the principal vehicles—sometimes the final and decisive one—whereby the others are articulated and effectuated within career systems."[11]

The major advantage in approaching this study was that for a number of years the author was *in* the foreign affairs culture, but not *of* the career. Serving as a staff member of the Committee of Foreign Affairs Personnel (the Herter

[10] *Ibid.*, p. 160.
[11] *Ibid.*, p. 162.

7

Introduction

Committee),[12] and subsequently as a member of the Department of State's Management Planning Staff, has offered an unparalleled opportunity for a close study—including scores of interviews, small-scale research, and observation of operations both in Washington and at more than 30 U.S. diplomatic posts abroad.

The author has produced two monographs on the FSO corps, which stemmed from research done while with the Herter Committee.[13] The data developed for one of them, vintage 1962, have been preserved and updated, providing the basis for longitudinal studies of the composition of the professional group (Chapter 4). Aside from this, the major formal research instrument was an opinion survey designed by the author and administered to a 20-percent sample of the FSO corps in the spring of 1966. Called "Survey of the Diplomatic Profession," the survey, for the sake of brevity, will be referred to throughout this study as the SDP, and is discussed in the Methodological Appendix. The SDP was also designed in part with an eye toward possible application in comparative research, in particular, a comparative self-ranking of several professional groups on 13 indices of professionalism (see the discussion in Chapter 7).

[12] The Herter Committee existed during calendar year 1962 and produced a major prescriptive report on foreign affairs management and personnel. See the discussion in Chapter 2 of this study.

[13] These two monographs, *The Anatomy of the Foreign Service* and *The Development of Careers in the U.S. Foreign Service*, were part of a series of six in a *"Foreign Affairs Personnel Study"* series published by the Carnegie Endowment for International Peace in 1965. All six monographs drew on Herter Committee research.

PART I

THE BACKGROUND AND FORCES
OF CHANGE

CHAPTER 1

THE PROFESSION: A NEW

DIPLOMACY?

....

IT IS CLEAR that there have been dramatic and far-reaching changes in the environment and conditions of great power diplomacy over the past generation. What is not so clear is whether these changes have in turn produced a change in the very substance of diplomacy as a profession. For more than 20 years there has been a running controversy about the question of the proper role and functions of the body of professional diplomats. It is a complex problem, appearing in many and shifting forms, and having many ramifications. In recent years the problem has been brought into sharper focus, but it has not been resolved.

The development of new functions or activities within the general area of interest of a professional group sooner or later poses a challenge to that group. Are the new functions to be legitimized and accepted as part of the substance of the profession? If so, what impact does the acceptance have on the profession? If not, is the professional group fully performing its expected role? What is the impact on the new functions?

In the case of the professional diplomat the problem is one of very real social and operational significance. Whether the problem is resolved, and how it is resolved, will influence how well overseas activities are coordinated and performed and how one organizes for the total conduct of foreign affairs.

Background and Forces of Change

The controversy over the proper role of the body of American professional diplomats in today's world permeates in greater or lesser degree every chapter of this study. Before examining the radically changing environment of diplomacy and the conflicting views about the nature of the profession that have arisen, it will be useful to consider the traditional view of the profession.

Sir Harold Nicolson has identified four schools of diplomacy, in chronological order—the classical, Italian, French, and American. By the French school, Nicolson means what is generally understood today as traditional diplomacy, which in his view was "originated by Richelieu" and "adopted by all European countries during the three centuries that preceded the change of 1919."[1] Its main characteristics were a sense of professionalism, a common basis in European civilization, emphasis on protocol and the rules of the game, private and continuing negotiation, honest reporting, and official representation among legitimate governments. This style of diplomacy reached its height in 19th-century Europe as the primary channel of communication among the great powers in their mutually understood role of maintaining a relatively stable international system, i.e., the Concert of Europe.

Nicolson characterized the French method as ". . . courteous and dignified; it was continuous and gradual; it attached importance to knowledge and experience; it took account of the realities of existing power; and it defined good faith, lucidity, and precision as the qualities essential to any sound negotiation."[2]

Two of the most often quoted definitions of diplomacy are those of Sir Ernest Satow and the *Oxford English Dictionary*. Satow defines diplomacy as "the application of tact

[1] Sir Harold Nicolson, *The Evolution of Diplomacy* (New York: Collier Books, 1962), p. 99.
[2] *Ibid.*, pp. 99-100.

12

The Profession: A New Diplomacy?

and intelligence to the conduct of official relations between the governments of independent states."[3] The dictionary definition is: "The management of international relations by negotiation; the method by which these relations are adjusted or managed by ambassadors and envoys; the business or art of the diplomatist." These definitions capture several of the elements of diplomacy that are stressed in all textbooks on international relations: diplomacy is concerned with official relationships between states; its essence is the art of negotiation; and it is an instrument of foreign policy, not a substitute for policy. Typically, other instruments of foreign policy are treated in separate chapters.

While there is consensus in the textbooks the precise view of diplomacy varies from a narrow one to a relatively broad one. Quincy Wright restricts diplomacy virtually to negotiation in a special sense, in defining it as "the art of negotiation, in order to achieve the maximum of group objectives with a minimum of costs, within a system of politics in which war is a possibility."[4] In this sense, negotiation may be carried out by many persons, as pointed out by Ernst Haas and Allen Whiting, including "heads of state, foreign secretaries, overseas staffs of ambassadors and career experts, special representatives, or military leaders."[5] In the "professional" sense of diplomacy, as it is carried out by men specifically designated as diplomats and accredited to foreign nations, several writers take a somewhat broader view and see four basic functions—representation, negotiation, reporting, and protection of interests.[6]

[3] Sir Ernest Satow, *A Guide to Diplomatic Practice*, 4th edn. (New York: Longmans, Green, 1957), p. 1.
[4] Wright, *The Study of International Relations* (New York: Appleton-Century-Crofts, 1955), p. 158.
[5] Haas and Whiting, *Dynamics of International Relations* (New York: McGraw Hill, 1956), p. 140.
[6] See, for example, Norman Pallmer and Howard Perkins, *International Relations*, 2nd edn. (Boston: Houghton Mifflin, 1957), pp. 98-100.

13

Background and Forces of Change

Richard Snyder and Edgar Furniss, Jr. apply the terms "symbolic, political, and legal" to these functions. "The diplomatic chief of mission in his person represents the head of his state," which accounts for the "privileges and immunities that attach to the person of the diplomat and to the establishment of which he is in charge," as well as for a great deal of participation in "formalities" and "ceremonial occasions." The political function encompasses negotiation and reporting in the diplomat's role of two-way channel of communication between his government and the government to which he is accredited. The legal function covers the legal obligations the diplomat must perform, the "duties laid down by the laws and statutes of his own country to which international law and usage have given application abroad."[7] These are the consular duties, including protecting the rights of individual countrymen and issuing or denying visas. It is possible to distinguish between diplomatic and consular practice historically and in terms of functions, but the general view is to see the consular field as a basic part of traditional diplomacy. As Elmer Plischke points out, the "two are so closely related and mutually contributory that for general purposes it is artificial to belabor the distinction."[8] Moreover, most countries long ago combined their diplomatic and consular services.

Throughout the literature, there is a strong association of diplomacy and peace, the settlement of differences by peaceful means such as accommodation, mediation, conciliation, negotiation. Hans Morgenthau maintains that "a diplomacy that ends in war has failed in its primary objective: the

[7] Snyder and Furniss, *American Foreign Policy* (New York: Rinehart & Co., 1956), p. 312.
[8] Plischke, *Conduct of American Diplomacy*, 2nd edn. (Princeton: Van Nostrand, 1961), p. 2.

14

promotion of the national interest by peaceful means."[9] Also, care has been taken in stressing that diplomacy and war are not entirely separable, but should be seen as alternative and often related methods. Quincy Wright points out that "diplomacy may function to create favorable conditions for war, to assist in winning war, to extract the maximum advantage from winning war, or to reduce the disadvantages from losing war." He concludes that "Diplomacy is a supplement to, as well as, on occasion, a substitute for, war."[10]

American participation in traditional diplomacy was marginal at best. "It is not much of an exaggeration to say that the United States during much of the nineteenth century used diplomacy scarcely at all, even in the affairs which brought it into contact with other states."[11] It is generally recognized that the United States entered the scene as a world power around the turn of the century, but that except for sporadic engagement the basic policy was isolationist until World War II. It is not surprising, then, that the United States was relatively late in joining the exemplars of the traditional diplomacy, the European powers, in improving the lot of its diplomatic and consular representatives by establishing a career service. A reform movement began about 1900, several decades after a comparable reform effort to improve the Civil Service had occurred. It culminated in a legislative charter for a career service in the Rogers Act of 1924.[12]

[9] Hans Morgenthau, *Politics Among Nations*, 2nd. edn. rev. (New York: Alfred A. Knopf, 1956) , p. 505.
[10] Wright, *Study of International Relations*, p. 159.
[11] Snyder and Furniss, *American Foreign Policy*, p. 314.
[12] Two excellent histories of the establishment of the career service are Warren Ilchman, *Professional Diplomacy in the United States, 1779-1939* (Chicago: Chicago University Press, 1961) and William Barnes and John Morgan, *The Foreign Service of the United States: Origins,*

Background and Forces of Change

Apart from the brief period following World War I, the limited American participation in diplomacy adhered very much in practice to the norms established by the Europeans. That is, American diplomats by and large were gentlemen of fortunate birth and superior education, engaging in careers that made them near-expatriates. Africa and substantial parts of Asia and the Near East were virtually unknown territory. Europe was the main arena, with lesser representation in Latin America and the Far East. One did more or less the same things regardless of the country to which one was assigned—consular affairs, reporting on matters of political and economic interest, occasional negotiating, and engaging in a continuing amiable representational life of a fairly high social order. Life was pleasant and relatively unchanging. There was little pressure. Most Americans scarcely knew their diplomats existed. Protocol was important. One dealt exclusively with representatives of the legitimate government currently in power. The interests one represented were narrow and inward-looking toward domestic concerns rather than outward to international involvements.

In an address to the American Foreign Service Association on May 31, 1962, President John F. Kennedy deftly sketched the pre-World War II environment:

> In the days before the war, we dealt with a few countries and a few leaders. I remember what Ambassador Dawes said, that the job was hard on the feet and easy on the brain. Theodore Roosevelt talked about those who *resided* in the Foreign Service rather than working in it. We were an isolationist country, by tradition and by policy and by statute. And therefore those of you who lived in the For-

Development, and Functions (Washington: Department of State, Historical Office, Bureau of Public Affairs, 1961) .

16

eign Service led a rather isolated life, dealing with comparatively few people, uninvolved in the affairs of this country or in many ways in the affairs of the country to which you may have been accredited.[13]

The catastrophe of World War I brought an end to the stable international system in which the traditional diplomacy had flowered. One immediate reflex was to blame diplomacy for the catastrophe, a view widely shared among leaders of the great powers except for the French.[14] But it was President Wilson who gave it memorable expression in the preamble to, and the first point of, his famous "Fourteen Points" address to Congress: "Open covenants of peace, openly arrived at, after which there shall be no private international understandings of any kind, but diplomacy shall proceed always frankly and in the public view."

Wilson's eloquence is what led Harold Nicolson to give the label "the American method" to what is variously referred to in the histories and texts as "Wilsonian diplomacy," "the new diplomacy," "open diplomacy," "democratic diplomacy," "parliamentary diplomacy." The "American method" was characterized by the extension of democratic ideals from the national to the international arena, egalitarianism, public negotiations, summitry, and attempts to influence and use public opinion.

Instead of a genuinely new school of diplomacy, the American variety was seen by Nicolson as a transitional phase, one result of the decline of the old order and the toppling of the dynasties. "Parliamentary" diplomacy continued to exist in the League of Nations, and today of course it is a major method of international relations in the United Nations and dozens of regional and specialized in-

[13] Taken from excerpts of the president's speech as printed in the *Foreign Service Journal* (July 1962), pp. 28-29.
[14] Haas and Whiting, *Dynamics*, p. 157.

17

ternational organizations.[15] But it has by no means supplanted traditional diplomatic methods. After the World War I peace conferences ended and the American relapse into isolationism occurred, diplomats resumed their business in much the same fashion as before the war. Yet it had become clear that the world was never to be the same again. If the American projection of democratic idealism onto the international scene was symptomatic of the end of the old order, the rise of the totalitarian states—and the extraordinary deviations from a stable international system that their foreign policies represented—provided the final proof.

World War II accelerated the forces of change that have affected the character and conduct of American foreign affairs. It is difficult to exaggerate the contrast in the situation of American diplomacy. In reminiscing about his pre- and postwar experiences, retired Ambassador Murat W. Williams captures something of the flavor of the change:

All has changed since those pre-war days . . . in Spain. There was a whole world between the early mornings when I elegantly took the Ambassadress' Pekingese for their morning walk on the dusty streets of Burgos—surrounded by war-stained soldiers—and the afternoons, decades later, when I wore shorts and sandals among my ex-Palmach friends, on a kibbutz in Israel. And there has been a world between those rich receptions in Madrid sparkling with the jewels of the duquesas of ancient names —and the simple meals we have today with eager, enthusiastic leaders of newly formed labor unions, imagina-

15 For a description and analysis of the rise and character of international organizations, see Inis Claude, *Swords into Plowshares* (New York: Random House, 1959). For a discussion of the relationship of traditional diplomacy and international cooperation, see Michael Cardozo, *Diplomats in International Cooperation: Stepchildren of the Foreign Service* (Ithaca: Cornell University Press, 1962).

tive new industrialists, and impatient students or Army officers—sincerely ambitious for social justice in their own countries.[16]

President Kennedy, in his address to the Foreign Service, drew the contrast to his picture of prewar American diplomacy in the following way:

> That is all changed now. The power and influence of the United States are involved in the national life of dozens of countries that did not exist before 1945, many of which are so hard-pressed.
>
> This is the great period of the Foreign Service, much greater than any period that has gone before. And it will be so through this decade, and perhaps even more in the years to come, if we are able to maintain ourselves with success.
>
> But it places the heaviest burdens upon all of you. Instead of becoming merely experts in diplomatic history, or in current clippings from the *New York Times*, now you have to involve yourselves in every element of foreign life—labor, the class struggle, cultural affairs and all the rest—attempting to predict in what direction the forces will move. The Ambassador has to be master of all these things, as well as knowing his own country.[17]

Writing about the postwar period to 1960, Gabriel Almond distinguishes three stages in the evolution of American foreign policy.[18] The pace of events can perhaps best be summarized within these stages, as well as in a fourth stage, from 1961 to the mid-1960s. The first stage occurred right after the war and unhappily was brief, lasting, in

---

[16] Murat W. Williams, "Life in the Diplomatic Service, 1939-1962," *American Oxonian* (July 1962) , p. 170.

[17] *Foreign Service Journal* (July 1962) , p. 28.

[18] Almond, *The American People and Foreign Policy* (New York: Frederick A. Praeger, 1960) , pp. xii-xv.

Almond's view, only into 1946. It was the time when the cornerstone of American foreign policy was the assumption that postwar reconstruction and prosperity would be achieved by the cooperation and leadership of the wartime great powers, largely through the instrumentality of the United Nations. It was at this time that an important restatement of the legislative charter of the Foreign Service, the Foreign Service Act of 1946, was drafted, steered through delicate negotiations, and passed by Congress. This was the beginning of the running controversy over the Foreign Service system, which is the subject of the next chapter. It suffices for present purposes to point out that the Act, though it has turned out to be remarkably flexible in practice, was designed by Foreign Service Officers themselves as an ideal vehicle for an elite corps of generalists who would carry on the traditional functions of diplomacy.[19]

During this early postwar period, the Department of State grew in size as large wartime civilian agencies were dismantled. Functions and personnel of some of them were transferred to State, including the Office of Coordinator of Inter-American Affairs, the Office of War Information (OWI), and parts of both the Office of Strategic Services (OSS) and the Foreign Economic Administration.[20]

The chill of the cold war soon emerged, dashing hopes for collaboration between the United States and the Soviet Union and ushering in the second stage, lasting in Almond's view from 1946 to 1949. He describes this period as one of a "responsible, imaginative, and generous confrontation of

19 This is brought out clearly in the excellent case study by Harold Stein, "The Foreign Service Act of 1946," in Harold Stein, ed., *Public Administration and Policy Development: A Case Book* (New York: Harcourt, Brace, 1952), pp. 661-737.
20 Lincoln Gordon, "The Growth of American Representation Overseas," in Vincent M. Barnett, Jr., ed., *The Representation of the United States Abroad*, published for the American Assembly, rev. edn. (New York: Frederick A. Praeger, 1965), p. 22.

a military, political, and economic threat."[21] The threat became plain—in the communist pressure on Greece and Turkey, in the Czechoslovakian coup, the Berlin blockade, the Soviet Union's attainment of a nuclear capability, the collapse of the Nationalist Chinese. The American response was a remarkable flurry of activity in assuming worldwide responsibilities, developing new instruments of foreign policy, proliferating new agencies, and articulating the "containment" policy. The National Security Act of 1947 created the National Security Council, the Central Intelligence Agency, and a unified Department of Defense. The Marshall Plan and the North Atlantic Treaty Organization were created. Large-scale economic assistance to the western European nations was followed by military assistance, authorized by the Mutual Defense Assistance Act of 1949, and by the idea of technical assistance to developing nations, first broached by President Truman in "Point IV" of his inaugural address of January 1949. The information program, which had dwindled and become nearly moribund after OWI functions were transferred to State, was energetically revived and given a new lease on life by the Smith-Mundt Act of 1948; its appropriation nearly tripled and it launched a "Campaign of Truth."

With all this growth, problems of coordination were inevitable. The body of professional diplomats, the Foreign Service Officer corps, remained essentially unchanged. It manned none of the new functions; indeed, it would have been impossible for it to do so in such a short time with its normal method of recruitment from the bottom. Moreover, there was a seemingly ephemeral aura about the events of the time and the new functions designed to cope with them. Intelligence and assistance functions were located in new agencies outside of State and no effort was made to assimi-

21 Almond, *American People*, p. xiii.

late the one large operating program within State, the information program. For these functions, whole new foreign services came into being, rivalling or exceeding the FSO corps in size. New functional bureaus came into existence within State, representing, in the case of economic policy and intelligence, State's needs for its own experts and for liaison with other agencies, and, in the case of international organization affairs, an area of interest with which the State Department had been closely associated since wartime planning for the peace to come. In all three cases these bureaus were manned largely by civil servants and not by FSOs. In addition to problems of coordination and State Department organization, the situation brought into question the role of the FSO corps and the character of the personnel structure for foreign affairs. The Hoover Commission of 1949 became the first of a series of major inquiries into this problem area.

Almond sees the third postwar stage of American foreign policy, the decade of the 1950s, in very negative terms—a period of "failure" and "deterioration" in which U.S. policy "turned into a hard shell of military production and deployments, security diplomacy, and a program of foreign aid that was assimilated into our security diplomacy." Almond sees as causative factors a failure to understand what was happening in the non-Western world, the deep internal distrust engendered by the McCarthy phenomenon, and a loss of bipartisanship.[22] It is not necessary here to pass judgment on this critical view to agree that the 1950s did represent a distinctive stage in the postwar evolution of American foreign policy, a stage that generally was more rigid and less creative than the one which preceded it and the one which succeeded it.

But the period was not without innovation. What came to

[22] *Ibid.*, pp. xiv, xv.

be known as the "Food for Peace Program" was made possible by the Agricultural Trade Development and Assistance Act of 1954, economic assistance increased greatly throughout the underdeveloped world, the Development Loan Fund was created in 1957, and toward the end of the Eisenhower Administration increasing attention was directed toward Latin America, as evidenced by the creation of the Inter-American Development Bank in 1959 and adoption of the Act of Bogota in 1960 which committed the United States to long-term assistance to Latin American countries. Attempts to break out of the apparently negative and status quo policy of containment, as evidenced by spasmodic summitry and ideas of massive retaliation, liberation of eastern Europe, and disengagement in central Europe, were frustrated. The ideological chill of the cold war remained pronounced, and awareness deepened that the situation was to last a long time and that it was not suited to the typical American crisis response of massive effort to overcome the crisis, followed by a return to normalcy.

Early in the Eisenhower Administration there was reconsideration of problems of coordinating the enlarged foreign affairs apparatus and of problems of role and organization of the new functions, the State Department, and its Foreign Service. A dominant view emerged that put these problems in a particular perspective. The view, which did not solve the problems so much as it provided a doctrine for living with them, was that a basic distinction between policy and operations was viable, and that it was not only possible but desirable to separate the two.[23] The State Department would concern itself with policy; the new functions would be operated by other agencies under the policy guidance of State. Following this logic, Reorganization Plans 7 and 8 of 1953 took the information program and various assistance

[23] Snyder and Furniss, *American Foreign Policy*, p. 342.

activities out of State and created two new agencies, the United States Information Agency (USIA) and the Foreign Operations Administration (FOA).[24] The following year, the Foreign Agricultural Service (FAS) was created for the Department of Agriculture, thus taking some overseas agricultural functions away from State. At this time, probably no other approach would have been less controversial or pleased more people. The White House and Secretary of State John Foster Dulles were firmly in accord, those representing "operations" were pleased with relative independence from State (particularly at a time when it was under fire from Senator Joseph McCarthy and others), and FSOs were satisfied inasmuch as the congruency between a State Department directly concerned only with policy and the traditional diplomatic role is obvious.[25]

Coordination of the numerous entities engaged in foreign affairs was to be assured in several ways. First, the foreign policy "primacy" of the Secretary of State was vigorously reaffirmed; words to this effect appeared in relevant legislation, Executive Orders, and statements of delegation of authority. Second, a network of interagency committees was built up; most importantly, an Operations Coordinating Board (OCB) was created as an adjunct to the National Security Council, specifically for the purpose of coordinating the multi-agency operations designed to effectuate policy. Third, the presence of multi-agency representation in U.S. embassies abroad gave rise to the "country team" concept,

[24] U.S. Congress, Senate Subcommittee on National Security Staffing and Operations of the Committee on Government Operations (hereafter referred to as Jackson Subcommittee), *The Ambassador and the Problem of Coordination*, 88th Cong., 1st Sess., 1963, pp. 20-22, 125-29. In 1955 the assistance program was transfered back into State by Executive Order 10,610 (May 9, 1955), in the form of the "semi-autonomous" International Cooperation Administration (ICA).

[25] These organizational issues and the rationale of the policy-operations dichotomy will be more fully discussed in Chapter 3.

in which the chiefs of the various agency programs and senior FSOs form a coordinating group "under the leadership of the Ambassador."[26]

A final point about the decade of the 1950s has to do with another in the series of major studies of the personnel system, this one by the Wriston Committee, so-called after its chairman, Dr. Henry M. Wriston. The study differed from most others in that its recommendations were vigorously implemented, bringing some 1,500 persons laterally into the FSO corps in a process that came to be known, inevitably, as "Wristonization." Again, this is a topic to be considered in the main in the next chapter; in the present context, it should be pointed out that, as important and controversial as the episode was, it did not basically alter the situation regarding interagency coordination, inasmuch as the entire operation was internal to the Department of State. That is, the persons brought into the FSO corps in this massive lateral entry program, lasting from 1954 to 1958, were already employed by the Department in categories other than the FSO category. They were persons engaged in such functions abroad as consular, commercial, and administrative work (the latter having greatly expanded as a result of the general growth in size of overseas missions), and, in Washington, persons mainly in the functional bureaus which, as was pointed out earlier, had been manned largely by civil servants rather than FSOs.

The Kennedy Administration brought to Washington a new ferment and energy in the foreign affairs field. Still more entities were created—the Peace Corps, the Arms Control and Disarmament Agency, the Office of the Special Representative for Trade Negotiation. The aid program received its most thorough overhaul to date in the Foreign Assistance Act of 1961, creating the Agency for Interna-

[26] Jackson Subcommittee, *Ambassador*, pp. 14-18.

25

tional Development (AID) within the State Department. A 10-year "Alliance for Progress" was proposed by President Kennedy and adopted in the Charter of Punta del Este of 1961. Trends toward longer-term development assistance and greater involvement were evident in W. W. Rostow's theories of "modernization" and Gen. Maxwell Taylor's espousal of "counter-insurgency." The geographic horizons of U.S. foreign affairs widened and deepened as Latin America received higher priority and as another 10 new countries achieved independence in Africa, following a surge of 17 new states in 1960. Major crises occurred in both regions, in Cuba and in the Congo.

Other characteristics of recent years could be enumerated at great length, but for the purposes of this study the most important was the abrupt reversal of the policy-operations dichotomy. In the words of McGeorge Bundy, "We have deliberately rubbed out the distinction between planning and operation. . . ."[27] President Kennedy dissolved the OCB, making it clear that he expected the task of coordination to be carried out by the Department of State.[28] In a letter to all chiefs of mission in May 1961, the president gave them sweeping authority and responsibility for supervision: "You are in charge of the entire United States Diplomatic Mission, and I shall expect you to supervise all of its operations. The Mission includes not only the personnel of the Department of State and the Foreign Service, but also the representatives of all other United States agencies. . . ."[29] Only military command forces were excluded.

A major interest in management in foreign affairs de-

[27] The full text of Bundy's letter to Sen. Henry Jackson appears in Jackson Subcommittee, *Administration of National Security: Selected Papers*, 87th Cong., 2nd Sess., 1962, pp. 5-8.

[28] *Ibid.*, p. 3.

[29] The full text of the Kennedy letter appears in Jackson Subcommittee, *Ambassador*, pp. 155-56.

veloped. The Jackson subcommittee discussed the multiple roles of the ambassador, as diplomat, as adviser, and as executive.[30] There was a certain fascination in the managerial strategy and methods of Secretary Robert McNamara in his reorganization of the Pentagon, particularly the programming system developed for this purpose.[31] Key members of the Administration began consciously to talk about "the new diplomacy." The latest of the major foreign affairs personnel studies, a blue-ribbon, privately sponsored committee chaired by former Secretary of State Christian Herter, used the phrase "new diplomacy" in the title of its report.[32] Its scope was considerably broader than the previous studies. Among many topics, it dealt with concepts of "the new diplomacy," with the need for executive talent, and the application of programming techniques to foreign affairs. The Johnson administration continued very much in the same direction as the Kennedy administration. In 1965 virtually all major agencies were instructed to develop "planning-programming-budgeting systems" (PPBS) similar to the Department of Defense system.[33] The Department of State had already been experimenting for more than two years with a foreign affairs programming system, following the recommendation of the Herter Committee. In 1966 the President, acting through the device of a National Security Action Memorandum (NSAM 341), gave the Secretary of State authority and responsibility in the strongest language for the "overall direction, supervision and coordination of

[30] Jackson Subcommittee, *Administration of National Security: The American Ambassador*, 88th Cong., 2nd Sess., 1964.

[31] See William W. Kaufmann, *The McNamara Strategy* (New York: Harper & Row, 1964), especially Chapter 5, "Cost Effectiveness."

[32] Committee on Foreign Affairs Personnel, *Personnel for the New Diplomacy* (New York: Carnegie Endowment for International Peace, 1962), hereafter cited as Herter Report.

[33] U. S. Bureau of the Budget, Bulletin 66-3 to the heads of Executive Departments and Establishments, "Planning-Programming-Budgeting," Oct. 12, 1965.

27

interdepartmental activities of the United States Government overseas" except combatant military. The NSAM established a Senior Interdepartmental Group (SIG) to be chaired by the Under Secretary of State, and five Interdepartmental Regional Groups (IRG) to be chaired by the five Assistant Secretaries of State in charge of the five regional bureaus.[34]

From this chronological overview of change over the past 20 years and more, it is possible to distill a list of the more significant changed conditions, or characteristics, of world politics and the conduct of U.S. foreign affairs. All are relevant to the question of whether the substance of diplomacy as a profession has changed, and probably all would be accepted as relatively objective descriptions of change by most adherents to either side of that question. Some items are so familiar that they have achieved the status of cliché, which, however, does not obviate their significance:

1. *We are in a revolutionary era in world politics.* Morton Kaplan holds that "there are portentous and momentous currents abroad in the world that can be described accurately only by the overworked and inexact term 'revolution.' "[35] Since the ending of the Concert of Europe, the international system has been basically unstable. Revolutionary tendencies can be seen in "the demands being made by masses, by elites, or by revolutionary organizations"; they can be seen in the uncommitted world, within the communist bloc as well as being espoused overtly by that bloc, and even within the Western world.[36]

[34] The text of NSAM 341 appears as Department of State Foreign Affairs Manual Circular No. 385 of March 4, 1966, in Jackson Subcommittee, *The Secretary of State and the Problem of Coordination: New Duties and Procedures of March 4, 1966*, 89th Cong., 2nd Sess., 1966, pp. 4-6.
[35] Kaplan, ed., *The Revolution in World Politics* (New York: John Wiley & Sons, 1962) , pp. xiii-xiv.
[36] *Ibid.*

28

The Profession: A New Diplomacy?

2. *The nature of military power has changed radically.* "There has now occurred, or is occurring, the most radical change in the nature of power and the characteristics of power units since the beginning of the modern state system or, perhaps, since the beginnings of mankind."[37] Although nuclear power can provide a veneer of stability in the "nuclear deterrent," it contributes to instability through such factors as the unpredictability of discoveries, rapid obsolescence leading to arms races, and the spread of nuclear weaponry to additional countries.

3. *The rivalry between the Communist nations and the Western powers is a dominating factor.* The view of the Herter Report, that this is "the most obvious, pervasive, and crucial element in the world situation," rings true even though we no longer have a rigid bipolar system: "While the United States and other nations in the past opposed and periodically warred against absolutism in one form or another, never before, short of all-out hostilities, have international energies been so mobilized and so committed to a struggle of this kind. This struggle motivates many international activities, and it colors virtually everything that is done in world affairs."[38]

4. *Both nationalism and internationalism are powerful forces.* Both the bilateral and multilateral spheres of diplomacy have expanded enormously. The number of nations with which the United States maintains diplomatic relations has nearly doubled—from 60 before World War II to 118 in 1967. The U.S. pays dues to 51 international organizations and participates in more than 400 major intergovernmental conferences each year.

5. *Ideology permeates international affairs.* If this is a

[37] John Herz, *International Politics in the Atomic Age* (New York: Columbia University Press, 1962), p. 22.
[38] Herter Report, p. 2.

29

revolutionary age in world politics, the inevitable corollary is strong ideological content. Clashing ideologies sharpen the lines of conflict and lessen the possibility of compromise. A favorite theme in the textbooks on international relations is to treat the prevalence of ideology as a major constraint on the traditional diplomatic reliance on patient negotiation.

6. *U.S. involvement in international affairs is very nearly total.* Isolationism appears to be dead as a policy. Events in what formerly could be considered insignificant countries may touch off worldwide repercussions. The U.S. must be concerned with the quality of its representation in every country.

7. *New instruments of foreign affairs have proliferated.* Partly because traditional diplomacy is so sharply restricted, there has been great ingenuity in developing new tools of foreign affairs to bring into play almost every conceivable method of affecting the course of events. The result is an extremely complex foreign affairs establishment.

8. *The style of U.S. diplomacy is interventionist and activist.* This is a controversial point, one often exaggerated both by proponents and critics. Intervention is not necessarily a mindless reflex—the Soviet crushing of the Hungarian uprising in 1956 and the abortive communist coup in Indonesia in October of 1965 are only two of the more prominent cases that the United States conspicuously stayed out of. But the exerting of influence whenever feasible, by all possible means, is undeniably a fundamental characteristic of U.S. diplomacy, one that is markedly in contrast to pre-World War II days.

9. *Diplomacy today is concerned not only with leaders, but with whole societies.* This is one of the most frequently cited changes that have occurred, probably, again, because it stands in such contrast to prewar days. As the Herter Report points out, concern with the larger society is not only

a characteristic of such programs as information and development assistance, but also of "traditional activities of foreign services," wherein "a great deal more attention must be paid than formerly to the many forces, factions, and interests on the local scene in addition to the government in power."[39]

10. *Crises are endemic.* If one were to list all of the significant international crises that have occurred over the past 20 years, the average rate might be as high as one per month. Before World War II it was possible for the United States to go for decades without a significant international crisis. This is an obvious manifestation of a "revolutionary" era in world politics; it is cited here to underscore the burden on the foreign affairs establishment, particularly on the Secretary and Under Secretary of State.

11. *Foreign affairs are more complex than ever before because of the continuing effort to influence the forces of change.* Former Under Secretary of State for Political Affairs George C. McGhee stated the point this way: "We must break with the passive role of the past, in which diplomats registered the changes that soldiers, explorers, and industrialists achieved. Now, diplomats themselves are the harbingers of change—among the innovators and leaders in the march toward progress."[40] The effort to influence change, rather than merely reacting to events, stands at the frontiers of knowledge; it means, in the words of Henry M. Wriston, that "both policy and performance require more subtlety and sophistication than heretofore."[41]

12. *Policy rapidly becomes obsolescent.* Policy-making is not a frozen, long-term process, despite the strong ideologi-

[39] *Ibid.*, p. 3.
[40] U. S. Department of State, "Address by the Honorable George C. McGhee," Press Release No. 371, June 8, 1963.
[41] Wriston, "Thoughts for Tomorrow," *Foreign Affairs*, Vol. 40, No. 3 (April 1962) , 374.

31

cal content of world politics. Rapid change in the world
at large presents many more problems than can be dealt
with adequately by merely a reference to basic ideology.
Harlan Cleveland, formerly Assistant Secretary of State for
International Organization Affairs, made the point as follows: "The longer I work at the business of diplomacy, the
more I am impressed by the rapid obsolescence of even the
most successful policies. On practically every important
question we try to handle in the State Department, there is
a race between the development of the objective world
around us, and the development of doctrine with which to
analyze and deal with that world."[42]

13. *The role of the military in foreign affairs is increasingly prominent.* Formerly, in the absence of war, military
representation abroad was limited to military attachés. In
the present era, military involvement abroad has changed
and expanded drastically—from providing occupation government in enemy countries right after the war to military
assistance programs, maintaining widely scattered bases and
forces, offshore procurement, coalition planning, intelligence, limited war, counterinsurgency, civic action programs.[43] This has given rise to many forms of interaction
between the Departments of Defense and State and to the
notion of a "national security" complex embracing both.

14. *The distinction between domestic interests and foreign affairs has lessened.* Before World War II relatively few
"domestic" agencies (for example, the Departments of Commerce and Agriculture) were concerned with activities
abroad. Today more than 30 agencies of the U.S. govern-

[42] U. S. Department of State, "Address by the Honorable Harlan
Cleveland," Press Release No. 249, April 13, 1962.
[43] For a description of all these activities see Paul C. Davis and
William T. R. Fox, "American Military Representation Abroad," in
Barnett, *Representation*, pp. 129-83.

ment have overseas operations of one kind or another.[44]

15. *There is need for both managerial talent and specialized skills in foreign affairs.* The greater size of the foreign affairs establishment, its varied tools and complex programs, all call for a variety of specialized skills and for managerial skill to direct programs. This contrasts sharply with prewar days when there was only one foreign affairs agency—the Department of State—and when its generalist corps of career officers performed all the tasks necessary abroad.

We may very well have entered a *fifth* postwar phase of American foreign policy, to add to the four that were described as the context for the changed conditions enumerated above. The fifth phase would have started when the Vietnam war reached unexpected proportions and duration, with a number of consequences—a strong protest movement in the United States, an increased drain on the balance of payments, a surge of neo-isolationism, revisionist theories on the origins of the cold war, greater awareness of the limitations of power. Over time, these forces, plus a much stronger concern for domestic problems, may well cause a measure of withdrawal and a general tempering of American foreign affairs, although a significant trend back to isolationism does not appear likely. But at the least, one suspects, U.S. policy-makers and the general public will become extremely cautious about becoming involved in situations that offer any prospect at all of coming to resemble the Vietnam engagement. There are many weathervanes pointing to declining interest in foreign affairs and height-

[44] For an examination of the varied overseas activities of some of these domestic agencies, see Robert E. Elder, *Overseas Representation and Services for Federal Domestic Agencies*, Foreign Affairs Personnel Study No. 2 (New York: Carnegie Endowment for International Peace, 1965).

ened interest in domestic affairs—the malaise surrounding the foreign aid program, program shifts of the major foundations from the international field to the domestic field, noticeably greater excitement on the working level in Washington over involvement in the newer domestic agencies rather than in the foreign affairs agencies.

Nevertheless, this shifting mood has not yet affected the 15 characteristics of American foreign policy listed above, nor is it likely to diminish the effect of more than one or two of them in any significant way; more likely, it will intensify several of them. We will return to the question of a "fifth phase" of postwar American foreign policy in the final chapter, when the accent will be on the future.

The responses to the severe pressures in the postwar years for deepseated and significant changes in the profession of diplomacy will occupy us in depth in subsequent chapters. A useful prelude is to draw the main lines of the controversy. First, the conservative viewpoint. An extreme reaction has been to view traditional diplomacy as dead, or nearly dead, chiefly as a result of the ideological content of the cold war:

> The old diplomacy of persuasion, compromise, and patient conciliation has come to a dead end, even if diplomats must pretend to the contrary. When the differences between the two parties are as profound as they are between the West and the Soviet world—when the political assumptions, economic beliefs, and the very modes of individual existence are so far removed as to be incomparable—then the very basis of this old diplomacy is abolished. It can only operate now within the alliances; between the two blocs, it falls freely in a vacuum.[45]

45 *Reporter*, Aug. 20, 1959, p. 2.

Some of those who see diplomacy thus sadly afflicted, or nearly so, hold out hope. Harold Nicolson states his belief "that the principles of sound diplomacy—which are immutable—will in the end prevail. . . ."[46] Hans Morgenthau stresses the crucial role of traditional diplomacy in maintaining peace and building toward a world state, and attempts to set forth the conditions for the "revival" of diplomacy.[47]

In the past 20 years the professional diplomats themselves have had no doubts about the continuing importance of the traditional diplomatic methods, and have been intent not only on preserving them, but also on maintaining their supremacy in the enlarged foreign affairs establishment. Often they have projected the image of an embattled band holding out against a host of unknowing and unprofessional critics and reformers. In particular, they have been intent on guarding the elitist concept of the career service from adulteration by the new specialists.

This conservative and defensive stance has dominated the FSO corps throughout the period of strong and growing pressures for change since World War II and remains important today, even though there is occurring a significant shift of opinion and a remarkable ferment within the ranks of the Service, as we shall see in detail in Chapter 7.

The conservative stance that has dominated the FSO corps for so long can be seen in its purest form in the memoirs and commentaries written recently by retired men who have spent most of their adult lives as professional diplomats.

One approach of the senior diplomats has been to question the need for new tools in foreign affairs and to decry

[46] Nicolson, *Evolution of Diplomacy*, p. 124.
[47] Morgenthau, *Politics*, pp. 526-35.

the expansion in staffs that has occurred. Perhaps the most extreme proponent of this view is Ellis Briggs who held seven ambassadorships before retiring. Briggs calls USIA, AID, and CIA the "propaganda, handout, and skullduggery agencies," but reserves his most biting sarcasm for the Peace Corps which he terms "an undertaking essentially irrational but wrapped in the irresistible pinafore of romantic endeavor." He suggests as its war cry (or perhaps peace cry is a better term): " 'Yoo-Hoo! Let's go out and wreak good on some natives.' "[48]

Even more temperate critics, such as John Paton Davies, Jr., appear to share this view. Davies calls himself a "defrocked diplomat," in reference to his ouster in the early 1950s as a victim of the controversy surrounding the United States' China policy. He writes: "By now the conduct of foreign relations is well established as everybody's business. With the Peace Corps in the act, butchers, bakers, and candlestick makers are eligible. There has never been such wide mobilization of if not talent at least bodies to deal with what has hitherto been regarded as a delicate and specialized undertaking—managing our relations with other countries."[49]

Henry S. Villard, a retired ambassador, expresses the fear that the new specialists are taking over: "In the same way that specialists in different branches of medicine are elbowing out the old-fashioned family physician, the specialists in the Foreign Service are displacing the old-time generalists." Further he states:

As in the case of Wristonization, the adulteration of the original Rogers Act by large doses of extraneous per-

[48] Briggs, *Farewell to Foggy Bottom* (New York: David McKay, 1964), pp. 165-67.
[49] John Paton Davies, Jr., *Foreign and Other Affairs* (New York: W. W. Norton, 1964), p. 185.

The Profession: A New Diplomacy?

sonnel cannot be expected to improve the morale of purists who have thought of diplomacy as one of the stricter disciplines. They see themselves inundated—yesterday by the home staff, today by a formidable information corps, and tomorrow, no doubt, by those who have made a career out of foreign aid.

As this process goes on, Villard fears, the generalists will disappear and with them will be gone "the assets of perceptiveness, sound judgment, panoramic understanding, and intuition tempered in the fires of practical experience."[50]

A related theme is to criticize the interventionist style of American foreign affairs, which in large part has created the need for new tools and specialists to staff them. Briggs says: "A more damaging doctrine than that which holds it to be the duty of the diplomat to accelerate someone else's social revolution would be impossible to imagine."[51] Davies sees the problem as follows:

> What is lacking in perception is more than made up in activity. Characteristic of the new intervention is a philosophy of activism, a belief in the efficacy of works. Since the results sought are amorphous, an indiscriminate range of activities can be and is represented as contributing to the desired ends. Uninhibited by deep understandings of the peoples affected, everything from dams and bazookas to home economics and Bach is held forth as efficacious against communism and so as contributing to the security of the United States.[52]

Special dislike is reserved for "professional administrators," a somewhat vague term covering virtually all those

[50] Villard, *Affairs at State* (New York: Thomas Y. Crowell, 1965), pp. 33-35, 175-76.
[51] Briggs, *Farewell*, p. 29.
[52] Davies, *Foreign*, p. 187.

37

who seem intent on changing the character of the diplo-matic corps. Included are administrators within the Foreign Service, senior administrative officials of the Department of State, members of special study groups, and administrators elsewhere in the federal government, particularly in the Bureau of the Budget and the Civil Service Commission. Briggs refers to the "administrative types" as "glorified jani-tors, supply clerks, and pants-pressers" who "yearn to get their fingers in the foreign affairs pie, and when they do, the diplomatic furniture often gets marked with gummy thumbprints."[53]

Referring to "professional administrators," Charles Thay-er writes:

> 'They seem to forget,' one Foreign Service officer said loud enough to be heard by the new men, 'that they are essentially valets. Instead of pressing our pants, they are trying to wear them.' Tactless though the remark may have been, it was not unjustified. The newcomers, many of them graduates of schools of government administra-tion, were unfamiliar with the objectives, problems, and methods of diplomacy. Yet, instead of confining their ef-forts to administrative problems, they rashly injected themselves into the substantive work of diplomacy.[54]

Villard echoes the threat: "In the State Department, the administrators are no longer the servants of the policy-mak-ers—they are rapidly becoming the masters."[55]

There is extensive argument about several other issues which are seen as areas of maneuvering by the administra-tors in their efforts to change the character of the profes-sion. One of these is training. Briggs sees "mid career and

[53] Briggs, *Farewell*, p. 29.
[54] Thayer, *Diplomat* (New York: Harper and Bros., 1959), p. 274.
[55] Villard, *Affairs at State*, p. 36.

38

senior training" as "frequently a waste of the officer's time and the taxpayer's money."[56] Thayer reports that the "mirth" of professional diplomats at such courses as "reading rate improvement" and "conference leadership" at the Foreign Service Institute gives way to "resentment when the institute expends some of its $5 million budget to improve senior American diplomats with courses in social psychology, cultural anthropology, and conceptual methods of analysis." His view of the correct background for the professional diplomat is the same as that espoused by Briggs and Villard: "thorough grounding in the basic disciplines of history, economics, and languages followed by active experience."[57]

A particularly sensitive issue is the appointing of non-career men to ambassadorial posts. All of the authors cited find it necessary to argue at length the wisdom of appointing career men.[58] Another threat is seen in the pressure to make the Foreign Service representative of American society, which is regarded as an effort to "lower the entrance requirements" and as "pressure toward mediocrity." The counterargument is a defense of the elitist concept, in the sense of representing the best of American life and not the average.[59]

The solutions posed by the senior diplomats are predictable, given the tenor of the arguments. There is a call for retrenchment. Davies sees it possible to cut the "staffs dealing with foreign affairs" to "a fraction of their present girth," and Briggs states: "Of over one hundred American

[56] Briggs, *Farewell*, p. 34.

[57] Thayer, *Diplomat*, pp. 280-81.

[58] Even though the percentage of ambassadorships held by career men has risen over the years, from a low of 35 percent in 1924 to over 70 percent in the Kennedy and Johnson administrations. See James L. McCamy, *Conduct of the New Diplomacy* (New York: Harper & Row, 1964), pp. 239-40.

[59] Davies, *Foreign*, p. 197; Thayer, *Diplomat*, pp. 281-82.

embassies in the world today a majority could perform *twice* as efficiently with *half* the persons now cluttering up the premises."[60]

There is a call for a resurgence of the best virtues of the traditional diplomacy to temper the "new diplomacy" of the New Frontier. Davies does not see a simple return to a golden past: "Notwithstanding its drawbacks, the new diplomacy is here to stay. It will, one must believe, mature." To mature, he feels that such qualities as "selective perception," "discrimination," and "moderation" must be applied.[61]

At the opposite pole from the conservative views of senior diplomats, which have dominated the FSO corps for so long, is the motion of the "new diplomacy" pressed by the Kennedy and Johnson administrations. President Kennedy issued the challenge to the FSO corps in his address to the American Foreign Service Association, already cited:

> I know that many Foreign Service officers feel (like former Marines, who believe that the old days were the best days) that the days before World War II were the golden days of the Foreign Service, that since then the Foreign Service has fallen on hard times and that there is a good deal of uncertainty about what the future may bring.
>
> I would like to differ with that view completely. In my opinion, today, as never before, is the golden period of the Foreign Service.

The president went on to say: "Those who cannot stand the heat should get out of the kitchen." And: "Personally, I think the place to be is in the kitchen, and I am sure the Foreign Service Officers of the United States feel the same way."

[60] Davies, *Foreign*, p. 195; Briggs, *Farewell*, p. 165.
[61] Davies, *Foreign*, pp. 193-200.

The Profession: A New Diplomacy?

Other administration spokesmen elaborated on the nature of the challenge. Under Secretary of State Chester Bowles wrote of the "sharply altered nature of diplomacy in our era," stressing the "challenge to our instruments of policy, to the organization, administration and operation of our efforts at home and abroad" which "has only recently begun to be appreciated and acted upon."[62]

The operational cast of the new diplomacy was also emphasized by Ralph Dungan, then special assistant to President Kennedy:

> We must know where we are heading, what we want to achieve, and how we can best achieve it. Foreign policy—the New Diplomacy—can, in short, no longer be only a matter of making policy by the cables, of playing it by ear, day-to-day. It requires planning and programming toward specific as well as general objectives, and it requires thinking through the contingencies and planning to meet them. In short, the New Diplomacy requires anticipation of, not reaction to, events.[63]

The most rigorous attempt to conceptualize the new diplomacy and spell out what needed to be done to meet the challenge can be found in the work of the Herter Committee. In reference to the traditional diplomacy, its report stated: "However effective this diplomatic model was in years gone by, it is clear that the old system, though still useful and even essential in its central elements, is inadequate by itself for the United States of today." Referring to the new diplomacy, the report said:

> One striking characteristic of the new diplomacy is the diversity of activities it encompasses and, therefore,

[62] Bowles, "Toward a New Diplomacy," *Foreign Affairs* (Jan. 1962), pp. 244-51.

[63] Ralph Dungan, "A Year of Substantial Progress," *Foreign Service Journal* (April 1963), p. 29.

41

the diversity of skills and knowledge it requires. It is no longer useful to think of foreign affairs as a single professional field. Rather, it is a broad spectrum into which a number of professions, some of the orthodox domestic variety and others peculiar to foreign affairs, must be fitted and modified. Equally striking is the premium this very diversity places on the capacity to coordinate activities, and to achieve a sense of unity and common purpose.[64]

On this view of the new diplomacy the Committee based many of its 43 recommendations dealing with the role of the Department of State and its Foreign Service and changes required in the personnel systems for foreign affairs.

The nature of the problem in the area of personnel systems has been analyzed incisively by James L. McCamy, arguing that a change not only in degree but in kind had occurred: "When the wartime changes were carried into the postwar years, something very significant had happened, a change so deep that we have not yet adjusted to it with a theory of personnel management that fits the startling circumstance." McCamy held that "without much notice the United States in a few years after 1945 displaced 500 years of the practice of diplomacy," with the changes adding up to a brand-new job both at home and abroad. The problem, however, has been the lag between the system and the need:

The expansion of diplomacy has had deep effect on the kinds of people we hire to work in foreign affairs, but our theory of personnel management has failed to change. We still act as if the new functions are the business of people who are not truly engaged in diplomacy. True careers in foreign affairs, the present theory goes,

[64] Herter Report, pp. 1, 47.

42

belong only to the Foreign Service Officers who are chosen
for their general ability and poise and who learn on the
job to be specialists in diplomatic and consular relations.[65]

One interesting feature of the articulation of a "new diplomacy" in the early 1960s was that no one pretended that
it had suddenly sprung into being, say, in the transition
from the Eisenhower administration to the Kennedy administration. The contrasts drawn—by President Kennedy,
by the Herter Report, by McCamy and others—were mainly
contrasts between the pre- and postwar situations. The 15
characteristics of change discussed earlier were operative
long before John F. Kennedy assumed office. Although there
was a new aura of activism in the Kennedy administration
and the creation of some new entities and programs, these
did not add up to a change in kind from the previous 15
years.

*The main difference, then, between the 1960s and the
earlier postwar years, was that a direct challenge was issued
by the White House to the bureaucracy (including the Foreign Service) to change itself to meet more adequately the
changed conditions that had already existed for a considerable time.*

In short, the view was that there had been a *lag* between
performance and need. Never before had the State Department and the Foreign Service been under such direct pressure from the White House to change their traditional ways
of doing business. And the rhetoric was backed up by some
strong measures, such as the Kennedy letter, the dissolution
of the OCB, the PPBS innovation, and NSAM 341. But, as
we shall see, there is often a very long and tricky path between the desire and the reality.

Insofar as the professional diplomats were concerned, the

[65] McCamy, *Conduct*, Chapter 11, "The New Diplomacy."

main lines of the controversy were now drawn. For the most part, they had successfully resisted reform pressures ever since the end of the war, but had been confronted with nothing like the force of the challenge now coming from the White House. At stake was the purity and distinctiveness of their view of the profession, drawn from a rich tradition of diplomatic history, emphasizing the qualities of tact, subtlety, sophistication, sensitivity used in representing the head of state in personal negotiations and activities that were largely political. These were the qualities that would produce sound foreign policy decisions, and they could be gained only by long experience in the traditional arts of the diplomat.

Ranged against this traditional view was the challenge of the "new diplomacy," a challenge calling for the State Department and the Foreign Service to *manage* the entire semi-chaotic spectrum of U.S. foreign affairs activities, a challenge emphasizing such alien themes to the professional diplomat as long-term planning, programming techniques, quantitative analysis, large-scale resource allocations, and the management of operational programs.

The next two chapters are concerned with the development of the controversy in two areas—the foreign affairs personnel systems and management and organization within the Department of State—and with efforts in both areas to meet the challenge of the "new diplomacy."

CHAPTER 2

THE SYSTEM

....

ONE MANIFESTATION of the period of rapid change reviewed in the last chapter is the remarkable series of efforts to change the personnel system for foreign affairs. A reform movement as persistent as this is not generated out of small and unimportant considerations. Typically, the parties involved have felt that issues of great moment are at stake, amounting basically to nothing less than the adequacy of the conduct of U.S. foreign affairs in extremely critical times. Thus, the reform movement is most revelatory about the attitudes of the professional group and the reformers, and most relevant to such questions as the proper role of the professional group and how best to meet the challenge of the times.

There is a great deal of documentary material available on all of the major reform efforts and their results, except the latest one—that represented by the Herter Report.[1] For this reason, the highlights of the reform movement will be discussed only in sufficient detail to distill the evolution of the significant issues and attitudes, with major attention reserved for the Herter Report and its aftermath. The necessary foundation is an overview of the creation of the career service and the important restatement of its charter which occurred in 1946.

[1] The monograph by Arthur G. Jones provides the most thorough coverage of the reform movement available in one volume: *The Evolution of Personnel Systems for U.S. Foreign Affairs,* Foreign Affairs Personnel Study No. 1 (New York: Carnegie Endowment for International Peace, 1965).

45

Background and Forces of Change

The modern Foreign Service was created by the Rogers Act of 1924. It was the joint product of two dedicated men, Congressman John Jacob Rogers of Massachusetts who labored in Congress for five years to produce the legislation, and Wilbur J. Carr, then Director of the Consular Service and subsequently Assistant Secretary of State for 13 years.[2]

The importance of the Act lay in two improvements which were the culmination of nearly 30 years of gradual reform. It combined the formerly separate Diplomatic and Consular Services into one service, officially called "The Foreign Service of the United States," and it created career conditions for that amalgamated service.

The Rogers Act designated permanent officers as "Foreign Service Officers" and confirmed the merit principle, including entrance by examination and a "suitable period of probation." Among other measures, it established titles and grades, provided for rank to be vested in the man and not in the position, called for maintenance of efficiency records, made allowance for a retirement system, and established a class of "non-career" vice consuls and clerks.[3] In short, the Act provided a fairly clear-cut charter for a permanent Foreign Service, free from political spoils. The salary scale, deliberately set higher than the Civil Service scale, represented a conscious effort to make it possible for a man to engage in a diplomatic career without the necessity of having a private income, an important step in the

2 Richard S. Patterson, "The Foreign Service: Four Decades of Development," *Department of State News Letter*, No. 39, July 1964, 3. This issue of the *News Letter* was devoted to commemorating "40 years of the Foreign Service." For the story of Carr's remarkable career see Katherine Crane, *Mr. Carr of State* (New York: St. Martin's Press, 1960).

3 For the text of the Rogers Act see U.S. Congress, House of Representatives, Committee on Foreign Affairs, *The Foreign Service Act of 1946, as amended to October 17, 1960.*

The System

"democratization" of the Service.[4] The merger of the two services into *the* Foreign Service clearly implied a monopoly in the foreign affairs field for the new entity and its home organization, the Department of State.

In a short time the Foreign Service Officer corps came to fulfill in most important respects the model of a career system the reformers had in mind. In Harold Stein's words, it became a "conscious and coherent group operating within but largely apart from the larger governmental structure. Usually called the 'Professional Service' or the 'Career Service' by its members, who look upon themselves primarily as 'political officers,' it has its own distinctive entrance and tenure procedures, its own salary system, its own traditions and group attitudes, its own sensitivity and code of privacy. It constitutes as it were a guild."[5]

There are other "career services" in the federal government. Frederick C. Mosher cites the Foreign Service, the military services, and the Public Health Service as representing the more pure examples.[6] They fulfill the "outward" characteristics of a career service as listed by Mosher: emphasis on entry at the bottom on the basis of a rigorous examination, selection based on career potential rather than on requirements for the first job, resistance to lateral entry, rank in the man rather than the position, career tenure and regular (if slow) advancement through the grades to the top if qualified, competition for advancement in the service with others of the same rank, a marked tendency

[4] For a discussion of the "democratization" of the Foreign Service see Warren Ilchman, *Professional Diplomacy in the United States, 1779-1939* (Chicago: Chicago University Press, 1961), Chapters 4 and 5. Also see Chapter 5 of this study.

[5] Harold Stein, "The Foreign Service Act of 1946," in Harold Stein, ed., *Public Administration and Policy Development: A Case Book* (New York: Harcourt, Brace, 1952), p. 664.

[6] Mosher, "Careers and Career Services in the Public Service," *Public Personnel Review*, Jan. 1963, pp. 46-51.

toward self-government, and strong esprit de corps. In addition to these outward characteristics, Mosher cites more fundamental ones: "historical backgrounds" that very often are ancient, "a rich body of tradition and a deep feeling of devotion on the part of members of the service toward the service," "a fairly strong resistance to disrupting factors that might upset revered traditions," an "element of risk attaching to the function" and a consequent stress upon discipline, and a "relatively heavy emphasis upon status distinctions."

Taken together, these characteristics begin to bear a strong resemblance to the characteristics of professional groups. Mosher completes the picture as follows: "One of the common features in the growth of career services has been the effort to look upon the work of the service as a professional enterprise, and to establish the image of the service itself as a legitimate, recognized profession, as diplomacy is conceived as a profession."

The Foreign Service has indeed taken on some of the symbolic trappings of the professional group, including the professional association (the American Foreign Service Association), the professional journal (the *Foreign Service Journal*), and such status symbols as Presidential commissions, diplomatic titles, and diplomatic passports.

Retired Ambassador Henry Villard captures much of the ambience of the Service in a single paragraph:

> The old service of the Rogers Act was frankly an elite corps. A superior education, a superior intellectual approach, a superior sense of responsibility and self-reliance, a superior flair for languages, all were important requisites for admission; those who made the grade took immense pride in their abilities and enjoyed a unique sense of

camaraderie, akin to that found in the congenial circles of a close-knit professional club.[7]

There are important differences between a career service and the general Civil Service. In the latter, entry can occur at any adult age and at any level, if qualifications are met, and rank adheres to the specific position, not to the individual. In a career service the individual normally enters at a young age and carries his rank with him to any job to which he may be assigned. The main reason why it was possible to adopt the career service concept—obviously the exception rather than the norm in the federal government—was probably the existence of a powerful example in the career diplomatic services of the European powers. In particular, the model the reformers had in mind was the British Foreign Service which possessed the strong generalist tradition of the British Administrative Class.

The idea of a unified Foreign Service to handle all U.S. foreign affairs abroad was broken in 1927 by creation of the Foreign Commerce Service for the Department of Commerce and in 1930 the Foreign Agricultural Service for the Department of Agriculture. But the concept was reaffirmed when these two services were transfered into the State Department's Foreign Service by President Franklin D. Roosevelt in Reorganization Plan No. II of 1939. This move brought 105 commercial attachés and nine agricultural attachés into the Foreign Service. On October 1, 1939 the Service numbered 833 career officers.[8]

A chaotic postwar situation and the recognition of inadequacies in prior legislation combined to generate the effort by Selden Chapin and a small group of other Foreign Service

[7] Villard, *Affairs at State* (New York: Thomas Y. Crowell, 1965), p. 152.
[8] Patterson, "The Foreign Service," p. 5.

Officers to achieve a new Act, an effort described and analyzed so thoroughly by Harold Stein in his case study. The
new Act was not the product of a reform movement as the
Rogers Act had been, and it in no way marked a significant
departure from the spirit of the Rogers Act. The effort was
more one of codifying previous legislation, of elaborating,
adding, perfecting. Although not without opposition, particularly from the Bureau of the Budget, the FSOs had their
way in nearly every important respect; in a "once and for
all" frame of mind, they achieved an Act which they felt
embodied the best of the past, incorporated changes regarded as necessary out of the 22 years of experience with
the career system since the Rogers Act, and equipped the
Foreign Service to deal flexibly with the future.

There also were important defensive reasons why the
FSOs felt that a vigorous restatement of the career service
in such an elaborate piece of legislation was necessary. The
Service had taken a distinct backseat during the war. Recruitment had ceased for the duration, and the bulk of expansion of civilian overseas activity in the intelligence, economic, and informational fields occurred in the temporary
wartime agencies, with the blessing of Secretary of State
Cordell Hull "who was anxious to preserve the Department
of State as a policy rather than an operating agency."[9] Stein
reports that career officers "widely believed that neither
Secretary Hull nor President Roosevelt had supported
them." Some 10,000 employees of the wartime agencies had
been transferred into State, compared to the 818 Foreign
Service Officers in the Service as of May 1, 1946. To these
FSOs, the "last crushing blow would be the blanketing in"
of the new people "who had not come up the 'hard way'
thus reenacting what one Foreign Service Officer described

[9] Stein, "Foreign Service Act of 1946," p. 665.

50

The System

as 'The Betrayal of 1939.' "[10] Finally, there was an under-
current of doubt discernible in Washington about the necessity of special status and a separate elite corps for foreign
affairs in the modern world.

Tangible evidence of the last point developed soon after
preliminary work of drafting the Act had been started by
the FSOs. James F. Byrnes became Secretary of State in July
of 1945 and immediately asked the Bureau of the Budget
for its advice on the organization of the Department. A report was delivered a month later, dealing largely with organizational questions and with the Departmental Service.
But its brief treatment of the Foreign Service was extremely
disturbing to the FSOs. Citing the "sharp distinction" between the Foreign Service and the "Departmental Service
in Washington, staffed by the regular Civil Service," the
report proposed steps that would lead to amalgamation of
the two to create "a thoroughly united organization." After
praising the Foreign Service, the report stated:

> Our government, however, has long since passed the
> stage in which a closed elite corps was the only alternative
> to patronage; and the staffing of a Foreign Service pre-
> dominantly with men whose whole career is spent abroad
> has revealed many serious weaknesses. Its members tend
> to lose touch with the views of the United States. Moving
> in restricted circles abroad, many have lost sensitivity also
> to some of the social forces and classes of peoples with
> whom they should be familiar in their role as the eyes
> and ears of the United States Government abroad. Many
> do not develop the specialized skills and the interest neces-
> sary to carry out the positive policies which our Govern-
> ment in the future may adopt. Moreover, differences in
> the character of the work performed abroad and at home

10 *Ibid.*

have been largely eliminated by the complete change in the character of world relations. Finally, the Civil Service today can provide adequate guarantees against patronage.[11]

The report had not been distributed within the Department, but its thrust became known to the FSOs. One can imagine the impact on a group characterized thusly by Stein: "To many Foreign Service officers, possibly to the majority, the need for a special corps was self-evident and needed no justification. The sense of dedication, of shared privilege and experience, was so strong, the feeling of participation in a profession set aside from the laity was so real, that the question of justification was frequently deemed unworthy of a reply."[12]

Attitudes similar to those in the Budget Bureau report and other reservations about the bill drafted by the FSOs were widely held by non-FSOs in the Department, such as the Assistant Secretary for Administration and the three assistant secretaries in charge of the new intelligence, economic, and information programs. There were serious reservations about numerous aspects in other Departments affected by the bill, notably Agriculture, Commerce, and Labor. Opposition in the Bureau to the general character of the bill and to many of its specific provisions was deepseated and severe. There was even opposition of another kind, from some FSOs who felt that some of the features of the bill were too liberal. How the FSOs who drafted the bill managed to steer it through these perilous waters to enactment, compromising only on relatively unimportant

[11] "The Organization and Administration of the Department of State," Report Submitted at the Request of the Secretary of State by the Director of the Bureau of the Budget, August 1945, p. 7.
[12] Stein, "Foreign Service Act of 1946," p. 674.

details and on none of the major features, makes a fascinating story in Stein's case study.

When it was all over, it was clear that two factors made their success possible. One was that the special subcommittee of the House Committee on Foreign Affairs got carried away with the project, adopted the bill as its own, and energetically worked for its passage. The other was that Secretary Byrnes had become identified with the bill, not so much through deep commitment and involvement, but because his new Assistant Secretary for Administration, an intimate friend, was determined to protect Byrnes and to "avoid any clash between the Secretary and the corps of Foreign Service officers."[13]

This was important throughout, but dramatically so at the last moment. After the bill had passed both houses of Congress unanimously right at the end of the session, with virtually no debate, President Harry S Truman seemed inclined to veto it on the basis of a memorandum from the Budget Bureau. The Bureau, still seriously in opposition and miffed at what it considered to be an end run by the FSOs, recommended approval but only after two pages of criticism of the bill. In the commemorative issue of the *News Letter* Byrnes told that he telephoned the President from Paris and urged him to sign the bill; the President "quickly agreed that Congress would react adversely if he vetoed a bill supported by his Secretary of State and adopted without a dissenting vote."[14]

The essentially conservative character of the Act is made clear in the following passage from the House report accompanying the bill:

The bill reflects an earnest re-examination by the Department of State of the place of a professional foreign service

13 *Ibid.*, p. 672.
14 *News Letter* (July 1964), p. 18.

in American foreign relations. It aspires to embody the best values selected from many judgments ranging from the one extreme, which postulates the progressive absorption of a separate service by the civil service, to the other, which adheres to the narrowest concept of "career" where participation or advice by other departments would be severely limited.

The bill is based upon the following fundamental principles:

The concept of a professional service should remain paramount.

A disciplined and mobile corps of trained men should be maintained through entry at the bottom on the basis of competitive examination and advancement by merit to positions of command.

Political influence should be excluded, while loyalty and esprit de corps should be sustained at a high level as essential elements in the efficient operation of the Service.

Compensation should be sufficient to attract able men regardless of the possession of private means.

These principles rest upon a foundation laid 40 years ago. They have been tested and proved by experience. It is the considered judgment of the Department that they afford the best basis for a sound and efficient service.[15]

Among the many modifications and changes, seven features of the Act may be singled out as having particular significance:

1. *The category system.* The Act created a category system of personnel organization in a more rationalistic and rigorous way than before. In addition to reconfirming the

[15] U. S. Congress, House of Representatives, *Reorganization of the Foreign Service*, Report of the Committee on Foreign Affairs to accompany H.R. 6,967, House Report No. 2,508, 79th Cong., 2nd Sess., July 12, 1946.

The System

FSO corps, two other categories were created—the Foreign Service Reserve (FSR) and the Foreign Service Staff (FSS), the Reserve for temporary specialists and the Staff for clerical, technical, and administrative personnel. The Reserve was given grades and pay identical to the FSO category but without tenure. The Staff picked up the old class of clerks, but went further in providing for higher-level technicians and specialists at grades and salaries analogous to the lower and middle FSO grades. This system not only protected the career principle but enhanced the elite character of the FSO corps by supplementing it with categories for temporary and subordinate employees.

2. *High-ranking positions.* Under previous legislation Foreign Service Officers had to resign from the career service if they were to be appointed ambassador or minister. The new Act changed the number of regular grades from eight to six and added a top rank of Career Minister, in order to "place the top rewards of a diplomatic career within the career itself rather than outside of it as at present."[16]

3. *Washington assignments.* There was a distinct shift in emphasis in regard to service by FSOs in the home office. Formerly they were near-expatriates. The Rogers Act provided only that FSOs "may be" assigned to Washington; the 1946 Act *required* that FSOs serve "not less than three years" of their first 15 years of service "in the continental United States." This shift may be attributed to a recognition of a need for greater "re-Americanization" of FSOs and probably to a view that, given the nature of decisions being made in Washington and the increased complexity of foreign affairs, more FSOs should be on hand to participate in Washington decision-making.

16 *Ibid.* In 1955 the Foreign Service Act was amended to add the topmost rank of Career Ambassador and to change the number of regular grades from six back to eight.

55

4. *Training*. Unlike the Civil Service, the Foreign Service was able to engage in in-service training as early as 1925 in its interpretation of the Rogers Act; indeed, there were sporadic and very modest training efforts prior to that time. But training remained very modest. It was not considered a necessary or even normal part of the traditional career development pattern of the FSO. As the House report accompanying the Act stated: "No training worthy of the name has been administered until recently; if the highly selected talents of the future Service are to be kept from atrophy a continuous program of in-service training must be directed by a strong central authority drawing on the best educational resources of the country."

The result was the Foreign Service Institute, created by the only title in the 1946 Act that represents in its entirety a clear innovation. The Institute was to be analogous to the military staff colleges; the FSOs rejected the military academy model as overspecialized.

5. *Selection-out*. Promoted particularly by Selden Chapin, the 1946 Act incorporated the rigorous approach to self-policing and pruning of a career service pioneered by the U.S. Navy in its "promotion-up or selection-out" system. The idea was that an officer would be "selected" for promotion to the next higher grade; if he was not so selected within a period of time to be determined administratively by the Secretary of State, he would automatically be selected-out.

6. *Lateral entry*. The resistance of a career service to lateral entry into the service at the middle or higher grades by outsiders has already been pointed out. Too much entry of this sort would do violence to the career principle, it was felt. On the other hand, all but the most pure of the careerists accept the need for at least minimal lateral entry

56

on several grounds—to avoid isolating the service from its environment completely, to help meet critics who charge creation of a privileged caste, and to provide flexibility in meeting new responsibilities that cannot be staffed quickly enough from the bottom. The 1946 Act spelled out the lateral-entry provisions more clearly than before, specifying examinations and a requirement of four years prior service in the "Service or in the Department or both" (reduced to three years if the applicant is over the age of 31).

7. *Internal administration.* Governing bodies of the Foreign Service were not set up by the Rogers Act but by executive order immediately following the Act. These included a Board of Foreign Service Personnel as the overall administrative entity and the Board of Examiners with jurisdiction over the entrance examination process. The considerably stronger provisions in the Foreign Service Act made it clear that the FSOs who drafted the bill "were thinking of a self-contained Career Service run by a special group within the Career Service, but equitably and efficiently."[17] The powers of the renamed Board of the Foreign Service were strengthened and the Board of Examiners was given a statutory basis. Most significant, active direction of the Foreign Service was entrusted to a Director General, to be appointed exclusively from among Career Ministers or Class 1 officers.

Aside from such issues as the wisdom of perpetuating a closed career system and the failure to move in a direction that would lead to amalgamation of Departmental and Foreign Service personnel, the self-government features of the 1946 Act were the most contentious. Summing up the Bureau of the Budget position, Stein says that the bill was seen as "objectionable because of its tendency to set up the

[17] Stein, "Foreign Service Act of 1946," p. 678.

Foreign Service as a quasi-independent organization for foreign affairs, when the need was for greater integration."[18] Despite the existence of sharply differing views on many issues, the issues were never really joined—there was no thorough confrontation, no great debate. Partly for this reason, as Stein points out several times, an atmosphere of suspicion and distrust grew up around many of the groups involved, particularly between the Foreign Service and Bureau of the Budget.

Views as strongly held as those discussed above were not likely to evaporate merely because the 1946 Act was passed. In a very short time, with the emergence of the cold war and the expansion of the foreign affairs establishment discussed in Chapter 1, the issues reemerged. If the 1946 Act had not been the product of a reform movement, as the Rogers Act had been, it helped generate a new reform movement that is still going on.

The reform movement has been so replete with major and minor studies and administrative actions that one can become quickly lost in a confusion of opinions and details. To help provide some guideposts, the major problem areas (all of them often interrelated) can be categorized as follows:

1. *A "unified" Foreign Service, problem no. 1.* The concept of a unified Foreign Service is applicable in two senses. The first refers to the amalgamation of all personnel in the Department of State, those in the Departmental Service (civil servants) *and* in the Foreign Service, into a single system. Short of amalgamation, the problem is one of the dual management of two quite different personnel systems within the same organization.

2. *A "unified" Foreign Service, problem no. 2.* In the second sense, a unified Foreign Service would be one em-

18 *Ibid.*, p. 725.

bracing all personnel engaged in overseas representation, not just those of the Department of State. This was the principle implicit in the Rogers Act, of which much was made when the foreign services of the Departments of Commerce and Agriculture were brought into State's Foreign Service in 1939. But, as we have seen, major new functions in foreign affairs have been established outside of State or have gravitated out. These functions can be said to participate in a "unified" system only in a marginal way. Whether inside or outside of State, they have been staffed by use of the temporary category (FSR) or the lower-status category (FSS) and have not been able to use the career category (FSO). While this issue was dealt with in the reform movement, it was not confronted in a major way until the Herter Report. The more salient issue in the earlier years was the amalgamation issue.

3. *Personnel requirements.* A great deal of attention has been paid in the reform movement to creating conditions that would attract and hold superior talent in all of the multifarious overseas activities of the U.S. in the postwar years. In the main, this has been a concern with functional specialization, with how to make a system in which the generalist concept has dominated into a suitable vehicle for varieties of specialized talents. Many proposals in such areas as recruitment, selection, training, career development, assignment, and promotion are basically addressed to the specialist-generalist issue. Area specialization has also been a prominent concern, and more recently (particularly in the Herter Report) the problem of developing managerial talent has been dealt with as a major issue.

4. *Organizational improvements.* Some of the studies have been as much concerned or more with the organization of the State Department and the foreign affairs community as they have been with the personnel system. Many times, the

two impinge upon one another in important respects. In the main, this area of concern is substance for the next chapter.

5. *Managerial improvements.* Here and there the studies deal with management problems, proposing improvements in such areas as interagency coordination, policy planning, programming methods, research, use of modern technology. This area is also reserved largely for the next chapter.

The first major study occurred as part of the first Hoover Commission's massive review of the executive branch in 1949. The commission was disturbed by "cleavages" in the Department of State—between the Departmental Service and the Foreign Service, headquarters and the field posts, functional bureaus and geographic bureaus. It was concerned that the provisions of the Foreign Service Act of 1946 separated the Secretary of State from a clear chain of command over the Foreign Service.

In the area of personnel its major recommendation was for amalgamation: "The personnel in the permanent State Department establishment in Washington and the personnel of the Foreign Service above certain levels should be amalgamated over a short period of years into a single foreign affairs service obligated to serve at home or overseas and constituting a safeguarded career group administered separately from the general Civil Service."[19]

The commission proposed a four-category system. It would have added another career officer category for specialists, keeping the FSO category intact for generalists and the Reserve for temporary specialists. The Staff would be cut down to strictly a clerical level category.

The commission took the view that the State Department

[19] *Foreign Affairs: A Report to the Congress by the Commission on Organization of the Executive Branch of the Government* (Washington: GPO, Feb. 1949) , p. 61.

60

should be concerned with policy and not with operations: "The State Department as a general rule should not be given responsibility for the operation of specific programs, whether overseas or at home."[20]

Organizationally, the commission termed the regional bureaus in State the "action units" and stressed that the Department's organization should be regional to the maximum extent possible, with the functional bureaus being reduced to small staffs. In its concern with transfering administrative power from the FSO corps to the Secretary of State the commission proposed abolishing the position of Director General of the Foreign Service and removing the statutory basis for the Board of the Foreign Service and the Board of Examiners.

The organizational recommendations were acted on quickly by the Department in what came to be known as the "Reorganization of 1949." The regional bureaus were strengthened, a single Office of Personnel was created, and administrative powers were vested in the Secretary of State by Public Law 73 of the 81st Congress. The law did not eliminate the office of the Director General, as recommended by the commission, but stripped it of power and reduced it to a staff advisory role. On the amalgamation issue, Deputy Under Secretary for Administration John Peurifoy explained to Congress that "authorizing legislation cannot be drafted until a more thorough study has been made and detailed plans prepared." He anticipated transmitting legislation to Congress "early in calendar 1950."[21]

In December 1949 Secretary of State Dean Acheson appointed a three-man committee to conduct a study and ad-

20 *Ibid.*, p. 32.
21 U. S. Congress, Senate, *Progress on Hoover Commission Recommendations*, Report of the Committee on Expenditures in the Executive Departments, Senate Report No. 1,158, 81st Cong., 1st Sess., Oct. 12, 1949, p. 129.

vise him if "fundamental changes are required in the personnel systems and relationships of the Department of State and the Foreign Service."[22] James H. Rowe, who had been one of the 12 members of the Hoover Commission, was designated chairman. The other two members were Robert Ramspeck, former Congressman and Chairman of the Civil Service Commission, and William DeCourcy, a career Foreign Service Officer.

A thorough report was delivered eight months later, with 20 recommendations aiming toward "a unified foreign affairs service and a positive personnel program." The report proposed "a single but flexible personnel system for the Department of State and the Foreign Service instead of the separate systems that exist at present." Two categories were proposed (instead of four as in the Hoover Report), a Foreign Affairs Officer category and a Foreign Affairs Clerical and Technical category. Temporary appointments would be possible, eliminating the need for the Reserve category. In contrast to the Hoover Commission, the Rowe Report stated that it was not necessary for everyone in the new system to be under an obligation to serve both at home and abroad. It estimated that there were about 1,500 Departmental positions for which overseas experience was essential or desirable. The system should be a nonpolitical career system administered outside of the Civil Service system, but the report said that this recommendation was made "without prejudice" to the possibility that improvement and development of the Civil Service system might make it suitable for foreign affairs at some future time. The report stressed the human factor, and indicated that the amalgamation should be done carefully and humanely over a substantial period of time.

[22] "An Improved Personnel System for the Conduct of Foreign Affairs," A Report to the Secretary of State by the Secretary's Advisory Committee on Personnel, August 1950, p. A-1.

The System

In its "positive personnel program" the Committee's recommendations displayed a concern for the need to attract and retain topflight specialized talent in such fields as economics, agriculture, public affairs, administration, and political affairs. The report proposed options in the basic examination process for these fields, occupational groupings in the promotion system, liberalized lateral entry procedures, and a systematic program of career development based on estimates of need for executives, generalists, functional specialists, and area specialists.

During this period the amalgamation issue became a subject of considerable debate. The Rowe Committee had commissioned the National Opinion Research Center to do an attitude survey on the question. The results showed that "81 per cent of the Civil Service officers, 76 per cent of the Foreign Service Staff officers, and 59 per cent of the Foreign Service officers" thought amalgamation "desirable from the viewpoint of the conduct of the foreign affairs of the United States." Looking at the issue from a personal point of view, however, "the number who are neutral or undecided rises sharply." The survey showed that "60 per cent of the total number of Departmental employees place some kind of restriction on their availability for overseas assignment." The pages of the *Foreign Service Journal* were replete with articles, editorials, and letters to the editor on the subject. There was no monolithic "group-think" operating in the FSO corps—FSOs lined up on both sides of the question. It seems fair to say, however, that opinion among the more senior officers who concerned themselves with running the Service was preponderantly negative, or at least extremely cautious. Some opposed amalgamation outright; others made proposals that would either make the amalgamation only partial or so slow to come to pass that it might pass away. A good example of this is a memorandum sent by the Executive Committee of the American Foreign Service Association to the Deputy Under Secretary for Administration. The memorandum urged meeting some of the Rowe Committee's criticisms and recommendations through more flexible use of the Foreign Service Act of 1946 which was based on "many years of experience" and should not be "jettisoned." The position was taken that "wholesale unification of personnel systems" would be "harmful" and that it would be "inadvisable for the Department to embark on a broad program of experimentation at this time."

After eight months of study of the Rowe Report, the Department announced a "Personnel Improvement Program" in the form of a directive from the Deputy Under Secretary for Administration to the Director of Personnel. It covered a great many points, but on the central issue of amalgamation it was clear that the Department had rejected the single service idea. Instead, it announced more liberalized opportunities for Departmental employees to enter the FSO corps laterally, aiming particularly for those employees who occupied positions regarded as interchangeable. It was the Department's position that the experience gained on this limited program would help determine whether any further steps were necessary and feasible. Rather than a clear and determined policy to achieve a single service, the matter was left to the voluntary decisions of individual employees. In the words of Snyder and Furniss, "From all the mighty rumblings emerged a timid mouse."[23]

An editorial in the *Foreign Service Journal* praised the program, paraphrasing the arguments of the Executive Committee memorandum cited earlier. The editorial said the decision was "courageous and realistic," and that it took the "only course which could be implemented without costly disruption of morale and efficiency in a time when all of

[23] Richard Snyder and Edgar Furniss, Jr., *American Foreign Policy* (New York: Rinehart & Co., 1956), p. 285.

64

The System

us in foreign affairs need to have undivided attention concentrated on our jobs."[24] In letters to the *Journal* many officers opposed even the limited program, particularly junior officers who felt that increased lateral entry would hold back their own advancement.[25]

The "Personnel Improvement Program" was viewed critically in editorials in the *New York Times* and *Washington Star*, by the Budget Bureau, by the Brookings Institution in a 380-page report on administration of foreign affairs prepared in 1951 for the Bureau, and by the Wriston Report.[26] Although more than 2,000 persons applied for lateral entry, the Wriston Committee found that three years later only 25 had actually been taken into the FSO corps, which it termed "a miserable showing."[27]

The Brookings study saw as the "main limitation" of the Hoover Commission recommendation for an amalgamated foreign service "its failure to take the whole problem of overseas personnel into account." The study said that the Rowe Report "shares the limitation of the Hoover Commission" because the Rowe Committee "interpreted its assignment as being limited to consideration of the personnel problems of the Department of State and the Foreign Service."[28]

Actually, the Brookings study had been contracted for by

[24] *Foreign Service Journal* (April 1951), p. 24.
[25] See various issues of the *Journal*: May 1951, pp. 11-12, July 1951, pp. 23ff., Sept. 1951, pp. 30ff.
[26] *New York Times*, Apr. 19, 1951; *Washington Star*, Apr. 18, 1951. The reference for the Brookings study is *Administration of Foreign Affairs and Overseas Operations*, Report prepared for the Bureau of the Budget, Executive Office of the President (Washington: GPO, June 1951), hereafter referred to as the 1951 Brookings Study (to distinguish it from a similar study made by Brookings in 1960).
[27] U.S. Department of State, *Toward a Stronger Foreign Service*, Report to the Secretary of State's Public Committee on Personnel, Department of State Publication No. 5,458, June 1954, p. 19, hereafter cited as Wriston Report.
[28] 1951 Brookings Study, pp. 298-99.

the Bureau of the Budget by way of following up on the Hoover Report. In a large sense, the Brookings study has its roots in the Bureau of the Budget's own 1945 study, taking the same basic view but with much more elaborate exposition. The Brookings approach on personnel is clear in the following: "There is need for development of a long-range program involving new basic personnel legislation, which would contemplate the creation of a foreign affairs personnel system inclusive of all, or nearly all, civilian foreign affairs staffs at home and abroad."[29]

In its chapter on personnel, the Brookings study develops this and related recommendations and discusses alternatives thoroughly. This, then, is the first major exposition of the idea of a unified Foreign Service in the sense of a system that would cover all significant civilian activities abroad as well as embrace both home and overseas staffs of all the agencies involved. However, as Arthur Jones points out, "There is no indication that the State Department modified its personnel practices to any significant degree as a consequence of the Brookings study, and no steps were taken to make statutory changes in existing overseas personnel arrangements."[30]

As noted in Chapter 1, the distinction between policy and operations, although not invented by the Eisenhower Administration, was highlighted as a rationale for separating operational programs from the State Department. When Reorganization Plans 7 and 8 of 1953 created the U.S. Information Agency and the Foreign Operations Administration, thus separating the information and aid programs from the Department of State, it was explicitly recognized that the matter of personnel systems was unfinished business. In his message to Congress accompanying the reorganization

[29] *Ibid.*, p. 325.
[30] Jones, *Evolution of Personnel Systems*, p. 122.

66

plans, President Eisenhower mentioned the need for a reappraisal of the personnel systems for foreign affairs.[31] For this purpose, a White House Personnel Task Force was constituted, drawing together experts from several agencies under the leadership of Philip Young, who served in a dual role as Chairman of the Civil Service Commission and the President's Adviser on Personnel Management.

Clearly the White House Task Force took a leaf from the Brookings study; in fact, the latter had specifically recommended a White House group:

> We therefore favor the designation or appointment, within the Executive Office of the President, of an administrative assistant to the President who would devote himself intensively to the problems of foreign affairs personnel administration for a period of 1 to 3 years, with the assistance of a small high-quality supporting staff. It would be the initial assignment of this unit to develop the necessary legislative proposals in consultation with interested agencies and to be of assistance during the period of the congressional consideration. Upon the enactment of basic legislation, the unit would concern itself with the preparation of such Executive orders and foreign affairs personnel regulations as would then be needed. Thereafter the future of the unit would be subject to reconsideration, taking into account such progress as may have occurred in the general development of the central personnel institutions of the Government.[32]

The last sentence is reminiscent of the 1945 Bureau of the Budget study and the Hoover Commission Report, in hinting at the possibility that eventual development of both

---

[31] Full texts of Reorganization Plans 7 and 8, plus President Eisenhower's letters of transmittal to Congress, may be found in U.S. Department of State, *Bulletin*, Vol. xxviii, No. 729 (June 15, 1953), 849-56.
[32] 1951 Brookings Study, p. 326.

foreign affairs and domestic personnel systems might make possible a merger of the two. Or, the "future of the unit" quite possibly could be as a kind of counterpart to the Civil Service Commission for foreign affairs. In fact, as an early step, Young wrote a letter to the heads of 14 departments and agencies, saying it was of "great importance that overseas employees be made an integral part of the whole Federal civilian career system." He expressed the need for "some central agency" to be designated to see that "standards are maintained and the system uniformly administered."[33] Also, the White House Task Force took the same route as did the Brookings study in proposing a unified foreign affairs personnel system which "would apply initially to the State Department, USIA, and the Foreign Operations Administration," and which could be extended by executive order "to new foreign affairs agencies, or to employees of other existing agencies engaged in foreign affairs work."[34] However, as Jones points out, not only was the report of the White House group never published, but "there is no indication that the Eisenhower administration took any action on the report."[35] The effort merely faded away. In retrospect, it seems rather clear that the White House effort was upstaged by the fast action of the Wriston Committee and of the State Department in implementing the Wriston Report, although Philip Young went on record to Congress as saying that the two efforts were not in conflict but were complementary.[36]

33 Young's letter appears in U.S. Congress, House of Representatives, *Foreign Service and Departmental Personnel Practices of the Department of State*, Hearings before the International Operations Subcommittee of the Committee on Government Operations, 83rd Cong., 1st Sess., 1953, pp. 96-97.
34 Jones, *Evolution of Personnel Systems*, p. 100.
35 *Ibid.*, p. 102.
36 U.S. Congress, House of Representatives, *Administration of Overseas Personnel*, Hearings before a subcommittee of the Committee on

The System

Because it was vigorously implemented, the story of the Wriston Report could easily fill a volume by itself. Indeed, it has been much commented on and written about.[37] For present purposes, it will suffice to recite the main facts and analyze briefly why the Report was implemented and what effects it has had.

Secretary of State John Foster Dulles established the Public Committee on Personnel, chaired by Dr. Wriston, in March of 1954, and asked that its report be submitted by May of the same year. The terms of reference signed by Under Secretary Walter Bedell Smith seemed to indicate determination to achieve action this time. The Committee was asked to make recommendations "to strengthen the effectiveness of the professional service to a standard consistent with the vastly increasing responsibilities in the field of foreign policy which have devolved upon the President and the Secretary." The terms of reference mentioned the Hoover Commission, the Rowe Committee, and "other groups," and the fact that despite the 1951 directive the earlier recommendations "have not been fully carried out." As its "primary objective," the new Committee was asked to review the prior studies, "particularly as they relate to the merging of Departmental Civil Service personnel into the Foreign Service to the end that the Department and its establishments abroad may be staffed to the maximum possible extent by career personnel, specially trained for the conduct of foreign relations and obligated to serve at home or abroad, thus providing a stronger and more broadly based Foreign Service." The Committee was also asked to keep

Government Operations, 84th Cong., 1st Sess., Sept. 14, 16, and Dec. 15, 1955, pp. 453-526.

[37] Perhaps the most thorough description is in Jones, *Evolution of Personnel Systems*, Chapter 6. Also see Zara S. Steiner, "The State Department and the Foreign Service," Memorandum No. 16, Princeton University Center of International Studies, Mar. 26, 1958.

Background and Forces of Change

its recommendations within the context of the 1946 Act rather than proposing a new charter for the Foreign Service.[38]

The Committee delivered its report in May, and its main proposals lay within its very limited terms of reference. In fairly strong language the Report castigated the State Department for failing to implement the 1951 directive, and for less than adequate recruitment, training, lateral entry, personnel planning, and assignment practices. It saw as major needs a larger service, more Washington exposure for Foreign Service Officers, a broadened base of recruitment, and much greater emphasis on specialization within the FSO corps.

Despite the critical tone, the Report delivered what the terms of reference asked for on the key issue of amalgamation. In its review of prior studies, the Report said that all had agreed on three fundamental points: (a) the diplomatic service should not be absorbed by the general Civil Service; (b) the Foreign Service should not be absorbed into a generalized "foreign affairs corps" staffing the 24 governmental departments and agencies that have American personnel abroad; and (c) above a certain level a single personnel system should cover all Departmental and Foreign Service personnel insofar as that is at all practicable.[39]

This is a somewhat spotty reading of the record. As we have seen, the 1945 Bureau of the Budget study, the Hoover Commission report, and the 1951 Brookings study at least hinted toward the first point above as an eventual possibility. More importantly, the idea of a single system for the *main* foreign affairs agencies, as proposed by the Brookings Study and the White House Task Force, was not mentioned. Finally, the qualifying phrase in the third point ("insofar

[38] Wriston Report, Appendix 1, pp. 59-60.
[39] *Ibid.*, p. 25.

70

as that is at all practicable," which echoes the qualification in the terms of reference—"to the maximum extent possible") differs basically from what the Rowe Committee said. It had recommended a single system for *all* State Department personnel and had specifically warned against a partial or limited program of amalgamation.

This, in fact, is what the Wriston Committee recommended—a limited program—and it quite accurately used the term "integration" rather than "amalgamation." Its proposal was essentially a restatement of the 1951 directive: "Integration as proposed by this Committee is a program for transferring many but not all Departmental, Reserve, and Staff Officers into the Foreign Service Officer Corps." This was to be done by designating positions in Washington which require foreign and domestic experience as "Foreign Service" positions and taking the Civil Service incumbents into the FSO corps. Abroad, Staff and Reserve personnel doing work that could be considered at the officer level would also be taken in. The FSS category would then be used for personnel "of lower than officer rank," the Reserve would be used primarily for temporary specialists "to deal with unique problems," and the Civil Service would be restricted to the nondesignated positions. At the same time, bottom-entry recruitment into the FSO corps would be expanded.

Minor legislative changes necessary to make the plan workable were quickly obtained and the Department vigorously implemented the recommendations. Bottom-entry recruitment was expanded and between 1954 and 1958 more than 1,500 persons entered the FSO corps laterally from the other three categories. By these means, the size of the corps was nearly tripled.

Much as the Rowe Committee survey had ascertained, most of the employees accepted the plan in general, but

71

there were individual misgivings. Some thought they would not be able to make full use of their specialized abilities in the FSO corps; others did not like the idea of class-wide competition for promotion and the possibility of selection-out; civil servants who had never intended to live abroad now found themselves obligated to do so; many FSOs thought the quality of the service was being diluted and that their own promotions would be held back. Nevertheless, most went along with the plan. The tenor of the Report and the vigor of its implementation made integration seem mandatory, or very nearly so. Those who resisted accepted a ceiling on promotions.

The reasons for large-scale action occurring this time and not before would seem to be:

1. Instead of disappearing, the reform pressure was building up, and it was doubtless concluded in the Department that something had to be done sooner or later. Particularly, the failure of the 1951 directive was an embarrassment.

2. The Department and the Service were in a dire situation. The budget had been cut and bottom-entry recruitment had ceased entirely for two years. A devastating reduction-in-force had just occurred. The Department and the Service were under attack from Senator Joseph McCarthy. Some of the problems that previously could be debated now seemed very real—constraints on specialization, inability to rotate FSOs into jobs held by civil servants, the small size of the FSO corps which had grown only in pace with the creation of new overseas posts and not in pace with the addition of new functions in foreign affairs.

3. The almost compelling conclusion is that the Wriston recommendations were rushed through to forestall what might have been much stronger medicine emerging from the White House Task Force.

The Wriston program was disruptive to many persons

The System

and controversial; yet, on the whole, it was undeniably beneficial to the State Department and the Foreign Service. The latter was at low ebb and the Wriston program clearly had a rejuvenating effect. In 1954, the Wriston Report stated, only 119 positions in Washington were occupied by FSOs. After Wristonization, more than 800 FSOs will be found serving in Washington positions at any given time. There has been much greater attention to specialization. Wristonization provided a much-needed source of executive talent to the FSO corps.[40]

Yet the controversy lingered. As recently as 1962 Senator Claiborne Pell of Rhode Island, a former FSO, could speak of "unscrambling the omelet of Wristonization." He entered into the *Congressional Record* a bitter attack on the Wriston program written by a retired FSO, William P. Cochran, Jr., entitled: "Our Third-Rate Diplomacy: Is it Good Enough?"[41] Cochran presented a picture of an FSO corps virtually destroyed by a massive infusion of mediocrity. He wrote: "Official apologists for Wristonization state that (like castor oil) it had to be swallowed, or the Foreign Service would have been destroyed. They aver that the Wriston program was a defensive, holding operation, and that nothing else would have been effective in the face of the high-powered campaign by the civil service to swallow and absorb the Foreign Service. Perhaps. But it is difficult to imagine how even complete abolishment of the Foreign Service could have been any more destructive to its morale and its structure."

Cochran may have been right about the essentially defensive character of the Wriston program, but he grossly exaggerated its impact. The FSO system and its dominant

[40] John E. Harr, *The Anatomy of the Foreign Service*, Foreign Affairs Personnel Study No. 4 (New York: Carnegie Endowment for International Peace, 1965), Chapter 6, "Foreign Affairs Executives."

[41] U.S. Congress, *Congressional Record*, Vol. 109 (Mar. 14, 1963), 3,977 and 4,193-96.

mores were not changed basically at all by the Wriston program, as we shall see in detail in later chapters.

Generally, a much more moderate attitude toward the Wriston program is now prevalent among FSOs, which might be summarized as follows: "The Wriston Program was probably necessary and it had some good effects, but it went too far." That is, too many persons were brought in without the educational background and experience necessary to compete successfully in the class-wide promotion system of the FSO corps. In the main, these were former Staff Corps personnel in the various administrative sub-specialties. Unable to move out of the low-status jobs, many employees had difficulty getting promoted thus exposing them to the danger of selection-out. To remedy this situation the Department has been engaged in an effort to "revitalize" the Staff corps and to bring back into it many former Staff people who were Wristonized.[42]

The Wriston effort did have the effect of buying time for the State Department and the Foreign Service by effectively dampening the reform movement. With all the energetic activity going on in the State Department during the Wristonization period, there would seem to be little point in proposing grander schemes. As noted, the White House Task Force faded away. USIA began a series of unsuccessful efforts to obtain legislation for its own career service, quite separate from that of the State Department's.[43] USIA's problem was that its overseas service of approximately 1,000 officers was staffed by using a category (FSR) limited by law to appointments of five years and reappointments of a second five years.

[42] U.S. Department of State, "New Staff Corps Policy Announced by Department," *News Letter*, No. 10 (Feb. 1962), 14.

[43] USIA's efforts in the 84th, 85th, and 86th Congresses are described in John E. Harr, "Key Administrative Problems of the United States Information Agency," unpublished Master's Thesis, Department of Political Science, the University of Chicago, 1961, Chapter 5, "The Problem of Personnel."

The System

By the mid-1950s USIA had hundreds of officers who had passed the 10-year limit. It kept these officers employed by the device of attaching a rider to its annual appropriations bill extending their appointments another year. For the aid program, this problem was ameliorated, if not solved by a clause carried in succeeding authorizing legislation allowing Reserve appointments "for the duration of operations under the Act."[44] In 1960 the Brookings Institution made its second major study of overseas operations, the personnel proposals of which were much milder than in its 1951 study. Although Brookings' main proposal was for an enlarged department of foreign affairs to include the information and aid programs, it supported the notion that these programs should seek their own career services "on a relatively independent basis" but with the "ultimate goal" of a "single service" in mind.[45]

Because the Wriston program did not solve the problem of administering two separate personnel systems in the State Department, did not extend career status to employees of the information and aid programs, and did not fundamentally alter the FSO system, it was inevitable that some of the problems it addressed would reemerge and perhaps inevitable that the reform movement would revive. A strong contributing factor was the aura of activism and ferment in foreign affairs brought in by the Kennedy administration. Scarcely anyone could doubt that the information and aid programs were now permanent fixtures. New programs were being created. Most important, the reversal of the "policy

[44] See, for example, Sec. 625 (d) (2) of the Foreign Assistance Act of 1961, in U.S. Congress, *Legislation on Foreign Relations*, joint committee print of the Senate Committee on Foreign Relations and the House Committee on Foreign Affairs, 89th Cong., 2nd Sess., Jan. 21, 1966, p. 55.
[45] H. Field Haviland, Jr. *et al.*, *The Formulation and Administration of United States Foreign Policy* (Washington: The Brookings Institution, 1960), p. 125; hereafter cited as 1960 Brookings Study.

operations" dichotomy and the clear indication that the president expected the State Department to manage both, and his clear expectation that ambassadors would fully manage their multi-agency missions, created a need for a new look.

These were the conditions that led to discussions in 1961, resulting in the establishment of the Herter Committee for the full calendar year 1962, at the end of which it produced its report. The Herter Committee differed from all the previous studies in that it was unofficial and privately sponsored, although its liaison with key officials in the three main foreign affairs agencies was very close. It was thought that private sponsorship would give the Committee greater freedom and its report greater impact. Three foundations supported the effort—the Ford Foundation, the Rockefeller Brothers Fund, and the Carnegie Endowment for International Peace. The latter was to actively administer the effort, with its President, Joseph E. Johnson, formerly a State Department official on the Policy Planning Staff, serving as one of the 12 members of the Committee. In Congressional testimony Johnson described the genesis of the effort as follows:

> In early 1961, at the request of Secretary Rusk, the Endowment undertook responsibility for a study of foreign affairs personnel, and I worked closely with Mr. William J. Crockett, then Assistant Secretary of State for Administration, in planning the study. Thanks to Mr. Rusk's support, I succeeded in persuading former Secretary of State Herter to accept the chairmanship of the Committee, the other members of which were chosen in consultation with Mr. Herter. I am glad to be able to say that every person whom we asked to serve shared with Secretaries Rusk and Herter and myself the view that this

76

was an important assignment and accordingly accepted the invitation to join the Committee. The Committee was very fortunate in obtaining the services of Prof. Frederick C. Mosher of the University of California at Berkeley as Staff Director. Dr. Mosher, who is here with me today, put together an excellent and dedicated staff.[46]

In addition to Herter and Johnson, other members of the Committee had extensive experience in foreign affairs. James Rowe had served on the Hoover Commission and chaired the Rowe Committee. John Hay Whitney had been Ambassador to the United Kingdom and a member of the Wriston Committee. George Allen was a retired Career Ambassador who twice had headed the information program. James H. Smith, Jr., was a former head of the aid program. Carlisle Humelsine had been Deputy Under Secretary for Administration in State at the time of the Rowe Report and the 1951 directive. Don K. Price and Milton Katz, both of Harvard, were recognized scholars and advisers in foreign affairs.

With a year in which to work, the Committee could be painstaking and thorough in its approach. It met, on the average, almost once a month, with the staff carrying on between meetings. Unlike most previous studies, its focus was on the entire field of foreign affairs instead of only the Department of State, but primarily on the three main agencies —State, USIA, and the Agency for International Development (AID). The Committee concentrated on personnel, but felt it necessary to go beyond this to questions of management and organization in several of its recommendations

[46] U.S. Congress, House of Representatives, *Foreign Service Act Amendments of 1965*, Hearings before the Subcommittee on State Department Organization and Foreign Operations of the Committee on Foreign Affairs, 89th Cong., 1st Sess., May 19, 20, and 25, July 13 and 14, 1965, pp. 33-34; hereafter referred to as Hays Bill Hearings, House.

in order to effectuate its major recommendations for personnel.

As noted in Chapter 1, the Herter Committee took the position that a new diplomacy had come into being; it consciously aimed its recommendations toward creating the conditions necessary to insure the best possible conduct of that new diplomacy. The report echoed the new Administration in stressing the leadership role of the Department of State over the whole spectrum of foreign affairs, including policy formulation and execution. The first of its 43 recommendations defined this leadership role and called for "strengthening" the Department to exercise it. Of the remaining recommendations, the major ones (with the Herter Report's recommendation numbers in parentheses) may be singled out as follows:

1. *Executive Under Secretary (2).* This new position, third in rank in the Department, was to provide continuity in management, and the incumbent was to concentrate on interagency coordination of policy and operations.

2. *A Programming System (3).* The Report recommended that under the leadership of the Executive Under Secretary the Department take the lead in developing a system to link policy, programs, budget, and manpower, as a major tool in the interagency coordination of policies and programs.

3. *A "Family" of Compatible Career Services (6).* Recommendations 4 and 5 proposed career services for the information and aid programs, and recommendation 6 proposed that these and State's Foreign Service constitute a "family" of compatible career services. It was clear that the Committee had in mind not rigid compartmentalizing, but rather very close relationships. The bulk of its later recommendations were devoted to insuring compatibility rather than compartmentalizing in such ideas as joint basic recruitment, provisions for interchange, a "pool" of senior officers from

the three services to fill executive posts, an interagency board chaired by the Executive Under Secretary.

4. *Amalgamation (8)*. The Committee had in mind a new personnel system, operating outside of the Civil Service system, to which all employees of the three agencies would belong. Civil servants to be brought into the foreign affairs system would not be obligated to serve abroad, but future recruitment would stress availability for overseas service. Close relationships with the Civil Service Commission were stressed, as well as the possibility of an interchange agreement between the two systems.

5. *Manpower planning (12)*. As a foundation for many of its other recommendations, the Committee urged that manpower planning machinery be devised, "a system for estimating, as far in the future and as specifically as possible, the numbers and kinds of people who will be needed by the foreign affairs agencies."

6. *A National Foreign Affairs College (32)*. The Committee proposed establishment of a graduate-level institution to replace the Foreign Service Institute, and to differ from the Institute in a number of ways, including "semi-autonomous" status, an image of representing the entire foreign affairs community instead of only the Department of State, a higher-level academic core group, and educational offerings better designed to meet the needs of the new diplomacy.

The Committee's final three recommendations constituted a "course of action" to bring its program into effect, calling for legislation, administrative action, and stepped-up interagency personnel research. The legislation would include a measure authorizing the position of Executive Under Secretary, a bill creating the National Foreign Affairs College, and a bill creating the personnel system, to be called the "Foreign Affairs Personnel Act of 1963."

There were to be major efforts to implement the Herter

Report, extending over a four-year period. The action was not to be clear and decisive as in the Wriston Program, but much more complex and difficult. One fundamental recommendation fell by the wayside almost immediately. In January 1963, just after the Herter Report was published, Secretary of State Dean Rusk hosted a luncheon for the Committee members. He congratulated the Committee on its work and said that he and his colleagues in the Department of State would study the Report and do their utmost to implement it. But he made it clear that he did not support the recommendation proposing the new post of Executive Under Secretary. He did not elaborate on the reasons.

Throughout most of 1962, the Herter Committee Staff Director and the key members of the Committee worked in very close association with the three State Department officials most directly concerned: Roger W. Jones, Deputy Under Secretary for Administration (fifth-ranking position in the Department) ; William J. Crockett, Assistant Secretary for Administration, who had been instrumental in starting the whole effort; and Herman Pollack, Director of Personnel. In the hierarchy, Pollack reported to Crockett, who in turn reported to Jones. Jones was so supportive of the effort that his unexpected departure in the fall of 1962 was disturbing to Committee members. His replacement, William H. Orrick, Jr., a San Francisco lawyer who had been active in the Kennedy campaign, was brought over to State from the Department of Justice. Orrick gave major responsibility for implementing the Report to Pollack, leaving Crockett to handle day-to-day administration of the Department.

Pollack set up a series of task forces organized around the Herter Committee recommendations, topped by a Steering Committee with himself as chairman, and a Policy Committee with Orrick as Chairman. There were representatives of other interested agencies on the task forces and committees. Throughout the spring of 1963 the task forces worked to produce their voluminous reports; for example, the report of the Task Force on Personnel Research (Recommendation No. 43) ran to 48 single-spaced pages.

Meanwhile, along other channels, the effort to create a new educational institution for foreign affairs proceeded. The White House was interested in this idea. In fact, President Kennedy had established a separate five-man committee in May 1962, which came to be known as the "President's Advisory Panel on a National Academy of Foreign Affairs," or the "Perkins Committee," after its chairman, James A. Perkins, vice president of the Carnegie Corporation. Two of the five members, Perkins and Don K. Price, were also members of the Herter Committee. This group produced its proposal for a National Academy on December 17, 1962, almost the same day the Herter Report, with its proposal for a National College, became available. The two proposals basically were similar, with the Perkins version being some-what more elaborate. The drafting of legislation began al-most immediately, springing more directly from the Perkins Report than from the Herter Report. Sen. Stuart Symington and 19 cosponsors introduced a bill for a "National Acad-emy of Foreign Affairs Act of 1963" on February 20, 1963, and presented a letter of transmittal from President Kenne-dy and a memorandum from Secretary Rusk, both of whom urged passage of the bill.[47] The bill was assigned to the For-eign Relations Committee, where it ultimately died, despite strong support during hearings by many prominent persons, including members of the Perkins and Herter Committees.

One reason for the bill's demise undoubtedly was that no further effort was expended by the White House. Presi-

[47] U.S. Congress, *Congressional Record*, Vol. 109 (Feb. 20, 1963), 2,459-62.

dent Kennedy was having difficulty getting anything passed by Congress during this period; the bill for an academy was necessarily given low priority. Also, Sen. Symington, because he preferred another kind of academy for foreign affairs— an undergraduate one on the model of the military academies—was not the ideal sponsor. He had introduced bills for such an academy in previous sessions of Congress and had found little support, none whatsoever from the executive branch.[48] The major reason for failure of the Academy bill, however, was probably the serious doubts entertained by Sen. J. William Fulbright of Arkansas and Congressman Wayne Hays of Ohio about the viability of academic freedom and semi-autonomous status for an institution to be subsidized by the Government and to be necessarily so close to foreign policy formulation.[49] These two powerful men, one the chairman of the Senate Foreign Relations Committee and the other chairman of the subcommittee of the House Committee on Foreign Affairs dealing with State Department organization and foreign operations, also felt strongly that most training could best be obtained on the campuses of American universities and that therefore the framework of the Foreign Service Institute was adequate and could be improved to meet other needs. Thus another of the major Herter Committee recommendations failed.

In the spring of 1963 an important change took place. Orrick had no previous experience in foreign affairs, and it had become clear that the man and the job were not suited to one another. He resigned and Crockett was moved up to

[48] For Symington's earlier views see his article in *This Week Magazine*, "Let's Have a West Point for Diplomats," Aug. 2, 1959, pp. 8-9.

[49] The Perkins Report had stressed that "faculty must be permitted to write and speak under their own names and responsibility on questions fraught with sensitive impact on U.S. international relations," pp. 6-7.

The System

take his place. The story of the implementation of the Herter Report becomes in large measure the story of Crockett's remarkable tenure in the important position of Deputy Under Secretary of State for Administration. A Foreign Service Officer, Crockett was not in the inner councils of the Service on two counts: his entire career had been spent in the low-status field of administration, and he had entered laterally during the Wriston Program. Crockett moved to the top on the strength of a charismatic personality, native political acumen, strong commitment to improving the State Department, and a reputation as a positive, innovative administrator who looked upon rules and regulations as opportunities to be tested rather than as restrictions. Specifically, his advancement to the post of Deputy Under Secretary came about because of his ability to get along well with the two most important men on Capitol Hill as far as the Department of State is concerned—Hays and Congressman John Rooney of New York, chairman of the appropriations subcommittee that handles State.

Crockett was not involved in the Herter effort for more than six months. The task forces set up by Pollack had concluded their work by the summer of 1963 and were disbanded. For a long time, Crockett's stance vis-à-vis the Herter Report was to push ahead on a number of minor changes coming out of the task force efforts and to work on one major recommendation, the proposal to create a foreign affairs programming system. He established a management planning staff as a small group to work on designing and installing a Comprehensive Country Programming System (CCPS), a three-year effort which will be discussed in the next chapter.

A description of administrative improvements in the Department of State over the period of 1961-64 was published early in 1965.[50] It lists a number of changes in the personnel area that can be traced to the Herter Report—the combining of State and USIA basic examinations, more interagency assignments, improved college relations for recruitment purposes, improvements in performance evaluation procedures. There also is a description of the CCPS effort. But there is no mention of any basic changes in the personnel system nor of any plans to go forward with legislation.

It was not until late in 1964 that Crockett's thinking began to jell on how best to make use of the opportunities for improving the basic personnel system offered by the Herter Report. Drawing on the thinking of a small working group on personnel policy he had established, on his management planning staff, and on his own consultations with key officials in other agencies, Crockett developed the main features of his plan. As described in a lengthy "information memorandum" to Secretary Rusk in March 1965, they were:

1. Amendments to the Foreign Service Act of 1946 that would establish the framework for a single foreign affairs personnel system to include all employees in the agencies involved.

2. Progressive involvement of other foreign affairs agencies in the benefits of the new system, beginning with USIA.

3. An interchange agreement between the Civil Service and Foreign Service which would make appointment from one service to the other easier (in that each service would accept the other's examination and appointment criteria so that qualified persons could cross over without undergoing reexamination).

4. Reconstitution of the Board of the Foreign Service as an interagency "board of governors" of the new system,

50 U.S. Department of State, *Improvements in Administration: 1961-64.*

84

acting under the general policy guidance of the Secretary of State.

5. Development of a sophisticated manpower utilization system that would identify and project position requirements and available skills for all participating "users" of the new personnel system.

6. Maximum decentralization of personnel authorities to "users" (bureaus within State, other agencies) of the personnel system, dependent in part on making the manpower utilization system operational.

7. Reorganization of the administrative area of State, including the Office of Personnel, to move from a hierarchical pyramid to a flatter type of structure in a concept of "management by objectives and programs." Layers of hierarchy would be stripped away, and "programs" would be identified with their managers reporting directly to the Deputy Under Secretary. This would have the effect of elevating some of the personnel and other functions and would make a measure of decentralization of personnel authorities immediately possible. Related to this was the rescuing of the Office of the Director General of the Foreign Service from symbolic status by placing it in the role of "coordinator" of the "semi-autonomous" personnel programs.

Crockett negotiated the interchange agreement which President Johnson put into effect on May 6, 1965 by executive order. The Management Planning Staff was directed to proceed with the design of the manpower utilization system. In June of 1965 the reorganization of State's administrative area took place.

On the personnel system, Crockett concurred entirely with the general thrust of the Herter Report, but he differed on two points: (1) he thought the necessary changes could be made within the framework of the Foreign Service Act of

1946 by amendment, and (2) he thought that a single career system was preferable to three "compatible" career services. One reason for this position was purely pragmatic —the belief that amendments to an existing Act to create the needed framework would be easier to achieve than an entirely new "Foreign Affairs Personnel Act." Another reason was Crockett's strong belief that the whole effort could be traced back to a principle inherent in both the Rogers Act and the Foreign Service Act, that of a single Foreign Service of the United States. If this were true, then what was involved was extending and modernizing an old charter, not creating a new one.[51]

In the first session of the 89th Congress, work began on two legislative fronts, one in the House and the other in the Senate. In the first, Crockett worked closely with Chairman Hays and John Macy, Chairman of the Civil Service Commission, to produce the package of draft amendments that came to be known as the "Hays Bill." On the other, Crockett worked with the leadership of USIA on a plan to integrate career USIA officers into the FSO corps. USIA identified 760 officers, and on April 13, 1965 President Johnson sent the list with his endorsement for the "advice and consent" of the Senate.

On May 6, 1965 President Johnson sent a letter to Speaker of the House John McCormack, citing the USIA list and the interchange agreement, and stressing the importance of the Hays Bill as "another vital step" in a program to strengthen the personnel capabilities of the foreign affairs agencies. The President characterized the bill as creating "a single Foreign Affairs Personnel system, broad enough to accommodate the personnel needs—domestic as well as over-

[51] The source for Crockett's opinions as described in the balance of this chapter is a tape-recorded interview the author conducted with Mr. Crockett on his last day in the Department of State, Jan. 30, 1967.

seas—of the Department of State, the Agency for International Development, and the U.S. Information Agency, and to cover appropriate personnel of other agencies engaged in foreign affairs." As described by the President, the main feature of the bill was creation of "a new category of professional career officers" to be called "Foreign Affairs Officers." This category would in all major respects be exactly like the FSO category except that it would be intended primarily for domestic service; in other words, it would replace the Civil Service in the foreign affairs agencies. There would be a transitional period of three years during which civil servants could decide whether or not to participate in the new system. If not, they would be "assisted in obtaining suitable employment in other Government agencies." Other measures would liberalize lateral-entry procedures, apply the selection-out principle to the entire Foreign Service (including the new FAO category and the FSS category, as well as the FSO category), and eliminate restrictions on the reappointment of FSRs.[52]

Hearings were held by the Hays Subcommittee in May and July of 1965. In addition to President Johnson's letter, strong support came from Secretary Rusk and John Macy. A number of members of the Herter Committee sent in letters endorsing the bill, and Joseph E. Johnson testified in person. There was stiff opposition from the Civil Service employee unions and veterans' groups. The FSO corps was conspicuous by its absence; as a group the corps expressed no point of view and no individual officers testified or wrote letters.

The Subcommittee made some changes in the bill, designed to placate the union opposition, and reported the bill out. It passed the House on September 9 and went to the Senate, where the session ended before it was considered.

[52] Hays Bill Hearings, House, pp. 2-4.

Background and Forces of Change

Meanwhile the USIA nominations had not been acted on by the Senate. The Committee on Foreign Relations reported favorably, but the majority leader failed to bring the list to the floor for a vote before the session ended.

In the new session, something the planners had never intended happened. The USIA list had to be resubmitted, and a special subcommittee of the Senate Foreign Relations Committee, chaired by Senator Albert Gore of Tennessee, took up consideration of the Hays Bill and the USIA list at the same time. Again Crockett carried the burden of testimony, with strong support from members of the Herter Committee, and representatives of USIA, AID, the Bureau of the Budget, and the Civil Service Commission.

Again the employee unions and veterans' groups opposed the bill, the latter because the Foreign Service system was exempt from veterans' preference. The unions were dismayed at the prospect of 10,000 persons leaving the Civil Service for another system which had no unions. Their representatives stressed the three-year time limit on transfer, the dangers of selection-out, the loss of Civil Service privileges, fear of centralized dictatorial power over the new system, and fear that this was an "opening wedge" to progressively exempt other groups from the Civil Service system.[53] Steadily throughout the hearings in the House and Senate, concessions were made to the opposing groups, but nothing would allay the last two fears mentioned.

Crockett argued long and eloquently to overcome the reservations of two Subcommittee members, Senators Hickenlooper of Iowa and Pell of Rhode Island. Hickenlooper saw the measure as creating a "colossus," a "gargantuan com-

[53] U. S. Congress, Senate, *Establishment of a Single Foreign Affairs Personnel System and Nominations of USIA Officers as Foreign Service Officers*, Hearings before a special subcommittee of the Committee on Foreign Relations, 89th Cong., 2nd Sess., Apr. 19, 20, and 28, 1966, p. 206.

plex," a "State Department here that is so big that it will run the entire Government of the United States." Repeatedly, Crockett argued that the bill added no new employees, that what was involved was an improved personnel system, not a merger of agencies, and that a basic point was to give career status to employees who had been denied it for years. The gap in thinking was never quite closed:

> *Mr. Crockett.* I am just disappointed I haven't been able to convince you so far.
> *Senator Hickenlooper.* Well, maybe I am sorry that you haven't been able to convince me. But as much as I like you, you haven't been able to convince me.[54]

As a former Foreign Service Officer, Pell had a traditional view of the FSO corps and felt in particular that it "should be an elite and relatively small corps with an outer corps of specialists." Crockett's answer to this was to agree with the idea of an elite group, but to point out that the best way to achieve an elite at the top, given the expanded needs of present-day foreign affairs, was by continuous sifting and continuous selection from an expanded base:

> Some people grow. Some people don't grow. Some people expand, their horizons expand, and so I think the elite corps is exactly the right concept. But it has to be broadly based so that you can distill the eliteness into the size that meets our needs, and I am convinced that from what my experience has been with the Foreign Service in the past 5 years—and I work with it intimately every day, finding people, selecting people, counseling people—my conviction is that it is still not large enough, the base is still not large enough to supply the depth of quality that we need at the top. There is no dearth of jobs for good people.

[54] *Ibid.*, p. 18.

Every day AID and USIA and ourselves want good people.[55]

Both Pell and Hickenlooper reported encountering opposition to the bill privately and in their mail from numerous Foreign Service Officers. Pell finally became exasperated:

> I would also like to go on record at this time that, in going through the witness list, I am very surprised that no Foreign Service officers or retired Foreign Service officers have chosen to come up and asked to speak. I am informed that everybody who has asked to be heard has been put on the witness list. I have heard all kinds of grumblings from the Foreign Service about this bill, received private letters and I am really surprised at the lack of gumption that is shown by this fact.
>
> If they are against it, as they say they are, why don't they come up and say so, but not grumble, and actually it takes no courage if they are retired, and I just think this should be a matter of record.[56]

Only three letters written by FSOs had come in, two by retired officers and one by an officer presently in the Service, all favoring the bill. Pell's challenge resulted only in the appearance of one man who had been selected-out of the Service and who testified in bitter opposition to the bill.[57]

The Board of Directors of the American Foreign Service Association wrote a letter to Chairman Gore which amounted to a rather lukewarm endorsement of the bill and a plea for "clear" expression of Congressional intent that many of its features be used conservatively. In particular, the board was concerned about lateral entry into the FSO corps, and called for this to be on "an individual and highly selective basis" rather than "large-scale integration." On the other

55 *Ibid.*, pp. 27-28.   56 *Ibid.*, p. 131.
57 *Ibid.*, pp. 253-57.

90

hand, the board was concerned that the FAO corps not "be permitted to evolve into a corps of officers parallel to but separate from the FSO corps, having access to all positions open to FSOs throughout the world, but not subject to the same obligations or governed by the same procedures for admission, assignment, promotion, or selection-out."[58]

These two concerns would narrowly restrict the possibilities of creating a single service out of the Hays Bill. The plan was to use the FAO category in place of the Civil Service in State, AID, and USIA. Some FSRs in the three agencies, those primarily oriented to domestic service would become FAOs. Others—the temporary specialists—would remain FSRs, and still others, a large group consisting of the career officers of AID and USIA not presently in career status, would become FSOs. The latter would not be possible if lateral entry were to be held to an "individual and highly selective basis," as proposed by the Board of Directors of the Foreign Service Association. In particular, they were concerned about AID officers becoming FSOs. Although the clear intent was that this would eventually happen, Crockett pointed out that no specific plans had been made. The emphasis was on the immediate integration of the USIA officers.

Ultimately, on August 18, 1966, the Subcommittee reported the bill out favorably, but it was tabled by the full Committee on September 15 and no further action was taken either on the Hays Bill or the list of USIA officers proposed for FSO status.

Probably the main reason the bill died is the unrelated atmosphere of dissent about the Vietnam war which had become very pronounced by this time. Chairman Fulbright and other key members of the Senate Foreign Relations Committee were not disposed to take any positive action in the foreign affairs field at a time when they were so deeply in dis-

[58] *Ibid.*, pp. 309-11.

agreement with the White House. In turn, the White House made no effort to push the Hays Bill and the USIA integration after the initial support when the measures were first introduced in 1965. Crockett's view was that more sustained support from the administration and better understanding of the bill within the FSO corps and support from the corps would have been enough to overcome the malaise stemming from the disagreements about the Vietnam war.

Soon after the demise of the bill ideas began to emerge about what to do in its place. The experience had been a traumatic one for USIA, with more than 700 of its best officers in a state of animated suspension for a year and a half. By the beginning of 1967 USIA was again at work on a draft of a bill to create its own career service.[59] In State, personnel specialists came up with an idea for legislation that would extend the FSS grades upward to a level equivalent to the top FSO-FSR grades. Their thought was that this would provide a career category that would substitute for integration of the FSRs of USIA and AID into the FSO corps, albeit a second-class category that smacks of Pell's "outer corps of specialists." Some senior FSOs in State began pushing the idea of reversing the policy of a decade or more and reviving the Civil Service system for domestic employment in State. At this point they became the curious allies of the employee union leaders.

Another possibility is the mounting of still another major study. This was the suggestion of Sen. Fulbright. The model he had in mind was the Plowden Committee which had studied the British Foreign Service in 1964 and reached conclusions remarkably similar to those of the Herter Com-

59 This effort succeeded when S. 633, introduced by Senator Pell in 1967, was passed into law in 1968, much to the surprise of everyone concerned in view of the potent opposition of Congressman Hays whose

mittee.[60] It differed from the Herter Committee in that it was an official body, appointed by the Prime Minister, with Members of Parliament among its membership.

Crockett resigned from the State Department in January 1967 to take a position in private industry. He left with confidence that the single service idea will prevail, "if not next year, then the year after, simply because it's basically right."

---

bill had been killed in the Senate the year before. At the last minute a compromise was achieved. Hays accepted Pell's concept of a "Foreign Service Information Officer Corps" for USIA when Pell accepted several amendments by Hays that went somewhat in the direction of the old Hays Bill—a provision for "unlimited tenure" for Foreign Service Reserve officers and a provision to include these officers under the Foreign Service retirement system. However, for these provisions to have any substantial effect in the manner of the Hays bill would require vigorous administrative action by the State Department; there has been strong pressure from the FSO corps to present such action.

[60] Great Britain, *Report of the Committee on Representational Services Overseas,* Cmnd. 2,276 (London: Her Majesty's Stationery Office, Feb. 1964).

CHAPTER 3

THE ORGANIZATION

....

IN A STUDY of the professional diplomat it may seem unnecessary to devote a chapter to the organizational home base of the diplomat, the Department of State. Yet, in my view, if there is a weakness in many studies of professional groups to date it is the failure to pay enough attention to the context within which the profession functions, where such a context exists. As Richard McArdle, former Chief of the U.S. Forest Service, has pointed out, a public agency "is not an amorphous mass"; it possesses "shape, character, individuality," and the "character of the agency . . . shapes the character of those who work there."[1] On the other side, it hardly needs pointing out that the professional group also has a profound impact on its parent organization.

This two-way impact is quite pronounced in the case of the State Department and the FSO corps. Although the latter constitutes less than 15 percent of total State Department employees, it is obviously the key group, the only one with a history and deeply ingrained traditions, a protected career service, high status, and the inside track to key jobs. FSOs provide the majority of ambassadors and almost all of the deputy chiefs of mission charged with supervising U.S. activities abroad.

A great many similarities between the professional group and the organization could be traced, including, most importantly, the critical problem of role identification and

[1] Delia and Ferdinand Kuhn, eds., *Adventures in Public Service* (New York: The Vanguard Press, 1963), p. 250.

94

performance that both now face. In Chapter 1 the challenge to the FSOs to redefine their profession to meet the requirements of the "new diplomacy" was discussed. In similar fashion the parent organization is challenged to assume active management of the entire spectrum of foreign affairs activities. The organization's problem and the professional group's problem obviously are very closely related, and one suspects that no significant progress will be made by one without comparable progress by the other.

Any adequate treatment of the total organization of State would require at least one large volume. Our concern here is less with the organization chart and the functions and procedures of the Department than with the role crisis it faces. In addition to reviewing the evolution of the problem in more depth than in Chapter 1, this chapter will examine recent efforts by the Department to meet the challenge.

The Staff Versus Line Controversy

Controversy over the proper role of the Department of State began virtually as soon as the Department lost its monopoly in foreign affairs, in the wartime and postwar expansion. In 1936 it was still possible for the entire staff of the Department of State to assemble on the steps of the Old State Building (now the Executive Office Building) to pose for a group photograph. By 1946 a similar photograph would have required a small stadium and an aerial view. Even as the process of growth went on, the dominant view was that the Department should remain as small an agency as possible, serving primarily as a staff agency to the Secretary of State and the President in the formulation of foreign policy.

Advocacy of this position by Secretary Hull and by the Hoover Commission has already been noted. Secretary Byrnes took the same position in his view of the State Department's role: "It must be a policy-making department. It cannot be run like one which is charged with conducting a variety of operations. The amount of time a Secretary of State must give to decisions on carrying out operating functions necessarily is taken away from the important questions of foreign policy."[2] As noted, Secretary Dulles held particularly strong views on the subject, which were echoed by President Eisenhower's Advisory Committee on Government Organization, headed by Nelson Rockefeller, the Committee that produced Reorganization Plans 7 and 8 separating the information and foreign aid programs from State in 1953. The logic of the plans eluded Congress, as shown by the following exchange between Congressman Charles Brownson of Indiana and Dr. Robert L. Johnson, new chief of the information program in 1953:

Mr. Brownson. This separation of policy and operations is a little disturbing. You see, we were asked last week— in fact, we voted on it this morning—to approve a Defense Department plan, the chief merit of the Defense Department plan, of which I approve highly, is that this plan brings policy and operations closer together.

Dr. Johnson. Yes.

Mr. Brownson. Then the next week and the next two plans in sequence, 7 and 8, we are asked to approve on the basis of their chief virtue, which is that we separate policy and operations. That is why we are probing this.

Dr. Johnson. I think, sir, I can help clarify that a little. Of course, the Defense Department has been traditionally an operating agency. The State Department has been traditionally a policy-making agency.[3]

2 James F. Byrnes, *Speaking Frankly* (New York: Harper and Bros., 1947). p. 244.
3 U.S. Congress, House of Representatives, Committee on Government Operations, *Hearings, Reorganization Plans Nos. 7 and 8*, 83rd Cong., 1st Sess., 1953, p. 174.

The Organization

State Department employees were informed of the reorganization in terms which made the policy-operations dichotomy emphatically clear:

One of the main results is to relieve the Secretary of State of supervising operating programs, freeing his time to concentrate on the important problems of foreign policy. The reorganization will relieve the Department of State of many duties extraneous to the main foreign policy problems. The administrative burdens falling upon the Secretary under the present arrangement where he is ultimately held responsible for personnel, budget, regulations, security of operating programs, such as the information program, cannot help but divert him and his principal assistants from concentrating on the primary role of the Department.[4]

Thus the policy-operations dichotomy remained dominant within the executive branch, but there was disagreement elsewhere. The 1951 Brookings Report said: "The assumed inconsistency of program operations with a policy role we believe to be fictitious." The report analyzed the staff versus line issue and concluded that the weight of tradition, probable Constitutional intent, and merits of the case all argued for the State Department being the general purpose agency concerned with both policy and operations in foreign affairs, rather than a small staff agency in the Executive Office concerned exclusively with foreign policy and planning. Pointing out that the larger role was essentially no different from the roles of Defense and Treasury, both very much concerned with policy and yet maintaining "immense" operations, the report held that the "creation of minor foreign affairs agencies should be avoided." It recognized that the

[4] U.S. Department of State, "Foreign Affairs Manual Circular No. 30" (June 4, 1953).

postwar expansion of foreign operations had occasioned the issue, and stated: "Now that the nature of foreign policy has changed, a form of organization under which the negative, passive, and minor operational aspects of foreign relations would be conducted by one foreign field service, while the positive, active, and major operational aspects would be conducted by another, would not appear to define a desirable jurisdictional basis. . . ."[5]

In this statement, the report was contrasting the traditional diplomatic and consular activities of State with the operations of the foreign aid program. It did not come down firmly in favor of any one pattern but indicated strongly that the desirable direction was toward an enlarged Department of Foreign Affairs which would include the foreign aid program.[6]

Only a year later, another outside group recommended that the Department of State be strengthened and extended to include all foreign operations except strictly military activities. This proposal would have upgraded the Secretary by including two subordinate secretaries below cabinet rank, one for foreign policy and the other for foreign operations. Particularly interesting is the fact that three of the persons involved in this study were to reappear in the 1960s—McGeorge Bundy and Arthur Schlesinger, Jr. on the White House staff of President Kennedy, and Don K. Price as Vice-Chairman of the Herter Committee.[7]

Although the policy-operations split remained doctrine throughout the Dulles era, the Department of State did not

[5] The Brookings Institution, *Administration of Foreign Affairs and Overseas Operations*, Report prepared for the Bureau of the Budget, Executive Office of the President (Washington: GPO, 1951), pp. 216-22.
[6] *Ibid.*, p.xix.
[7] *United States Foreign Policy: Its Organization and Control*, Report of a study group for the Woodrow Wilson Foundation (New York: Columbia University Press, 1952).

The Organization

go so far as to shed its traditional operations abroad in the consular and reporting areas. Outside critics continued to differ. In 1953 Arthur MacMahon proposed a "Department of Foreign Affairs" concept.[8] The 1960 Brookings study proposed a "Department of Foreign Affairs" with three component departments—the Department of State, the Department for Foreign Economic Operations, and the Department of Information and Cultural Affairs. Each would be headed by a secretary of cabinet rank and the three would be presided over by a Secretary of Foreign Affairs of senior cabinet rank to be "the President's chief deputy on matters of foreign policy."[9]

A proposal tending in the same direction, but going somewhat further, was made by New York Governor Nelson Rockefeller in a speech on June 21, 1960, a time at which it was still unknown whether or not he would make a sustained bid for the 1960 Republican Presidential nomination. Criticizing "government by committee," which he termed likely to take the "least bold or imaginative position," Rockefeller called for the creation of the position of "First Secretary of the Government" to "assist the President in the exercise of his authority in the whole area of national security and international affairs." The holder of this super-cabinet post would be "Executive Chairman of the National Security Council" and would operate on "the Prime Ministerial level."[10] Such a proposal would place a governmental official other than the President in authority not only over all of the foreign affairs agencies but over the military as well.

[8] MacMahon, *Administration in Foreign Affairs* (University, Ala.: University of Alabama Press, 1953), Chapter 2.
[9] H. Field Haviland, Jr. et al, *The Formulation and Administration of United States Foreign Policy* (Washington: The Brookings Institution, 1960), pp. 3-4.
[10] *New York Times*, June, 1960, p. 22.

99

Background and Forces of Change

The Management Challenge

The Kennedy administration put an end to the policy-operations dichotomy, but no master plan or blueprint was forthcoming from the White House on how the State Department should manage its enlarged role. In a statement President Kennedy made when he abolished the Operations Coordinating Board on February 19, 1961, he said the abolition was "part of our program for strengthening the responsibility of the individual departments" and that much of the responsibility for the Board's work would devolve on the Secretary of State: "He expects to rely particularly on the Assistant Secretaries in charge of regional bureaus, and they in turn will consult closely with other departments and agencies. This will be our ordinary rule for continuing coordination of our work in relation to a country or area."[11]

The President's Special Assistant for National Security Affairs, McGeorge Bundy, attempted to explain more fully in a letter to Sen. Henry M. Jackson the "other ways" in which coordination could be achieved better than by the OCB. "The most important of these other ways is an increased reliance on the leadership of the Department of State," he said. Furthermore, ". . . the President has made it very clear that he does not want a large separate organization between him and his Secretary of State. Neither does he wish any question to arise as to the clear authority and responsibility of the Secretary of State, not only in his own Department, and not only in such large-scale related areas as foreign aid and information policy, but also as the agent of coordination in all our major policies toward other nations." In this regard Bundy stressed that he and others in the "closely knit" White House staff were serving strictly as staff officers to the president and not in any way interposing

[11] The Kennedy statement appears in full in Jackson Subcommittee, *Administration of National Security*, 87th Cong., 2nd Sess., 1962, p. 3.

100

themselves between the president and his line officers, the heads of departments and agencies.[12]

Secretary Rusk, in an address to "policy-making" officers of the Department of State the day after the OCB was abolished, echoed the views of Bundy and the President: "We can no longer rely on interdepartmental machinery 'somewhere upstairs' to resolve differences between this and other departments. Assistant Secretaries of State will now carry an increased burden of active formulation and coordination of policies." Rusk stressed that State must be concerned with foreign policy "in its total context," including defense, trade, and fiscal policy, and that its role was one of "leadership of change" in a world in which change was the "dominant theme." Overseas, Rusk said, ambassadors should "take charge" in an "active, operational, interested, responsible fashion"; at home, the Department was "entering a new phase in its existence," in which "we are expected to take charge."[13]

Neither in this nor in later statements did Rusk elaborate any more of a master plan for "taking charge" than had the White House, although elements of his approach to management came through. He expressed a preference for informal arrangements rather than "elaborate machinery" for coordination, and for reliance on his senior line officers instead of a large personal staff. His principal prescription for vitality in a large organization was urging people to live up to the horizons of their responsibility. "The heart of the bureaucratic problem is the inclination to avoid responsibility," he said. "One of the reasons that organization seldom gets in the way of a good man is that if a man

[12] The Jackson-Bundy exchange of letters appears in full in *ibid.*, pp. 4-8.
[13] The text of the Secretary's remarks appears in *ibid.*, pp. 23-29.

demonstrates that he is willing to make judgments and decisions and live with the results, power gravitates to him
because other people will get out of his way." This was
related to Rusk's identification of the major organizational
problem, that of "layering," of burying action beneath layers of supervision so that communication and creativity became stifled. He saw the problem as particularly crucial for
the country desk officer:

> I think we need to do something about layering, and
> one of the ways to do this is to upgrade the desk officer
> level. It seems to me that the man in Washington who
> spends all of his time brooding about a country like Brazil
> ought to be a man comparable in competence to the man
> who is Ambassador to Brazil. We then clear the way for
> him to get quickly to the Assistant Secretary or the Secre-
> tary.[14]

In sum, the White House and the Secretary gave the mandate for leadership to the Department of State, gave responsibility to the Assistant Secretaries in charge of the
regional bureaus and to Ambassadors, and exhorted people
to live up to their responsibilities, in such forms as President
Kennedy's letter of May 1961 to all ambassadors, cited
earlier, and Secretary Rusk's views quoted above.

It should be observed that there was a considerable gap
between the Kennedy administration's pronouncements that
the State Department should be in charge, and its organizational innovations in foreign affairs. President Kennedy's
letter of May 26, 1961, transmitting the foreign aid bill to
Congress, not only referred to the "separate identity" of the
Peace Corps but also made it clear that AID would be sub-

[14] These points, which repeated much of what the Secretary said
to the policy-making officers, were brought out in his subsequent
testimony to the Jackson Subcommittee: *Administration of National
Security, Part 6*, 88th Cong., 1st Sess., Dec. 11, 1963, pp. 386-412.

102

ordinate only to the Secretary of State, not to other officers of the Department. The letter said: "Economic development assistance can no longer be subordinated to, or viewed simply as a convenient tool for meeting, short-term political objectives."

There are several possible explanations for the gap. It may simply have reflected ambivalence and uncertainty as to whether State was able to take charge; the higher policy may have given way to parochial pleadings when specific organizational issues arose; or some Rooseveltian theory of bureaucratic competition may have been operative. The only thing that is clear is that the injunction to State to manage both policy and operations was not supported by any reorganizations or mergers designed to give State more direct control over operations. In fact, the tendency was in the opposite direction.

Apparently there was no thought of a major reorganization, of moving toward an enlarged Department of State, as some outside critics had been recommending for the previous 10 years or more. Much of the flavor of the approach of the White House and the Secretary can be found in a 1960 study done by the staff of the Jackson Subcommittee, which specifically opposed solving problems by "radical organizational changes." Arguing particularly against the Rockefeller proposal for a "First Secretary of the Government," the burden of the study was that the necessary improvements in the foreign affairs area could come about by unclogging the administrative channels, relying on the American governmental system (particularly the line departments and the budgetary process), and steadfastly working toward better performance in key areas.[15]

[15] Jackson Subcommittee: *Super-Cabinet Officers and Superstaffs*, 86th Cong., 2nd Sess., 1960.

Background and Forces of Change
Problems in Meeting the Challenge

Only a little more than two years after the abolition of the OCB, and the clear expectation of the White House that the State Department would assume the leadership role in foreign affairs, a recognized and astute observer of the national security scene, Dr. Richard Neustadt, said to the Jackson Subcommittee:

> So far as I can judge, the State Department has not yet found means to take the proffered role and play it vigorously across the board of national security affairs. The difficulties here may be endemic; the role may ask too much of one department among others. But I think it is decidedly too soon to tell. State, I conceive, should have the benefit of every doubt and more time for experiment.[16]

In retrospect, the gap between expectation and reality obviously was very large. The State Department was not in good enough shape to assume vigorous leadership and management in foreign affairs. While growth and expansion were occurring in foreign affairs, the Department had clung to a narrow view of itself as a policy agency and not an operating agency. Its key group of employees, the FSO corps, was dominated by a conservative view of diplomacy. The corps had not engaged significantly in the new functions; consequently, FSOs on the way up had virtually no opportunity for command experience. The chaotic personnel system for foreign affairs, as we saw in the last chapter, was a divisive rather than unifying force. There was a radical cleavage in the organization between "substance" and "administration," with the former meaning political and economic work and the latter the most mundane kind of service and support. What fell in between was management.

The net result of these traditions was an almost total lack

16 Jackson Subcommittee, *Administration of National Security*, Part *1*, 88th Cong., 1st Sess., Mar. 11, 22, and 25, 1963, p. 81.

of preparation for the new managerial role, and an environment within the Department that was highly resistant to change. For example, in the midst of a technological era, the Department did not obtain a computer until late in 1962, and then used it almost exclusively for administrative purposes such as the payroll. Its worldwide communications network, of World War II vintage, had proved inadequate during the Cuban missile crisis.[17] The handling of information was and is extremely antiquated. A study in 1963 of all information available in the Department on one country revealed 17 different repositories, none related to any other. There is no R & D tradition in State. Its large Bureau of Intelligence and Research emphasizes intelligence, principally the sifting and analyzing of thousands of reports from the overseas posts and other sources. In fiscal 1964 State spent $83,000 on research, compared to almost $13 million by AID and $7.5 billion by Defense.[18] Sophisticated, newer modes such as contingency planning, simulation, gaming, and programming were unknown in State. There was no attempt in State to create policy plans covering all U.S. operations in given countries until 1962 when W. W. Rostow became Counselor of the Department and Chairman of the Policy Planning Council.

A very serious constraint on managerial vitality in the Department is that its top leaders have played almost no managerial role—virtually a tradition in State. Alexander DeConde has pointed out that "no Secretary of State has left a mark on history because of his administrative talents."[19] Another factor is that men are not normally selected for

[17] Jackson Subcommittee, *Administration of National Security: Basic Issues*, 88th Cong., 1st Sess., 1963, p. 19.

[18] The White House Conference on International Cooperation, "Report of the Committee on Research on Development of International Institutions," Washington, D.C., Nov. 28-Dec. 1, 1965, p. 10 and p. 16.

[19] *The Secretary of State*, Report of the Occidental College American Assembly, July 26-29, 1962, pp. 18-19.

Secretary or Under Secretary of State because of their reputations as executives, but rather for their knowledge and experience in the substance of foreign affairs. Finally, there is the crushing burden of the top few jobs in State. The dilemma has been stated well in a staff study by the Jackson Subcommittee:

> The modern Secretary of State is thus adviser, negotiator, reporter of trouble, spokesman, manager, and coordinator. This is all too much. Yet somehow he must handle it. He cannot take just any one piece of his job. He has to do the best he can with all his several duties. None can be sacrificed—or wholly delegated to others. As a result some duties are bound to be shortchanged. Some things that need doing, by him, will be left to others—or left undone, for they will not have sufficient priority to crowd other things off his schedule.[20]

Probably no one would disagree that the role of manager gets the lowest priority, not only for Secretaries of State but for their Under Secretaries as well. It would be a truly extraordinary performance if a man came into an agency where the weight of tradition is that he must devote his energies to matters of high policy, where he himself is predisposed to do exactly this, and where the pace of events reinforces this practice, and break through all of this to assert himself vigorously as a manager—and yet not at the expense of inadequate treatment of high policy.

This sort of performance was not to occur in the Department of State under the Kennedy and Johnson administrations, in spite of the emphasis on management. Secretary Rusk's style became clear fairly early; like previous Secretaries, he did not assume an active managerial role over

[20] Jackson Subcommittee, *Administration of National Security: The Secretary of State*, 88th Cong., 2nd Sess., 1964, p. 3.

the full spectrum of foreign affairs policy and operations. Rusk did his share of exhortation for change and he was generally permissive of change efforts mounted at a lower level, but he did not himself take active leadership.

Because few people expect a Secretary of State to play such a role, there tend to be great expectations focused on the No. 2 man, the Under Secretary of State. Writing in the *New York Times*, Victor S. Navasky quotes former Secretary Dean Acheson as saying: "The Under Secretary of State should be like the executive officer on a ship. . . . He should run things. The Secretary is the captain." There have been three Under Secretaries since 1961—Chester Bowles, George Ball, and Nicholas Katzenbach. Navasky sums up their performance as managers as follows: "Nicholas deBelleville Katzenbach, in office a little over a year, is the latest in a distinguished line of Under Secretaries who haven't run things. . . . Bowles tried unsuccessfully to engineer departmental ideology through a combination of imaginative ambassadorial appointments and enlightened memoranda, while Ball operated primarily as an *ad hoc* troubleshooter. Katzenbach has spent a year 'getting a fix' on the department."[21]

Both chroniclers of the Kennedy years, Theodore Sorenson and Arthur Schlesinger, Jr., describe the President's gloom over the unresponsiveness of the State Department and the extensive personnel changes he made in an effort to get things done.[22] But none of the new men and troubleshooters sent over from the White House were to lead a sustained effort for change, with the exception of Rostow

[21] Navasky, "No. 2 Man in State Is a Cooler-Downer," *New York Times Magazine*, Dec. 24, 1967, p. 3.
[22] Sorenson, *Kennedy* (New York: Harper & Row, 1965), pp. 287-90; Schlesinger, *A Thousand Days: John F. Kennedy in the White House* (Boston: Houghton Mifflin, 1965), Chapter 16, "The Reconstruction of Diplomacy."

in the policy-planning area. Thus in the era of the "new diplomacy" and the managerial challenge to the Department of State, there was no sustained leadership, involvement, or guidance from the top, with respect to change.

Because, in the words of the 1951 Brookings Report, State had not embraced the "positive, active, and major operational aspects" of foreign relations, it was in a situation in which the mechanics of governmental process in a multi-agency situation were stacked against it in attempting to assume a managerial role. The point is not that authority was lacking, but that the tools for exercising it in any systematic way were nonexistent. Both AID and the Peace Corps technically are part of State, with authorities delegated by the Secretary. In practice they are almost completely autonomous, especially the Peace Corps, where the ethos is that the operation is nonpolitical. The Arms Control and Disarmament Agency is a separate agency, but its director reports to the Secretary of State. The Secretary has important latent controls over the military assistance program, the P.L. 480 program, and USIA. But because the planning, programming, and budgeting for all these operations are carried on within the individual agencies concerned, State Department officers are in an extremely weak position to influence the character of the activities. Typically, the officers are asked for concurrence on a program plan late in the day, when the plan is solidified or is perhaps already in the budget, so that they are reduced to a negative or pro forma position rather than a creative one. If they differ, their only powers are the powers of persuasion, unless they are prepared to buck the problem up the laborious chain of command to where the power is—in the Secretary's office. Few officers are willing to do this very often. The point of diminishing returns is quickly reached.

The dilemma exists even in the field, where State is in

its strongest coordinative position. The ambassador is not only an employee of State, he is also the personal representative of the president, and he clearly has authority over all operations in his country of assignment, except combatant military, by virtue of the Kennedy letter. One problem lies in the traditions of the Foreign Service—many ambassadors are interested only in policy matters and high-level political reporting, scarcely moving beyond the Foreign Ministry and their own political sections, and pretty much allowing the large operational programs to run themselves. Where an ambassador is disposed to manage, and many are, he faces formidable problems. He may have authority on the scene over representatives of other agencies in his mission, but they still must report back to their parent agencies.

For example, each of the large operating programs puts together some form of a yearly program plan related to its budget. But many times, much of the program plan will be ready-made at agency headquarters in Washington. The ambassador is asked to concur in these program plans, but they come to him at different times during the year because the budgetary cycles of the agencies differ, and they come to him late in the game. All of the plans are stated in different terminology, with information organized in different categories. They are often voluminous. It is virtually impossible to compare activities in one plan against those in another plan because of timing and terminology differences. The ambassador thus finds himself in almost as weak a position as the State Department desk officer or Assistant Secretary in Washington, the very people to whom he would appeal for help if he had a major problem with one of the program plans.

This situation is not the product of any particular obstinacy on the part of officers in the other agencies, especially in the field where the impulses for collaborative effort normally are strong, but rather the product of the system. And it takes more than a mandate and exhortation to change a system such as this.

Still another problem is the general unwieldiness of State's organization. It is as much afflicted with the pathology of the classic bureaucratic structure as any other large organization, but in addition it has developed a kind of organizational sprawl, born out of the erratic history of expansionism in foreign affairs. This was described in trenchant, if somewhat exaggerated, prose by a White House staff member:

> The State Department is not an organization in the usual sense. It is a constellation of small power centers—some moving, some standing, some competing, some hiding, some growing, some decaying, a few coalescing, but more breaking apart into smaller fragments which soon develop all the organs and physiology of their parents. There is no central nervous system. It is an anti-organization. A few of its problems are . . . problems of *identity and role, attitude, organization, budgeting and programming,* and *personnel.*

Because the author cannot be cited, no importance is claimed for this point of view, other than that it is generally symptomatic of still another problem for the State Department, one that in a sense is a sum of all the other problems: it has a very poor reputation in management. One can see this as far back as the 1945 Bureau of the Budget study and the 1951 Brookings study, which said: "The Department's administrative record is better than it is frequently supposed to be, but the distrust of the Department's administrative competence is sufficiently widespread at present to limit the possibility of making assignments that would otherwise be justified and desirable."[23]

The criticism has been most pronounced over the period of the expectation-reality gap—1961 to the present. There will be occasion to examine some of this criticism toward the end of this book. For the present, it suffices to point out that although the criticisms are often exaggerated, usually attack symptoms (overstaffing, too much paperwork) rather than causes, and are somewhat weak on positive solutions, they nevertheless exist and have more than a little foundation in fact. A poor reputation, in the case of State, can become a serious obstacle to efforts aimed at improving the situation.

Blueprints for Change

In 1962 the existence of a gap between presidential expectations for the State Department to assume a vigorous management role in foreign affairs and the Department's ability to do so was sensed by the Herter Committee. The committee was also aware that no one in the White House or the State Department was coming forth with a blueprint on how to get there from here. For these reasons, as noted in Chapter 2, the committee moved beyond its narrow terms of reference in the personnel area to set forth the broad framework of what needed to be done.

The committee's report identified the problem, defined the Department's role, and set the cornerstone for the balance of the report in the first recommendation. Holding that the Department had "not developed adequately either the attitudes or the machinery needed to relate policies to the operations required to carry them out," the report said that "The Committee is convinced that the Department's capacity to assist the President in coordinating the programs

[23] The Brookings Institution, *Administration of Foreign Affairs*, p. 222.

111

and operations of the entire Federal Government in the field of foreign affairs must be strengthened. Likewise the tendency within the Department to view what is called 'administration' as separate, subordinate, and of little relevance to the foreign policy function must be corrected."[24] The recommendation for the new position of Executive Under Secretary was specifically designed to fill the management gap. As the No. 3 man in the Department, the Executive Under Secretary would be the manager, responsible for interagency coordination and assuring that "foreign affairs personnel and machinery are adequate to the nation's international responsibilities." On the machinery side was the committee's recommendation for Departmental leadership in establishing a programming system for relating policy plans, programs of action, and the resources needed to carry them out for the entire foreign affairs community. On the personnel side, the committee recommended an improved career personnel system and manpower planning, and numerous proposals designed to insure that the new personnel system would be unifying rather than divisive.

As we have seen, the White House set the mandate for change in the foreign affairs area, a mandate that was explicated in detail by the Herter Committee. The Kennedy letter to ambassadors was an important move, as was the order giving comparable authority to the State Department in Washington (NSAM 341) issued by the Johnson administration in 1966. Beyond these measures, White House tactics for actually achieving change consisted of exhortation and the shuffling of personnel near the top of State. All this was important, but it was only a beginning toward effective change, for the top leadership of the State Department did not follow through in any sustained way.

In this situation, it is remarkable that a major and sus-

24 Herter Report, p. 10.

112

tained effort to implement the Herter Report occurred at all. But such an effort did occur, and it was mainly the work of William J. Crockett, fifth-ranking man in the State Department.

In November 1963, six months after his promotion to Deputy Under Secretary, Crockett testified before the Jackson Subcommittee and displayed a grasp of the problem and the beginnings of an operational blueprint for change derived largely from the general framework established by the Herter Committee.

Crockett was candid and clear about the basic problem— the lack of preparation of the State Department for its new managerial role. After describing the "dignified past of diplomacy" to the subcommittee, he said:

And because of this traditional mode of operation, we —the Foreign Service and the Department of State— hesitated to realize or acknowledge the postwar broadening of the scope of foreign affairs and the rapid multiplicity of factors that could affect our national security. We did not "recognize" many of these factors; we did not consider them within the diplomatic realm, and we consequently did not bother to develop among ourselves the capabilities to deal with them—be they agricultural in nature or, for example, of an intelligence or military character. In short, the diplomatic profession was not about to redefine its role nor was the oldest bureaucracy in the Government about to make any major changes in its structure.[25]

Crockett also discussed problems that must be overcome for significant progress to be made—"fundamental organizational problems in Washington," attitudinal problems in

[25] Jackson Subcommittee, *Administration of National Security, Part 4*, 88th Cong., 1st Sess., p. 273.

113

the Foreign Service in terms of fully understanding and accepting the new mandate for leadership, problems in the mechanics of interagency coordination. On the disparate authority patterns in the field, compared to those in Washington, Crockett foreshadowed NSAM 341 which came more than two years later:

> Another thing that I personally think would be useful would be to endow an Assistant Secretary with some of the responsibility and prerogatives that an Ambassador has in his country of assignment. An Assistant Secretary might be given the same kind of charge of authority by the President that the Ambassador has been given and told officially and formally and the whole Government advised that Mr. X, the Assistant Secretary, is going to be the coordinator of all the Government activities for this area and these countries.[26]

There was another major problem:

> There is another thing that leadership implies, and which we, in the State Department, have not really recognized, nor really projected successfully to Congress. That is that leadership costs money.[27]

In his testimony Crockett described specific efforts started by others and by himself aimed at building State's capacity to lead in foreign affairs on behalf of the president. He described other efforts that were in the planning stage. At a later time, still other projects bent in the same direction were to emerge.[28] Taken together, these projects and

[26] *Ibid.*, p. 318.
[27] *Ibid.*, p. 290.
[28] A description of many of the management improvement efforts may be found in a September 1966 publication entitled: "A Management Program for the Department of State," produced by the Office of the Deputy Under Secretary for Administration.

changes, major and minor, which Crockett and many others worked on over the next three years, could be itemized literally by the score.

The Change Efforts

For purposes of this discussion, it will be necessary to describe only the efforts at major changes, relating briefly what has occurred in each case, before pulling the threads together to assess the over-all fate of the reform movement generated by the Kennedy administration and the Herter Report. All of the following major projects were sponsored by Crockett, except the Rostow policy planning effort and the issuance of NSAM 341.

One starting point for Crockett in mapping out his change strategy was the realization that any large-scale reorganization or merger to create an enlarged Department of State had been ruled out. Therefore change programs would have to be designed with an eye to compensating for this by overcoming problems of parochialism, stereotyping, and poor communication that are likely to exist when a number of agencies are working in the same general area, i.e., foreign affairs. The Hays Bill obviously tended in this direction by envisioning a common personnel system which all foreign affairs agencies could use on an equitable basis.

The same intent was also true of another major project, the effort to create a planning-programming-budgeting system that would encompass *all* overseas operations of the United States government except command military forces.[29] The specific impetus was Herter Committee Recommendation No. 3, and an important model was the successful Department of Defense programming system.

---

[29] This effort is described in detail in a forthcoming case study: Frederick C. Mosher and John E. Harr, *Program Budgeting Visits Foreign Affairs*, in preparation, to be published by the Inter-University Case Program, Syracuse University.

Crockett's staff aide, Richard W. Barrett, regarded as the "architect and prime mover" of State's programming effort, first articulated his thoughts in early 1963.[30] He proposed a "country programming system" to "provide the Ambassador with the action-forcing process he needs to focus the total spectrum of U.S. programs on a set of agreed-upon goals and objectives." He set the purpose of the effort as providing "a much-needed management tool" that would "assist the Department and its officers in discharging the enormous managerial responsibilities inherent in the new diplomacy." The basic idea was to overcome the problem, discussed earlier in this chapter, of the mechanics of governmental process being stacked against the State Department in attempting to coordinate foreign operations. This was to be done by creating and installing a management information system that would provide information to State Department decision-makers on the present and projected activities of all agencies operating abroad. The information would be provided in a common terminology and at the same point in time, so that activities could be compared meaningfully.

The real utility of the system would come when program data could be linked to policy objectives (where State had acknowledged supremacy) and to the budgets formulated independently by each agency. The idea was not to give State authoritarian control of all operational decisions, but to make it possible for the Department to influence those decisions and thus play the coordinating role that was expected of it.

Barrett envisioned this happening in the form of a "coun-

[30] Stanford Research Institute, "Documents Compiled for Second Meeting of the Advisory Group to the Secretary of State on Foreign Affairs Planning, Programming, and Budgeting," Sept. 19, 1966, Document II, pp. 12-13.

116

try program" in which an ambassador, working with all of the agency representatives in his country of assignment, would use the information available in the system in relationship to policy objectives to create a total country program for the next budget year. This program would then be reviewed in Washington and final decisions would be reflected in the budgets of all the agencies concerned.

Out of these considerations was born the unwieldy name of the system, "Comprehensive Country Programming System" (CCPS). In terms of interagency relationships, decision-making procedures, and the operating styles of State Department officers, the implications were revolutionary.

Beginning with a rudimentary system design in 1963, Barrett assembled a small staff composed of Reserve officers and a number of young Foreign Service Officers. In two years four major revisions of the system took place, based on repeated field tests. Data processing was computerized. By early 1965 an advanced design of the system had been installed in some 30 U.S. Missions abroad.

Except for the junior officers involved in the effort, and other scattered interest, the programming system was not popular with FSOs. An extreme example is Ellis Briggs' reference to "ravening bureaucratic termites" who "have chewed their way into the woodwork of the Comprehensive Country Programming System, as the latest revelation of the professional planners is labeled."[31] In general, the attitude of personnel of other agencies was one of wary cooperation. There was widespread interest, particularly in the field, in an improved method of collaboration. This interest coexisted with some concern over the possibility of losing a measure of autonomy. Some of the wariness, on

[31] Briggs, *Farewell to Foggy Bottom* (New York: David McKay, 1964), p. 29.

117

the part of both FSOs and other agency personnel, stemmed from uncertainty whether the experimental effort was "for real," as far as the State Department was concerned.

There was close collaboration between the programming effort and Rostow's National Policy Paper effort, so that good prospects existed for closing the gap between policies and programs. An excellent opportunity for testing the link between programs and budgets came in March 1965 when President Johnson instructed the State Department and Bureau of the Budget to collaborate on an experimental review of programs in 10 to 15 countries. The President specifically related the experimental review to "allocations of funds and resources for the ensuing year" and to "better management in the fuller utilization of our resources."[32]

Thirteen missions with an existing CCPS data base were selected for the experiment, which was labeled the "Executive Review of Overseas Programs" (EROP). Guidance papers were sent out; CCPS data was updated; ambassadorial review sessions were held in the field; and for the first time total country programs were submitted for review to Washington.

While the 13 country programs were being reviewed in Washington during the fall of 1966, the fascination with Secretary McNamara's programming methods, mentioned earlier, suddenly had government-wide impact. President Johnson instructed the Budget Bureau to see to it that every major agency created a "planning-programming-budgeting system" (PPBS).

Some months later the cooperation between State and the Bureau in the EROP exercise dissolved as the International Division of the Bureau, instead of co-opting the existing State Department effort, took the position that each foreign

[32] U.S. Office of the President, "Statement by the President to the Cabinet, March 25, 1965," press release dated Mar. 25, 1965.

affairs agency should develop its own PPBS. In early 1966 this view gradually hardened into outright opposition to State's comprehensive approach, and a classic bureaucratic stalemate ensued. One result was that the EROP experiment was never completed; no report ever went to the President.

Crockett was faced with the choice of referring the stalemate to Secretary Rusk for resolution, or finding some other way to ease the tension. So strong is the tendency in State to protect the Secretary from all but the most crucial problems that Crockett chose another way out. His solution was to create an "advisory committee" to Rusk to make recommendations on a foreign affairs PPBS. The committee was a distinguished group; it was chaired by Charles Hitch, architect of the Department of Defense programming system. The State Department's CCPS effort went onto a standby status. In October 1966 the Hitch Committee delivered its report to Secretary Rusk. The report said that State should indeed proceed energetically with the creation and implementation of a comprehensive foreign affairs PPBS. Conscious of the fact that there had not been any commitment to a programming system above the level of Crockett's job, the Committee recommended that the effort be headed by an established expert in programming who would report directly to a higher level than the administrative area of the Department.

Implementation was assigned to Nicholas Katzenbach who in the meantime had succeeded George Ball as Under Secretary of State. A search was launched for the right man to head the effort, to be hired as an Assistant Secretary of State directly under Katzenbach. Within a few months a candidate was chosen—Thomas C. Schelling of Harvard University. After studying the situation for several months in advance of his appointment, Schelling withdrew in May

1967 on the grounds that the problems were too large for him to make any significant impact in the 12 to 18 months he would be able to devote to the job.

When W. W. Rostow became Chairman of the State Department's Policy Planning Council in 1962, he studied previous policy-planning efforts and learned that with rare exceptions the policy papers drafted in previous years had had no real tie to actual operations abroad. All too often they were the product of the compromises that can occur in a committee situation. In particular, the OCB efforts suffered from this malady. Every agency engaged in foreign operations provided policy guidance of one form or another to its field representatives, sometimes informed by State Department viewpoints, sometimes not. Possibly because other agencies had their own policy documents, the latest pre-Rostow State Department effort, the drafting of relatively brief "Policy Guidelines" papers for all countries, was virtually restricted to political guidance for ambassadors, DCMs, and political sections, making no attempt to cover the full range of mission activities. One result of this situation was a tall stack of policy documents in many missions abroad, coming from half a dozen different agencies, with frequent overlaps and gaps and no comprehensive view. Another result was a reinforcement of the natural tendency of many FSOs to dislike the attempt to project policy ahead in the form of guidance papers; they could point to the current situation and to examples in the past to show that it was not a productive exercise.

Rostow regarded it as essential to overcome these problems and to create authoritative, comprehensive policy papers. The result of his thinking was the National Policy Paper concept. The NPP was to include a study in depth of a given foreign country's situation, and the situation of the U.S. vis-à-vis the country, in all of the key sectors—

political, economic, social-cultural, security, and so on. Based on this analysis, the NPP would conclude with long-range objectives, short-range objectives, and specific courses of action. The latter were intended to be programmatic statements, including specifying which components of the mission were to carry out the course of action.

To avoid the perils of drafting by committee, Rostow decided to make one person responsible for each NPP, usually a member of the Policy Planning Council. Part of this person's responsibility would be working with appropriate officers of the agencies concerned, to get their thinking and hopefully begin establishing a consensus. There was also stress on getting the views of the Country Team in the field, which would often involve a trip to the field by the principal drafter and the representatives of the other agencies.

Because creating even one NPP required a formidable effort, there was no intention of producing one for every country, but only for countries of particular interest and concern. To make the papers authoritative, Rostow succeeded in having a National Security Action Memorandum issued which stated that NPPs signed by the Secretary of State would be binding on all agencies.

In his Jackson Subcommittee testimony in November 1963 Crockett reported that 15 NPPs were "in process." Rostow became an avid supporter of the CCPS effort precisely because he saw in it the link to operations and the feedback mechanism that would help avoid the air of unreality which had pervaded past policy paper efforts.

Although it is impossible to evaluate the NPP effort very precisely because of the high security classification placed on the papers, it is clear that the effort has not made nearly the impact Rostow had hoped for. One problem is that with the programming system effort becoming moribund, the connection with real world of operations does not exist, so that the NPPs are not much more immune to the ivory tower cast than previous papers. There are problems of organization and format of the papers, of the level of generality of the objectives, and of the length of time involved in creating an approved NPP. However, the NPP effort continues to exist.

The chief architect of NSAM 341 was Gen. Maxwell D. Taylor. Formerly Chairman of the Joint Chiefs of Staff, military adviser to President Kennedy, and Ambassador to South Vietnam, Taylor (along with Attorney General Robert F. Kennedy) was the apostle of counterinsurgency in the Kennedy Administration. He had been instrumental in setting up the top-level, interagency "Special Group for Counter-Insurgency" after the Bay of Pigs disaster in 1961. On Taylor's return from Saigon, as he related the story in an address to the Foreign Service Association, President Johnson asked him "to review all of the activities of our Government in the Counter-Insurgency field, both at home and abroad, and to make appropriate recommendations."[33]

Possibly because of his experience in Saigon, Taylor's perspective had broadened. He saw "subversive insurgency" as a potential danger "in most of the 90-odd emerging countries" and, more importantly, he saw it as a function of other problems. Taylor's study led him to consider the government's organizational framework for dealing with these broader problems. He noted his surprise at discovering "how little specific authority" the Secretary of State "had for the management of inter-departmental business." Taylor said he "found that the only special authority that the Secretary of State had in this field had been given by President

[33] Taylor's speech appears in Jackson Subcommittee, *The Secretary of State and the Problem of Coordination, New Duties and Procedures of March 4, 1966,* 89th Cong., 2nd Sess., 1966, pp. 17-23.

122

Kennedy rather casually in the public relations release made at the time of the abolition of the OCB."

This then became the focal point of Taylor's work, to provide a specific and clear mandate of authority to the Secretary of State as the president's agent in managing foreign affairs. He felt that the mandate in NSAM 341 was even stronger than that given to ambassadors:

> To assist the President in carrying out his responsibility in the conduct of foreign affairs, he has assigned to the Secretary of State authority and responsibility to the full extent permitted by law for the over-all direction, coordination and supervision of interdepartmental activities of the United States.

As noted in Chapter 1, the NSAM created the Senior Interdepartmental Group (SIG), with the Under Secretary of State as executive chairman, and five Interdepartmental Regional Groups (IRG), with the regional Assistant Secretaries of State as executive chairmen, to assist the Secretary in this responsibility. The concept of "executive chairman" is central to the problem of avoiding committee compromises. According to Taylor, "That title is defined as a chairman who has not only the authority but also the responsibility for settling any issue on the agenda of his committee." As Taylor pointed out, appeal channels existed. An agency representative on the SIG who disagreed with a decision of the executive chairman could appeal to the Secretary of State and beyond him to the president.

At Secretary Rusk's instruction, Crockett appended the Country Director reorganization within State to the issuance of NSAM 341. This eliminated the position of Office Director in the regional bureaus, the title for an officer supervising a number of country desk officers. It upgraded the desk officers. In theory, there would be one Country Director for every country, a high-ranking, highly competent man who would function vis-à-vis other agency personnel concerned with the country, much as an ambassador is related to a Country Team in the field. In practice, the idea of one Country Director per country became true only for the medium to large countries. In the case of the smaller countries, a Country Director is responsible for more than one. The Country Director reorganization will be discussed in more depth in Chapter 8.

One of the most obvious areas of need in the State Department, to outside critics at least, is for the Department and the Foreign Service to recognize the knowledge explosion adequately and begin building programs and competence in such areas as social science research and information technology.

As indicated earlier, the State Department's expenditures on research have been miniscule compared to those of other Federal agencies. The need for more research was a major consideration in the recommendations by the Herter and Perkins Committees for a national academy for foreign affairs, the image being one of a research-oriented academic facility in contrast to the Foreign Service Institute which operates strictly as a training facility. Of the many outside pleas for the State Department to modernize its research, one of the most eloquent is that of Robert E. Elder:

The government is pouring millions of dollars into theoretical research in the physical sciences and billions into the application of such research findings to practical projects, i.e., Vanguard, Thor, Polaris, Jupiter. Research and experimentation in the physical sciences are recognized as ways to win the cold war, to preserve peace in our time, to maintain American security. There is missing from the government and among its leaders any compar-

124

The Organization

able recognition of the value of theoretical and applied research in the social and behavioral fields as related to the formulation and conduct of American foreign policy. There is no encouragement from high sources for this type of research—in psychology, sociology, anthropology, economics, political science, even semantics and group dynamics—so that America can better learn how to control the weapons of destruction which we assume will help us preserve the peace, but which will also prove useful for war. Nowhere in the Department of State nor in the National Security Council structure is there an attempt made either to stimulate social research or to bring its findings to bear directly in any integrated way upon the formulation and conduct of American foreign policy.[34]

Clearly, State Department leadership and the FSO corps have not as yet been receptive to significant efforts in the social science research area, or, as Elder points out, they simply have not recognized the need. The culture has not been outward-looking, positive, experimental. The Project Camelot debacle, in which a multimillion-dollar Pentagon-sponsored social science research project in Latin America was cancelled in the face of Chilean antagonism, offers a case in point. To begin with, the fact that the military instead of the State Department was behind such a project *in foreign affairs* is significant in itself. One commentator offered an explanation:

It is an old story that between the State Department policy sections and the American academic community there is, and for long has been, distrust founded upon the State Department's lack of confidence in the concrete

[34] Elder, *The Policy Machine: The Department of State and American Foreign Policy* (Syracuse: Syracuse University Press, 1960), pp. 166-67.

125

results of social science research and the academic community's belief—best expressed by Professor Gabriel Almond to a reporter for *Science*—that the State Department is a "conservative institution dominated by a foreign service which is trained largely in the law, in history, in the humanistic disciplines. They believe in making policy through some kind of intuitive and antenna-like process."[35]

When Camelot exploded, the State Department's negative position came through in the Congressional hearings that followed. Secretary Rusk brushed aside questions about why the State Department was not the sponsor of such a project instead of the military and why State never asked Congress for any significant appropriation for research. Rusk indicated that the Department had no objection to others engaging in social science research—all it wanted was to be in a position to veto projects which might upset delicate relationships and create problems in foreign affairs.[36]

It was in this atmosphere that Crockett created the Center for International Systems Research (CISR) in 1965, with the hope that somehow it would stimulate interest and concrete activity in both social science research and systems development. Outside talent was imported to head up the program on the assumption that FSOs could not be found with the necessary experience and interest. This assumption was probably valid, but it also may have functioned as a self-fulfilling prophecy. At any rate, the managers of CISR expended a great deal of effort over an ex-

[35] Robert A. Nisbet, "Project Camelot: An Autopsy," *The Public Interest*, No. 5 (Fall 1966), 45-69.

[36] U.S. Congress, House Committee on Foreign Affairs, *Behavorial Sciences and the National Security*, Hearings before the Subcommittee on International Organizations and Movements, 89th Cong., 1st Sess., 1965, p. 126.

tended period in a fruitless attempt to interest FSOs in serving in the program.

The purpose and program of CISR were never fully stated. Whether for this reason or not, jurisdictional friction points cropped up between CISR on the one hand and the Foreign Service Institute and the Bureau of Intelligence and Research on the other.

The most serious problem of CISR was inadequate funding. Since 1964 there has been strong and persistent cost-cutting pressure in the federal government. Even though the State Department, next to the Department of Justice, has the smallest budget among Cabinet agencies, Secretary Rusk made it clear that he would approve no requests for increases in positions and funds except under the most compelling circumstances. With the sole exception of improvements in communication technology, Crockett had to find support for the new change programs within existing ceilings.

CISR was awarded a complement of approximately a dozen positions, but its managers had to engage in a continuing struggle to obtain even the most minimal operating funds. One of the most promising projects, a fairly advanced plan for a series of highly professional case studies on foreign policy crises, never came to life, largely because of lack of money. There was an interesting simulation project developed by CISR in cooperation with Wayne State University, and two symposia were organized. A series of "occasional papers" was launched, but only two papers were published. Very few of the CISR projects ever got out of the planning stage.

In the case of information technology, there were three Crockett efforts: the Substantive Information System (SNS) effort, the Manpower Utilization System and Techniques

Background and Forces of Change

(MUST) effort, and physical improvements of the Department's worldwide communications network.

The problem of applying modern technology to improve the flow, storage, retrieval, and display of substantive information in foreign affairs has received some attention since the early 1960s. Largely under the stimulus of the Bureau of the Budget, an interagency program was mounted, known as FAIME (Foreign Affairs Information Management Effort). Considerable money was spent by the Bureau in supporting the interagency group, with indifferent results. The effort was scaled down, and there was an understanding that the State Department would take on the role of interagency leadership. FAIME has become the tiny nearly-forgotten staff with no budget known as SNS. In a manner analogous to CISR, the SNS staff tends to think in terms of large-scale systems design and avoids small concrete projects. The program represents something of a dilemma for State. Given the interagency history of the effort, State cannot afford to abolish the program. On the other hand, it has not been able to afford the money necessary to give the program any significance.

Calls for improved career-planning procedures and personnel data within State go back as far as the first Hoover Commission Report of 1949, and were repeated in the Rowe, Wriston, and Herter Reports. A serious effort was made when the Career Development and Counseling (CDC) staff was created in 1957, but by 1962 it had expired.[37] Profiting from the CDC experience, the MUST concept was developed early in 1965. Its basic elements included (1) an inventory of worldwide position requirements, projected ahead up to 10 years; (2) development of

[37] The history of recommendations and the CDC experience are described in John E. Harr, *The Development of Careers in the Foreign Service* (New York: Carnegie Endowment for International Peace, 1965), Chapter 4.

128

The Organization

an assignment profile for each officer, projecting his tentative assignments and training ahead for up to 10 years; and (3) a computer program that would compare the inventory and the assignments at any point in time and report out imbalances. One of the early steps was the consolidation of more than 1,200 position titles in the Civil Service and Foreign Service systems into less than 100 titles. Experience and training prerequisites were tentatively set for each successive grade level in each position series.

Aside from the advantage of improving State's inadequate data on jobs and people, a major purpose of MUST was to make possible greater decentralization of personnel authorities to the operating bureaus, the "users" in MUST terminology. The assignment profile developed on the individual officer would represent the "contract" between central personnel and the using bureau, but since the profile would set the assignment only in general terms, the bureau would have considerable leeway in designating the specific assignment. For example, the profile might say only that an officer's next assignment should be in an overseas political section in a large mission in Latin America. The Latin American bureau would make the decision as to which mission and which specific job. MUST was designed to serve the needs of the State Department, but was also to be expandable to the larger foreign affairs community if a uniform personnel system is achieved.

In concept and design MUST was as sophisticated as any manpower system in the Federal Government, and it won a measure of acceptance. The regional bureaus in State liked the decentralization prospects, and the Budget Bureau became a strong supporter. A large number of FSOs worked on MUST, particularly in developing the assignment profiles, so that it was better understood within the Service than most of the other major change efforts. Still, it has not become operational, although it was designed and ready for implementation by 1966.

In the third effort in the area of information technology, Crockett sponsored improvements abroad and a highly sophisticated "Automated Terminal System" at home to modernize the Department's worldwide communications network. This one example of success in the change efforts is illustrative. The problem of inadequate communications facilities reached the proportions of a crisis for State; therefore energetic action simply could not be avoided. The need became clear at high levels, and, as noted, Crockett was able to get support for a budget increase for this purpose. It is extremely doubtful that improvements of this magnitude would have occurred had not events literally forced them upon the Department.

Partly out of frustration over little or no progress in the other change efforts, Crockett initiated a new program concerned specifically with the processes of organizational change, in particular, the interpersonal dimension. Called ACORD (Action for Organizational Development), it was based on applying the knowledge of the behavioral sciences to the actual workings of a complex organization.

The creation of Richard W. Barrett, ACORD is difficult to evaluate since it coalesced as a program only in the spring of 1966. It was also a complex program, and cannot be fully described here.

There were several antecedents, including the experimental use in 1965 of the group dynamics training method known variously as "sensitivity training," "laboratory training," or "T-group" training. Basically this is a learning-by-experience method in which a group is assembled, usually in a retreat setting, without a structured program. A trainer is present who attempts to help participants learn, through the group's own experiences, about such human processes as community formation, leadership, communication, trust, and so on.[38] The early State Department groups were limited to senior officers. One result was a provocative study on conformity in the "living system" of the State Department, which is discussed at length in Chapter 6.

Another antecedent was the 1965 "management by objectives and programs" reorganization of the administrative area of the Department in which Crockett attempted to overcome some of the inhibitions to communication and responsibility-taking inherent in the classic bureaucratic structure, by applying some of the ideas of such theorists as Douglas McGregor and Rensis Likert.[39]

Drawing on these experiences, the ACORD program was conceptualized in 1966 when it had become abundantly clear that the managerial and technological change efforts had been launched with insufficient consideration given to the human relations dimension of the organization. The ACORD concept attracted a good deal of attention throughout the government. A great many industrial firms and government agencies employ the T-group method or variations of it, but only rarely is there a program that helps transmit something of the T-group learning experience back to the life of the organization itself. The term "organizational development" has grown up to denote these few programs.

Aside from the T-group method itself, the basic elements of the ACORD program were development of an internal staff to serve as a focal point for the program, a long-term relationship with the T-group trainers who also serve as consultants to managers, pairing of internal staff members

[38] A useful source among the many available on the T-Group method is Leland P. Bradford, Jack R. Gibb, and Kenneth Benne, ed., *T-Group Theory and Laboratory Method* (New York: John Wiley & Sons, 1964).

[39] McGregor, *The Human Side of Enterprise* (New York: McGraw-Hill, 1960) ; Likert, *New Patterns of Management* (New York: McGraw-Hill, 1961).

and consultants and assigning pairs to specific parts of the total organization, and working with varieties of groups in brief "off-site" meetings for problem-solving or team-building purposes. A major emphasis throughout was focusing the activities on real problems and relationships within the organization that otherwise might not be dealt with adequately.

ACORD was given a complement of 10 positions and sufficient funds to put on the T-groups and contract for the consultant services. More than 200 State Department officers elected to attend the T-groups, and the program became quite a conversation piece both within and outside the State Department.

With Crockett's departure in January 1967 there is no longer a driving force in the State Department to sustain the change efforts. Administration in the routine, noninnovative sense is now supreme. Crockett's successor has largely reversed the reorganization of the administrative area; he eliminated CISR in mid-1967, the CCPS staff in the fall of 1967, and ACORD in early 1968. MUST has not fulfilled its original promise. Merged into a routine personnel services area, it has lost its identity. There has been no new initiative in the personnel area comparable to Crockett's efforts in regard to the Hays Bill and the USIA integration plan. Only SNS in the information technology area continues to exist, and there is an effort to generate financial support for it.

Perhaps the most disastrous failure was the case of the programming system and its relationship to NSAM 341, since this combination offered the strongest and most direct promise of overcoming the barriers to effective State Department leadership of foreign affairs. The most immediate cause of failure was the Bureau of the Budget's flat opposition to State's three-year effort to develop a comprehensive system opposed by the Bureau in favor of its own individual-agency approach.

Ironically, this bureaucratic struggle reached its climax in March of 1966, just at the moment when the State Department received its strongest mandate ever for leadership in foreign affairs in the form of NSAM 341. But as the NSAM was issued Secretary Rusk had this to say, among other comments: "There can be no room for parochial viewpoints or petty bureaucratic 'in-fighting.' Each of us must recognize at all times we are, in a real sense, acting for and on behalf of the President, and through him, serving all the people of the United States."[40]

At this critical juncture Crockett felt that he could not buck the problem up to Secretary Rusk in the form of a bureaucratic stalemate, so the programming operation went into standby status while he sought to involve the Secretary by another means—through a high-level committee chaired by Charles Hitch. The Hitch report clearly supported the State Department approach over the Budget Bureau and urged that momentum not be lost. But since it did not comment on the adequacy of the past efforts, Katzenbach's position, when he was given responsibility for implementing the report in the fall of 1966, was not to seek any link-up with the talent pool and body of experience which then existed in State. Instead, he embarked on his effort to find a top man to lead the effort, which ultimately failed when his candidate withdrew in May 1967. No effort has been made to find a candidate since then. Throughout this period of more than a year, the programming staff languished, having little to do. It was able to cooperate in mounting a new comprehensive programming system within the Latin American bureau of State, a discrete effort that was not

40 U.S. Department of State, *News Letter* (Mar. 1966), p. 3.

related to Katzenbach's attempt to implement the Hitch Report. There had been more than 20 highly motivated persons with several years of experience on the State Department programming staff; by mid-1968, none remained in the employ of the State Department.

Possibly because he wanted to solve the programming problem first, Katzenbach did not activate the potentially powerful Senior Interdepartmental Group, of which he was Executive Chairman, for a long time. Not until nearly nine months after becoming Under Secretary did Katzenbach call his first SIG meeting. It is now a rule that no two-week period shall pass without a SIG meeting.

A development over the winter of 1967-68 has made the picture even more dismal. Because of the costs of the Vietnam war and the gold flow problem, the White House ordered the foreign affairs agencies to cut back their overseas personnel and resources by 10 percent. With a coordinated framework for decision-making, such as would have been provided by a comprehensive planning-programming-budgeting system in foreign affairs, this sort of cut can be handled reasonably well, and indeed can be beneficial in forcing a hard rethinking of priorities. Without such a framework, it can become a morale-damaging across-the-board slash.

With benefit of hindsight, some of the reasons can be identified for the general lack of success of the imaginative and daring change efforts of the period 1963-67. An obvious one was the shortage of money. Another was the generally inert and unexperimental nature of the larger State Department culture. A reflection of this was lack of understanding and commitment to the change efforts within the greater part of the FSO corps. Some of the responsibility here, however, must be laid to the sponsors of change. Until late in the game there was inadequate recognition of the need to work for the involvement of the FSOs.

The Organization

Another problem was that the Crockett-sponsored change program was encumbered with a large number of minor projects and tinkerings. (Only the major projects have been described in this chapter.) The result was that the strength of the over-all change impulse was dissipated and lacked coherence. The objectives never quite came through, and to some extent the whirlwind of activity tended to generate mistrust and defensiveness.

A related weakness was that the major projects were never quite connected together, or in some respects were out of synchronization with one another. For example, the ACORD program was born largely out of the frustrations of trying to impose a major managerial and technological change—the CCPS—on a puzzled and unwilling bureaucracy. If the two efforts had been started simultaneously, or preferably ACORD first, the story might have been quite different.

In the same manner, five years separated the Kennedy letter, which gave strong authority to ambassadors in the field, and NSAM 341, which gave comparable authority to State Department line managers in Washington. The absence of the decision-making framework made possible later by NSAM 341 was one of the critical barriers to the success of the comprehensive programming effort.

All things considered, the fundamental difficulty in the way of effective change in the Department of State is the lack of a strong, concerned managerial focal point above the administrative area of the Department. There is no evidence that anyone at this level appreciates the magnitude of the change that is being asked of the Department, nor believes that anything more than issuing instructions and exhorting people to live up to their responsibilities is required to bring the change about.

The problem of the top leadership in State is a particularly knotty one. The split between substance and administra-

135

tion is not simply an invention of the FSO corps, but goes right to the summit of the organization and is gravely dysfunctional. Holding that the Department remained a puzzle to President Kennedy to the end, Arthur Schlesinger wrote: "No one ran it; Rusk, Ball and Harriman constituted a loose triumvirate on the seventh floor and, passing things back and forth among themselves, managed to keep a few steps ahead of crisis."[41] There is no management team in the Department. In a real sense, Crockett and others attempted to devise a management strategy for something that did not exist—management. Whether or not things must always be this way is still an open question. As we have seen, the widespread view is that the Secretary and the Under Secretary are too busy with policy and crises to manage the Department. Others dispute that this need be so, and a favored model for those holding this view is the performance of Robert McNamara in the Pentagon.

Although in most tangible respects, the change program failed, it nevertheless has left an impact. For example, the new attempt to create a programming system in the Latin American bureau continues to exist; though limited, it may provide continuity and a seedbed for a larger effort later. The change program also has had a decided impact on the FSO corps, even though most FSOs at least passively resisted the change efforts while they existed. In the next five chapters, I undertake a depth examination of the FSO corps—the composition of the Service, social origins and characteristics, attitudes toward change, and leadership within the Service. In the concluding chapter, we will return to the question of an over-all management strategy for change and to the crucial interrelationships between the FSO corps and the larger organization, with respect to the role challenge.

[41] Schlesinger, *A Thousand Days*, pp. 446-47.

PART II

THE PROFESSIONAL GROUP

CHAPTER 4

COMPOSITION OF THE CORPS

....

THERE IS a natural tendency to see FSOs as a highly homogeneous group. What is readily apparent about the FSO corps can easily lead to the erroneous conclusion that there is not much more to be learned about the corps. But there is quite a bit more. One may learn, for example, that the FSO corps constitutes a unique institution within the larger organization of the Department of State. Although technically it is but one of several large personnel groups within State, it is soon apparent that it occupies a special position not enjoyed by the other groups such as the Civil Service employees who fill many of the domestic jobs, the Reserve officers, the Staff corps, and the foreign nationals (locally employed at overseas posts). The FSO corps lays claim to professional status. It has its own legislative charter and is constituted as a "career system," in contradistinction to the general Civil Service. One of the pronounced characteristics is well-developed norms of behavior which to a considerable extent are self-enforced in the manner of professional groups. This includes, for example, a quasi-military sense of discipline and a readiness to serve anywhere in the world.

The familiar image is one of a relatively small, elite group, whose members are carefully chosen to spend most of their careers abroad practicing the somewhat esoteric art of diplomacy, which in turn consists basically of representation, negotiation, reporting, and consular services. But the reality behind this image has changed substantially in recent years.

139

The Professional Group

Most FSOs do share a number of attributes, and, as we shall see in detail in subsequent chapters, there are fairly strong pressures for conformity and homogeneity in the career experience. Yet in important respects, there are differentiating characteristics. Two very important areas of differentiation are found in the functions FSOs perform and the methods by which they enter the Service. The full-scale involvement of the U.S. in foreign affairs following World War II created a need for new functions. In order to staff these functions one of the expedients resorted to over the past 20 years has been bringing some persons into the FSO corps by unorthodox methods, that is, other than entrance at a young age on the basis of a rigorous examination process.

In a previous work the author studied the composition of the FSO corps as it existed in mid-1962, in terms of such indices as function and method of entry, as well as others.[1] This provides a basis for comparisons to the mid-1966 composition of the corps and for analyzing trends in the four-year timespan. The points of comparison and the changes of the 1962-66 period will have greater meaning if they are set against the background of the prevailing pattern of career development in the Foreign Service.

Career Development in the Foreign Service

In an earlier work I described the classic career development pattern in the Foreign Service as follows:

The aspiring diplomat would enter the Service at a young age, on the basis of competitive examination of an

[1] John E. Harr, *The Anatomy of the Foreign Service*, Foreign Affairs Personnel Study No. 4 (New York: Carnegie Endowment for International Peace, 1965). Aside from a few tables drawn from the "Survey of the Diplomatic Profession" (which was designed and administered by the author in 1966), the tables in this chapter are based on the author's independent computer analysis and comparison of his 1962 data with 1966 data obtained from a number of offices in the Department of State.

essentially generalist character. For a number of years, he would be assigned consular duties in different parts of the world. This would provide ample opportunity for testing his competence, devotion to the Service, and general performance and adaptability as an American representative in foreign environments. If judged capable, he would then move on to economic and political work in his middle years, and would have every reasonable prospect of reaching the top ranks in his later years.[2]

The four major functional fields were and still are the political, economic, administrative, and consular fields. In a somewhat special category are the commercial and labor fields, representing the interests of the Departments of Commerce and Labor as performed abroad by FSOs. A third group consists of a number of small, specialized fields, representing positions filled by FSOs mainly in Washington—public affairs, cultural affairs, intelligence and research, and international organization.

The highest-status field, the one that most young persons join the Foreign Service to engage in, is the political field. The economic field has been rising steadily in status over the years, although it includes a number of highly specialized subfields (civil aviation, atomic energy, international finance, petroleum, fisheries, minerals) which are regarded by many FSOs as potential dead ends for career purposes. Taken together, the political and *general* economic fields are referred to by FSOs as the "substantive" fields of diplomacy, as contrasted to administration, by which is meant low-level support of other activities, not management.

The relatively low status of the consular field may be attributed to its use historically as a testing ground for new officers. Another indication of the low status of the

[2] John E. Harr, *The Development of Careers in the Foreign Service*, Foreign Affairs Personnel Study No. 3 (New York: Carnegie Endowment for International Peace, 1965), p. 8.

consular field, and of the administrative field, as well, is the fact that before the Wriston program substantial numbers of Staff employees worked in these fields, whereas Staff personnel would almost never be found in political and economic jobs.

The political and economic fields, in the parlance of FSOs, constitute the "mainstream" of a Foreign Service career. They are closer to policy considerations and are better rewarded in the promotion system, thus providing the most direct track to the top. Being deficient in this regard, the other fields are less prestigious, outside of the "mainstream." They are more narrowly specialized; once assigned to one of them, many officers believe, it is difficult to get out.

Therefore, the rule for the young examination-entry officer has been either to avoid assignment to the low-status fields altogether or to serve in one of them early in one's career and rotate into the political and economic areas as soon as possible. This is the classic generalist pattern, although the terms *generalist* and *specialist* do not have very precise meanings in the Foreign Service context. An officer may be just as specialized in the political field as the consular or administrative fields. An important element of the generalist-specialist debate over the years in the FSO corps is status—high-status versus low-status fields.

The obvious result of the classic pattern is difficulty in staffing all of the functional fields except the political field, with the difficulty easing in the economic field over time. A number of measures have been taken to correct the situation, the most visible being a resort to lateral entry. The need to solve the problem of specialization was one of the Wriston Report's major arguments in support of the large-scale program for bringing into the FSO corps hundreds

142

of persons in the administrative and consular fields, and others with experience in the smaller functional fields.

Most of the incoming lateral entrants, therefore, found themselves in a low-status position on two counts: as lateral entrants they were entering the corps in unorthodox fashion; and the functions most of them represented (and in a great many cases were to continue to perform) were of low status within the FSO corps. The result was that those lateral entrants who were well-equipped to compete with examination-entry officers, in educational background and level of professional experience, made haste to move into the higher-status fields. In the main, they were officers who had been in the Civil Service in the Department before Wristonization. By 1962 more than half of the FSOs serving in executive positions were lateral entrants, one of the reasons being that many had had supervisory experience in their domestic jobs before entering the FSO corps laterally.

On the other hand, many of the lateral entrants less qualified to compete with FSOs for the higher-status jobs found themselves in difficulty. For the most part, these officers had been in the Staff corps before Wristonization, and were engaged mainly in consular work and the sub-specialities of administration, such as budget and fiscal, disbursing, general services, personnel. They were unable to move from these fields, and did not fare well in the FSO promotion system. Some were selected-out and many others faced the serious threat of it.

The fact that many lateral entrants fled their specialized fields and that new examination entrants for the most part were not interested in these fields made it necessary to continue to use lateral entry to staff these fields. In the period 1958 to 1962, for example, 97 of the 247 officers who entered laterally were administrative specialists.

After 1962 the situation improved somewhat as a result of the Herter Report and the State Department's decision to "revitalize" the Staff corps (mentioned briefly in Chapter 2). The import of this decision was that lower-level specialized jobs in such functions as administration and consular affairs were gradually to be removed from the FSO corps, as incumbents either left State Department employment or were persuaded to convert to another personnel category, principally the Staff category. This, in effect, was a partial reversal of the Wriston program (the success of the effort will be discussed in a later section).

Cognizant that the Wriston integration program had not solved the problem of specialization, the Herter Committee made a number of recommendations for correcting the imbalance among the functional fields. These included manpower planning, career development, options for the functional fields in the written entrance examination, a concept of "functional career lines," and changes in the procedures of the promotion panels to help insure greater consideration of specialized competences. There have been efforts to implement all of these recommendations. Options are now included in the basic examination for the commercial, economic, and administrative fields, in addition to Option A (history, government, the social sciences, and public affairs). Counseling and assignment services for the mid-career group are organized around the major functional fields, and the promotion panels go through a two-step process, the first step being consideration of officers as grouped by their major functional fields.

In addition, the practice of automatically assigning young officers to two-year tours in consular sections has ended. All new entrance examination officers are now under the jurisdiction of the Junior Officer Program for their first several tours. For their first two years abroad, the normal pattern

144

is rotation among the four major fields, six months each in the political, economic, administrative, and consular sections of an embassy. The result of these measures is that there are probably more capable officers in the undernourished functional fields than there were even four or five years ago. The generalist-specialist issue is not nearly as hotly debated as it was during the 1950s.

This is not to suggest that all of the functional fields are neatly balanced, but merely that there has been some improvement of a serious imbalance. The specialized options in the basic examination still attract small numbers of applicants.[3] The trend toward positions with status among the functional fields described above is still very strong. It is still true that FSOs rarely gain experience in such major fields as overseas information and development assistance. Generally, however, there is better acceptance and understanding of the need to staff the specialized fields, and more readiness on the part of most officers to take their turn in doing so.

Some of these points will be touched on again in examining the data comparing the 1962 and 1966 FSO corps. A useful starting place is to present background information on the size of the corps and method of entry.

Size of the Corps

Table 1 shows the size of the corps by grade level at four points in time, from 1954 to 1966. As discussed in Chapter 2, in 1954 the corps was at a low point as a result of McCarthyism and budget cuts. There had been no normal

[3] For example, in the period September 1963 (when the options were first employed in the written examination) to June 1966, 88 percent of the applicants chose Option A. Three percent chose B (Administration), 8 percent chose C (Economics), and 1 percent chose D (Commerce). See U.S. Department of State, "Department of State Manpower," Fiscal Year 1966 Report of the Management Reports Staff, pp. 11-12.

145

TABLE 1

FSOs by Grade, 1954-66

Grade	March 31, 1954 No.	Percent	June 30, 1958 No.	Percent	June 30, 1962 No.	Percent	August 1966 No.	Percent
Career Ambassador	—	—	4	0.1	7	0.2	8	0.2
Career Minister	46	3.6	64	1.9	48	1.3	54	1.5
1	103	8.0	188	5.5	220	6.0	297	8.5
2	143	11.1	372	10.8	404	11.0	435	12.4
3	232	18.0	531	15.5	603	16.4	654	18.6
4	250	19.5	570	16.6	718	19.6	632	18.0
5	308	24.0	585	17.0	572	15.5	446	12.7
6	203	15.8	611	17.8	322	8.8	475	13.5
7	—	—	126	3.7	380	10.4	345	9.8
8	—	—	381	11.1	396	10.8	161	4.6
Totals	1,285	100	3,432	100	3,670	100	3,507	100

bottom-level recruitment for two years. The Personnel Improvement Program had flopped, setting the stage for the Wriston program. As the table indicates, three grade levels did not exist at the time—the topmost level of Career Ambassador and the bottom two grades, 7 and 8; among several legislative measures designed to make the large-scale lateral entry proposed by the Wriston Report more nearly feasible, these grade levels were added.

By 1958, when the Wriston program ended, the corps had grown enormously, from 1,285 to 3,432, which was accomplished by implementation of two Wriston recommendations: lateral entry of more than 1,500 persons from other personnel categories within the Department of State (Civil Service, Reserve, and Staff), and vigorous renewal of the orthodox bottom-level entry process. The latter is represented in the 1958 column by all of the officers at levels 7 and 8 and by most of those at level 6.

The corps increased slightly in size from 1958 to 1962, and declined slightly from 1962 to 1966, presenting a picture of relative stability. As we shall see later in this chapter, however, there have been significant shifts of emphasis within the numerical boundaries. In 1954 the shape of the corps resembled the classic organizational pyramid, with smaller numbers at each ascending grade level, except for the bottom grade. In subsequent years the corps became more nearly diamond-shaped, with the largest numbers in the mid-career grades. The specific cause was the large lateral influx; the general cause was increasing specialization within the corps, which called for proportionately more persons at mid-career levels.

Method of Entry

Analysis by method of entry is fairly complex because of the number of special lateral-entry programs, particularly in

The Professional Group

the postwar years. Organized by the major modes of entry over the years, Table 2 shows the numbers in each category in 1962 and in 1966. First on the list is the basic entrance examination method which has been considered the orthodox method since creation of the modern Foreign Service by the Rogers Act.[4] The first item of interest is that the proportion of examination entry officers has risen significantly, from 54.3 percent of the total corps in 1962 to 65.7 percent in 1966.

TABLE 2

FSO Corps by Method of Entry, 1962 and 1966

Method of Entry	Operative Dates	1962	1966
Basic entrance examination	1924 to present	1,992	2,303
Section 5, Rogers Act	1924-1946	8	5
Reorganization Act	1939	9	5
Manpower Act	1946	96	57
Section 517, Foreign Service Act	1946-1954	97	76
Personnel Improvement Program	1951	18	13
Direct lateral entry	1954-1958	18	13
Wriston program	1954-1958	1,185	757
Continuing lateral entry	1958 to present	247	278
Totals		3,670	3,507

A brief explanation of each of the remaining methods in Table 2, all of them lateral entry methods, will be useful:

Section 5, Rogers Act. As an indication that the main emphasis was to be on the basic examination method, the Rogers Act provided for lateral entry in very restrictive terms—the only persons eligible were Department of State employees in executive or semi-executive positions.

Reorganization Act. The merging of the overseas services of the Departments of Commerce and Labor into the FSO corps by Reorganization Plan No. 2 of 1939 added 114 officers to the corps; by 1966 only five remained.

[4] Since 1924, of course, the nature of the basic examination process has changed a number of times.

Composition of the Corps

Manpower Act. Shortly before the Foreign Service Act was passed in 1946, Congress passed the Manpower Act which was intended to compensate for the cessation of recruitment during the war. The Manpower Act provided for the entry of "not more than 250" qualified persons into the FSO corps, but only 166 were actually taken in under this authority. Of this group, only 57 remained as of 1966.

Section 517, Foreign Service Act of 1946. This is the basic legislative authorization for lateral entry which replaced Section 5 of the Rogers Act, and which liberalized the eligibility requirements. All of the remaining lateral entry methods are based on this provision, but are shown separately because of their character as special programs of emphasis at the various times.

Personnel Improvement Program. A limited effort of the Department of State, described in the last chapter, to implement the Rowe Report. Only 25 persons were brought in laterally under this program, of whom in 1966 13 remained.

Direct Lateral Entry Program. During the time of the Wriston program the Department was authorized by Congress to take laterally into the FSO corps up to 40 persons whose prior government service was not in the Department of State. This quota was later raised to 175, and in 1960 the quota restriction was removed entirely.

The Wriston Program. Of the 1,525 persons brought into the FSO corps in the Wriston program, attrition had cut the number virtually in half by 1966, to 757 persons.

Continuing Lateral Entry Program. The Department of State considered the Wriston program terminated by the beginning of 1958. All lateral entry since that time has been regarded as coming under the "continuing lateral entry program," which is not so much a program as an administrative effort to make lateral entry routine and stabilize it

149

The Professional Group

at a reasonable annual figure, to avoid large-scale integrations. The level has been approximately 20 to 30 entrants per year. The legal authority is still Section 517 of the Foreign Service Act, as amended.

Continuity and Turnover

A convenient way to view method of entry, one that was employed in the 1962 study, is according to time of entry in four-year blocks. Because of the magnitude of the Wriston program the four-year blocks in this study are built around the period 1954-58. Tables 3 and 4 show first the examination entry time groups and then the lateral entry time groups, comparing the population of each group for 1962 and 1966.

TABLE 3

Population of Examination Entry Groups, 1962 and 1966

	Time of entry			
	Pre-1954	1954-58	1958-62	1962-66
1962 FSO corps	806	466	720	—
1966 FSO corps	687	403	569	644
Percent of decrease, 1962 to 1966	14.8	13.3	21.0	—

TABLE 4

Population of Lateral Entry Groups, 1962 and 1966

	Time of entry			
	Pre-1954	1954-58	1958-62	1962-66
1962 FSO corps	246	1,185	247	—
1966 FSO corps	169	757	160	118
Percent of decrease, 1962 to 1966	31.3	36.1	35.2	—

The decrease in the pre-1954 group is attributable almost entirely to retirements, since this is the most senior group. Retirement would not be a possibility in the case of the

150

other two groups, so that the reductions must be attributed mainly to selection-out and voluntary resignation. At first glance, it might seem surprising that the younger group had the greatest proportionate decline; the explanation is that this is the period of adjustment. It is during the first or second tour of duty abroad that the individual officer and the Foreign Service learn something about the extent to which the newcomer is able to adjust to the rigors of living abroad, the constraints of bureaucratic life, and the real world of international politics, as compared to the more romantic notions that neophytes are inclined to have.

The lateral entry groups show much greater turnover than the examination entry groups, for several reasons. One is that the lateral entrants as a whole are older than the examination entrants, and therefore are more prone to retirement. Another is that many lateral entrants face a more difficult adjustment problem than examination entrants, therefore are more vulnerable to selection-out. The third reason is the concerted effort in recent years to convert to other personnel categories those officers relatively less well qualified to compete in the FSO system.

As Table 5 indicates, 157 of the 180 officers who converted from FSO status to another personnel category were lateral entrants. In effect, the table shows what has happened to the 1962 FSO corps (organized in the four-year blocks) in the period between 1962 and 1966. Of the 1962 total of 3,670 officers, almost 75 percent are still in the Service. Almost 5 percent have converted to other personnel categories, and slightly more than 20 percent have left State Department employment entirely (attrition). This compares with the Department of State's official figure of approximately 5 percent attrition annually in the FSO category. The voluntary resignation rate (as contrasted to selection-out, separation for cause, resignation on marriage

TABLE 5
Attrition, Continuity, and Conversion
of FSOs by Personnel Category, 1962 to 1966

	Lateral Entry						Examination Entry							
	Pre-1954		1954-58		1958-62		Pre-1954		1954-58		1958-62		Total	
	No.	percent	No.	percent	No.	percent	No.	percent	No.	percent	No.	percent	No.	percent
Attrition	77	31.3	321	27.1	35	14.2	113	14.0	59	12.7	139	19.3	744	20.3
Continuity	169	68.7	757	63.9	160	64.8	687	85.2	404	86.7	569	79.0	2,746	74.8
Conversion	—	—	107	9.0	52	21.0	6	0.8	3	0.6	12	1.7	180	4.9
Totals	246	100	1,185	100	247	100	806	100	466	100	720	100	3,670	100

Composition of the Corps

or transfer to another category) at the junior levels has been constant at about 2 percent per year.[5]

As Table 6 shows, attrition, in the main, has occurred at higher grade levels than the conversions, due to the higher incidence at these grades of normal retirement after a full career. Again, the attrition at the lower grades is due to selection-out and voluntary resignation.

TABLE 6

FSO Attrition and Conversions by
Grade Level, 1962 to 1966

1962 grade	Attrition		Conversions	
	no.	percent	no.	percent
Career Ambassador	3	0.4	—	—
Career Minister	14	1.9	—	—
1	72	9.7	1	0.6
2	103	13.8	1	0.6
3	101	13.6	16	8.8
4	126	16.9	38	21.0
5	118	15.9	60	33.1
6	63	8.5	25	14.4
7	66	8.9	34	18.8
8	78	10.4	5	2.8
Totals	744	100	180	100

A closer examination of the 180 FSOs who converted to other personnel categories shows that they come preponderantly from the group discussed earlier in this chapter— officers relatively less well-equipped to compete in the FSO system, primarily former Staff corps personnel in the lower status functions. Table 7 shows the personnel status of the convertees *before* they became FSOs and the new personnel status to which they have converted upon leaving the FSO corps.

The great majority of the converted officers came from the Staff corps in the first place, and an even greater majority

[5] U.S. Department of State, "Department of State Manpower," Fiscal Year 1966 Report by the Management Reports Staff, p. 15.

153

The Professional Group

TABLE 7
Prior and Present Personnel Status
of Converted FSOs

	Prior status	Present status
Foreign Service Staff	134	156
Foreign Service Reserve	5	18
GS (General Schedule of the Civil Service)	26	6
Not in government employment	15	—
Totals	180	180

converted to it. The category "not in Government employment" would apply to those examination entry officers who came directly into FSO status without an interim appointment in another category.

Viewing the 180 officers in terms of their major functional category in the FSO corps (Table 8), it is clear that the great majority come from the administrative and consular fields.

TABLE 8

Functional Fields of Converted Officers

Function	New Personnel Status Group		
	FSS	FSR	GS
Administration	95	3	—
Consular	41	2	2
Public Affairs	—	2	1
Economic/Commercial	4	6	1
Political	3	2	1
Special Technical	—	—	1
Unknown	13	3	—
Totals	156	18	6

Apparently the conversion policy has been reasonably successful. Combined with attrition and the rebuilding of the Staff corps, it has effectively removed from the FSO purview a great many of the more narrowly specialized jobs in the administrative and consular functions.

Composition of the Corps

Age and Grade

Referring now to the 2,745 officers in the "continuity" group—those 1962 officers still in the FSO corps in 1966— Table 9 shows their grade progression over the four-year period. The numbers of officers at each grade level in 1962 add vertically, and the numbers for the 1966 grades horizontally. Underlined numbers represent officers who have not been promoted during the four-year period. For example, of the 147 Class 1 officers in the Service in 1962, 123 are still at Class 1 and 24 have been promoted to Career Minister.

Obviously promotions occur more frequently at the lower grade levels. For example, only four of the 280 officers at FSO-7 in 1962 were still at that level in 1966, while 16 of them had gone as high as FSO-4. The average rate of promotion over the four-year period was one promotion per officer, which compares with the annual rate of approximately 25 percent of FSOs being promoted. The average grade of the "continuity" group in 1962 was 4.5; by 1966 it was 3.5.

TABLE 9

Grade Progression of FSOs, 1962 to 1966

1966	CA	CM	1	2	3	4	5	6	7	8	Totals
CA	4	3									7
CM		30	24								54
1			123	144	10						277
2				157	246	11					414
3				230	374	28					632
4					169	322	100	16			608
5						44	129	189	56		418
6							4	71	210		285
7								4	47		51
8											—
Totals	4	33	147	301	486	554	394	233	280	313	2,745

155

The Professional Group

The average-age-by-grade is widely viewed among FSOs as an important measure of career progress, and as the most tangible evidence of "success." An officer who is consistently younger than the average age for his grade obviously is moving ahead quickly and will enjoy greater rewards and probably better assignments than the officer who is consistently and significantly older than the average. Most officers are aware of the average age for their grade. Table 10 compares the figures for 1962 and 1966 of the average age per grade of the total FSO corps, the examination entry officers, and the lateral entry officers.

TABLE 10

Comparisons of Average Age Per Grade of
FSOs, 1962 and 1966

Grade	1962			1966		
	Total service	Exam. entry	Lateral entry	Total service	Exam. entry	Lateral entry
Career Ambassador	59.1	59.1	—	60.6	60.3	63.0
Career Minister	55.7	55.5	56.5	56.0	56.5	55.3
1	51.2	49.7	51.8	51.5	50.3	52.2
2	48.6	46.9	49.5	48.9	47.0	50.3
3	45.4	42.8	47.1	46.1	43.6	48.1
4	42.3	38.4	45.0	42.5	38.8	46.9
5	40.5	34.6	45.0	36.1	34.9	41.7
6	35.7	32.7	44.4	31.5	31.3	41.4
7	31.6	30.6	39.0	27.8	27.8	—
8	27.3	27.3	36.0	25.3	25.3	—
Over-All average	40.6	35.7	46.6	40.4	36.2	48.5

The most striking fact in the comparisons is that at every grade level except one (Career Minister in 1966) the average age of the examination entrants is younger than the average for the total service, while the average for lateral entrants is older. In most cases, the variance is pronounced, narrowing only at the very high grade levels. This, of course, is a function of the status problems of the lateral

156

entrant mentioned earlier, both in entering the Service in an unorthodox way and working for the most part in the less favored functional fields.

Two patterns of the four-year period are discernible in the figures—the continuing high level of intake of young examination entrants and the outgo of many lateral entrants via attrition and conversion. Note that at grades 5 through 8 the average ages of both examination and lateral entrants are significantly lower in 1966 compared to 1962. Comparing the total service columns, there has been some stretch-out of average ages in the intervening time; the senior officers are slightly older in 1966 compared to 1962, and the junior officers are significantly younger.

Functional Assignments and Interests

Table 11 shows the deployment of the FSO corps according to the functional fields discussed earlier in this chapter. Included in the table are assignments to managerial roles and to several special categories, so that the full complement of 3,507 officers is shown.

During the 1962-66 period the Department of State decentralized position classification authority, reduced the number and variety of position categories, and made other changes in its personnel data operations in line with the development of its manpower utilization system. Since that system is not operational, the data here were culled from a number of available data sources in the Department and should be regarded as broadly rather than precisely indicative of deployment. The same point holds for comparisons of this data to the 1962 data.

Under the "managerial" heading the term "executive" refers to presidential appointments—for example, as Ambassador or Assistant Secretary. The term "program direction" refers to other managerial positions such as Deputy

TABLE 11
Functional Assignments of FSOs, 1966

	CA	CM	1	2	3	4	5	6	7	8	Total	Percent of total	Percent above FSO-4
MANAGERIAL													
Program Direction, Exec.	8	45	151	113	52	31	10	11	4	—	425	12.1	87.0
FUNCTIONAL													
Political		4	35	108	199	157	123	100	29	—	755	21.5	45.8
Economic		—	18	46	107	97	80	54	7	—	409	11.7	41.8
Administrative		3	24	52	96	92	37	26	9	1	340	9.7	51.6
Consular		—	6	8	29	83	47	91	53	1	318	9.1	13.5
Commercial		—	1	9	29	33	19	14	2	—	107	3.1	36.4
Labor		—	1	10	9	9	7	4	—	—	40	1.1	50.0
International Org.		—	11	16	26	17	12	17	4	1	104	3.0	51.0
Intelligence & Research		—	2	7	9	15	17	20	16	—	86	2.5	20.9
Cultural Affairs		—	—	3	3	6	6	10	3	—	31	.9	19.4
Public Affairs		—	2	3	7	6	1	3	3	—	25	.7	48.0
SPECIAL													
Junior Officer		—	—	—	—	—	—	—	185	143	328	9.4	—
Training		1	16	24	25	21	36	42	13	11	189	5.4	34.9
Detail		—	17	22	30	23	20	19	17	4	152	4.3	45.4
Special Technical		1	6	6	5	4	—	1	—	—	23	.7	78.3
Other		—	7	8	28	38	31	63	—	—	175	5.0	24.6
Totals	8	54	297	435	654	632	446	475	345	161	3,507	100	41.3

Composition of the Corps

Chief of Mission abroad or Office Director in Washington. The number of officers in managerial roles has risen slightly over the four-year period, from 402 to 425.

The political field was the largest in 1962, with 669 assignments; it is still the largest and has increased substantially to 755. The economic field has declined by about the same margin, from 503 to 409, reflecting more a shift of job titles rather than a real change.

As one would expect from the analysis earlier in this chapter, the administrative and consular fields have declined, substantially, in numbers, particularly the former, from 592 assignments in 1962 to 340 in 1966. The two fields accounted for almost one-third of all assignments in 1962; in 1966 they accounted for less than one-fifth. The fact that the lower-level administrative positions are the ones that have been sorted out is indicated by the percentage of administrative jobs occupied by officers in grades above FSO-4. In 1962 this percentage was 24.2; in 1966 it was 51.6. Looking at the far righthand column of the table, it can be seen that the fields staffed predominantly by the lower-ranked officers are consular affairs, intelligence and research, and cultural affairs.

Among the smaller fields commercial work and cultural affairs have declined since 1962, and international organization affairs and intelligence and research have increased. Labor and public affairs have remained almost constant. The group of special assignment categories is largely self-explanatory. The junior officers are those on the central complement roster of the Junior Officer Program. "Training" includes only those officers on relatively long training assignments of more than three months duration. "Special technical" includes doctors, lawyers, engineers, science advisors, and other small groups of highly specialized persons.

The Professional Group

The "other" category includes officers between assignments or on the medical complement.

A comparison of the functional assignments of examination and lateral entrants is given in Table 12. Slightly more than one-third of FSOs are lateral entrants. If this can be used as a rough basis for comparison, it can be seen that the greatest area of overrepresentation for lateral entrants is still the administrative field. The pattern is almost exactly the reverse of that in the political field, where more than three-fourths of the jobs are occupied by examination entrants. In the remaining fields lateral entrants are over-

TABLE 12

Functional Assignments of Examination
and Lateral Entrants, 1966

	Exam. entry		Lateral entry		Totals	
	no.	percent	no.	percent	no.	percent
MANAGERIAL						
Program Direction and Executive	222	52.5	202	47.5	425	100
FUNCTIONAL						
Political	576	76.3	179	23.7	755	100
Economic	274	67.0	135	33.0	409	100
Administrative	85	25.0	255	75.0	340	100
Consular	184	57.6	134	42.4	318	100
Commercial	52	48.6	55	51.4	107	100
Labor	22	55.0	18	45.0	40	100
International Org.	61	58.7	43	41.3	104	100
Intelligence and Research	76	88.4	10	11.6	86	100
Cultural	24	77.4	7	22.6	31	100
Public Affairs	14	56.0	11	44.0	25	100
SPECIAL						
Junior Officer	328	100.0	—	—	328	100
Training	145	76.7	44	23.3	189	100
Detail	99	65.2	53	34.8	152	100
Special Technical	10	43.4	13	56.6	23	100
Other	130	74.2	45	25.8	175	100
Totals	2,303	65.7	1,204	34.3	3,507	100

Composition of the Corps

represented significantly in management, consular, commercial, labor, international organization affairs, public affairs, and special technical positions. The very large proportions of examination entrants in intelligence and research and cultural affairs are largely the result of the recent trend toward assigning young officers to the bureaus representing these functions during their first assignments in Washington after service abroad.

There have been increasing efforts in recent years to assign FSOs to tours of duty with other agencies, chiefly the foreign affairs agencies. Most FSOs, however, continue to regard such assignments as outside the mainstream, and therefore tend to resist them. On the other hand, the minority viewpoint, that operational experience with another agency can be a positive aid to the career progress of an officer, seems to be growing. Table 13 lists the number of officers assigned to other agencies in 1962 and 1966. The total has grown from 116 to 152, with the most striking in-

TABLE 13

FSOs on Detail to Other Federal Agencies, 1962 and 1966

	1962	1966
AID	19	57 (55)*
USIA	3	25 (20)
Peace Corps	7	10 (5)
Arms Control & Disarmament Agency	17	11
Commerce	34	21
Labor	2	2
Defense	13	4 (4)
White House	5	7
National Security Council	2	2
National Aeronautics & Space Admin.	3	6
Treasury	3	3
Agriculture	1	1
Interior	1	1
Health, Education and Welfare	1	1
Misc.	5	1
Totals	116	152

* Numbers in parentheses are officers serving overseas.

161

The Professional Group

creases in assignments to AID and USIA, the two major foreign affairs agencies apart from State.

When FSOs are asked their preferences for the functions in which they would most like to serve, political work and program direction emerge as the two favorites. This question was asked in the Survey of the Diplomatic Profession (SDP), given in the spring of 1966 to 588 FSOs. Table 14 shows the response.

TABLE 14

Functional Preferences of FSOs

Function	Number	Percent
Consular	15	2.6
Administrative	45	7.7
Political	175	29.8
Economic	57	9.7
Commercial	1	0.2
Labor	3	0.5
Program Direction	218	37.1
No one field—would rather rotate	60	10.2
Other	14	2.2
Totals	588	100

Almost 30 percent of the respondants preferred political work and 37.1 percent program direction. This again highlights the strong attraction of the political field for the FSO, particularly the examination entry officer. Among the latter group in the SDP, the proportion desiring political work rises to 38 percent, compared to 16 percent for the lateral entrants. Those desiring the administrative field are almost all lateral entrants, 19 percent of that group expressing preference for administrative work compared to one percent among examination entrants. Representing the top jobs that the FSO can aspire to, program direction is equated with success, thus is naturally attractive to officers, examination and lateral entrants alike.

162

Composition of the Corps

Area Specialization

One of the pronounced trends in the Foreign Service since World War II has been toward increasing interest in area specialization. Expertise in a particular area was not unknown before the war, but it was the exception. The Service was strongly Europe-oriented, and the ideal FSO type was the generalist in both function and area. With the much greater involvement of the United States in foreign affairs after the war, and the spread of the geographic horizons of the Foreign Service virtually to all parts of the world, the growing interest in area specialization developed.

The famous early Soviet specialists, George Kennan and Charles Bohlen, became the models for many young FSOs. The trend was accelerated in the 1950s when the Foreign Service Institute, under some prodding by Congress, greatly expanded its capability for training in the lesser known languages of the world. Another boost came with the realization of many officers that area specialization, since it is mainly associated with political and economic work rather than consular and administrative work, is highly useful if not essential to success.

An SDP question asked officers to indicate their area of specialization if they regarded themselves as area specialists or were so regarded by colleagues. As Table 15 shows, only about 58 percent saw themselves as area specialists, compared to about 70 percent who described themselves as functional specialists in another SDP question.

The responses are fairly well distributed among the major areas, with the Latin American and Atlantic Affairs specialists as the largest two groups. Taken together, the Soviet and Eastern European specialists total almost 9 percent, and the Arabic and other Near Eastern or South Asian specialists total almost 10 percent. The three Far Eastern

163

The Professional Group

TABLE 15

Area Specialization in the FSO Corps

	Number	Percent
I am not an area specialist	250	42.6
Latin America	67	11.4
Arabia	23	3.9
Other Near East or South Asia	34	5.8
Atlantic Affairs	48	8.2
Soviet	20	3.4
Eastern Europe	31	5.3
Chinese	19	3.2
Japanese	11	1.9
Southeast Asia	24	4.1
Africa (south of the Sahara)	39	6.6
Other	22	3.6
Totals	588	100

groups also total almost 10 percent. Given the recentness of Africa's emergence on the world political scene, the fact that 6.6 percent of FSOs regard themselves as African specialists is surprising.

Examination entry officers were much more likely to see themselves as area specialists than were lateral entrants— nearly two-thirds of the former, as against less than half of the latter said they were area specialists. The high point of area specialization seems to come at grade levels 3 and 4, where two-thirds of the officers said they were area specialists, compared to half or less than half at levels 1 and 2 and 5 and 6.[6]

These results, of course, are self-descriptions. Adequate independent measures of the extent and depth of area specialization in the FSO corps do not exist. In *The Anatomy of the Foreign Service*, I attempted to identify area specialists in the 1962 FSO corps by screening all officers in

[6] Throughout this study, where SDP results are discussed in terms of subgroups distinguished by grade levels, the grade levels are grouped to cut down the number for convenience. Thus grades FSO-1 and FSO-2 are grouped together, as are 3-4 and 5-6.

terms of two criteria: five years or more of working experience abroad in selected areas, matched with professionally useful speaking ability in a foreign language relevant to the region.[7] Only a little more than 10 percent (374) of the FSO corps fulfilled the two criteria. The results are only broadly indicative, since the criteria are somewhat arbitrary and restrictive. For example, it is clear that an officer could fulfill both criteria and still not be considered an area specialist, while another officer who failed to fulfill one or the other criterion might very well be a genuine area specialist. Western Europe was excluded from the study because it was felt it was too easy to satisfy the criteria in the case of this popular region with its more familiar languages.

There are many who believe that the State Department has not gone nearly far enough in developing deep area expertise among at least a substantial proportion of the Foreign Service. The tour of duty policy, which periodically rotates FSOs not only among functions but also among regions, is an inhibiting factor. FSOs appear somewhat ambivalent, since they favor the rotation policy as much as they favor area specialization. The difficulty, of course, is that many of the areas of specialization are also hardship areas— for reasons of health, climate, education, inflation—which tends to place real limits on the length of time an officer can serve in any one of them. The Herter Report strongly urged the development of a "consciously designed program" to stress area specialization.[8] There has been progress made in the decentralizing of some personnel authorities to the regional bureaus in State and in the conceptual framework

[7] Harr, *Anatomy of Foreign Service*, pp. 60-66.
[8] *Ibid.*, pp. 58-59. The problem of area specialization is thoroughly examined and a number of recommendations are made toward what might constitute a "consciously designed program," in Edward R. Brandt, "Regional Specialization in the Foreign Service," unpublished Master's Thesis, School of Government, Business, and International Affairs, The George Washington University, 1965.

The Professional Group

of the manpower utilization system. But until the latter is fully operational and successful it cannot be said that the State Department has a consciously designed program for area specialization.

Organizational Location

Table 16 compares the 1962 and 1966 Services in terms of broad deployment, showing the numbers of officers overseas in the five geographic regions of the world and in the major categories of domestic assignments.

TABLE 16

Organizational Location of FSOs, 1962 and 1966

Location	1962 No.	1962 Percent	1966 No.	1966 Percent
Overseas areas				
Latin America	412	11.3	429	12.2
Europe	934	25.4	662	18.9
Far East	413	11.2	346	9.9
Near East, South Asia	387	10.5	318	9.1
Africa	286	7.8	288	8.2
Subtotals	2,432	66.2	2,043	58.3
Domestic: regional bureaus				
Latin America	58	1.6	101	2.9
Europe	111	3.0	114	3.2
Far East	67	1.8	76	2.2
Near East, South Asia	54	1.5	59	1.7
Africa	58	1.6	69	1.9
Subtotals	348	9.5	419	11.9
Domestic: executive offices and functional bureaus	478	13.0	703	20.0
Special assignment	412	11.3	342	9.8
Totals	3,670	100	3,507	100

It is apparent that over the four-year span there has been a significant drop in the number of officers serving abroad and a corresponding increase in the numbers serving in

Composition of the Corps

Washington, particularly in the executive offices and functional bureaus. Overseas, Europe is still the largest region, but the number of officers there has declined substantially since 1962; clearly, it can no longer be said that the Foreign Service is a European service. Table 17 provides a better view of the distribution of the officers serving overseas among the five regions.

TABLE 17

FSOs Serving Overseas, 1962 and 1966

	1962		1966	
Region	No.	Percent	No.	Percent
Latin America	412	16.9	429	21.0
Europe	934	38.4	662	32.4
Far East	413	17.0	346	16.9
Near East, South Asia	387	15.9	318	15.6
Africa	286	11.8	288	14.1
Totals	2,432	100	2,043	100

Proportionately, the European area has declined, while the Far East and the Near East have remained very nearly constant. The two areas of significant proportionate increase are Latin America and Africa.

In Washington all five regional bureaus increased their staffs, the Latin American bureau by the widest margin. The "special assignment" category in Table 16 includes officers on detail, in training, and on the medical complement.

Education

A typical characteristic of an elite group is a relatively high level of educational attainment. The Foreign Service is no exception. A major study of Federal executives in 1963 shows that 88 percent of Foreign Service executives have bachelor's degrees or higher, compared to the same percentage for military executives and 78 percent for career

167

The Professional Group

Civil Service executives.[9] The author's 1962 data showed that 85.8 percent of *all* FSOs were college graduates. The data also showed that 106 of the 164 FSOs with high school diplomas or less were former Staff corps Wristonees.[10] The departure or conversion of many of these officers in the intervening time doubtless has raised the over-all percentage of college graduates in the Service, inasmuch as the entry by examination of a recruit without a college degree is extremely rare. As an example, only one of 65 persons in an incoming class in June of 1966 lacked an undergraduate degree, and 37 of the 65 had attended graduate school.[11]

An SDP question asked respondents to report their educational majors in both graduate and undergraduate education. In the 1962 data the fields of history, political science, international relations, and economics accounted for approximately 60 percent of the college graduates. The same is true for the 1966 FSO corps, although history and political science show larger percentages than before and international relations and economics show smaller percentages. The same four fields are evenly distributed among graduate students, totaling more than 60 percent of the total. As an undergraduate major, English is up considerably from 1962 to twice the previous percentage.

Examination entrants are more likely than lateral entrants to have studied history, political science, international relations, and English, while lateral entrants are more likely to have studied economics, accounting, public administration, and business administration.

9 W. Lloyd Warner, Paul P. Van Riper, Norman H. Martin, and Orvis F. Collins, *The American Federal Executive* (New Haven: Yale University Press, 1963), p. 354.
10 Harr, *Anatomy of Foreign Service*, pp. 14, 39.
11 U. S. Department of State, "Department of State Manpower," p. 13.

Composition of the Corps

TABLE 18
Undergraduate and Graduate Majors of FSOs, 1966

Educational field	Percent of under-graduate majors N-540	Percent of graduate majors N-363
History	24.5	16.0
Political Science	19.0	16.5
International Relations	8.2	16.5
Economics	8.2	16.5
Accounting	.8	0.0
Public Administration	1.7	4.4
Business Administration	4.2	3.0
English	9.3	3.5
Language	5.4	3.9
Physical Science	4.1	.9
Social Science (other than those named)	4.6	2.8
Humanities (other than those named)	5.3	1.9
Other	4.7	14.1
Totals	100	100

Summary

While the total number of FSOs has remained relatively stable since 1958, it is clear that there has been a recent and decisive shift away from at least some of the effects of the Wriston program. Officers whose experience is in what is regarded as the subprofessional fields of administration have been or are being separated or converted to another personnel status.

The great majority of those converted were lateral entrants to the FSO corps, and the great majority of these came originally from the Staff corps. By and large, they were less qualified to compete in the FSO system than the former civil servants, many of whom now occupy executive roles in the FSO corps. Almost half of the FSOs in executive and program direction assignments are lateral entrants.

Attrition and conversion have taken a heavier toll of

169

The Professional Group

lateral entrants than of examination entrants, so that lateral entrants now represent slightly more than one-third of the total Service, compared to more than 45 percent in 1962. They are still heavily identified with the administrative and consular fields and several of the smaller specialized fields, while the examination entrants account for the great majority of assignments to the political and economic fields, regarded as the two major "substantive" fields of the Foreign Service. The average age of lateral entrants is still much higher than that of examination entrants at all except the top grades.

The political field is still the dominant one, both in number of positions and interest among FSOs as a career field. There is more consideration of specialization within the personnel system than in past years; yet the long-standing generalist mores of the FSO corps continue very much in evidence. The administrative positions still encompassed by the FSO corps are, in the main, the high-level ones. The open question is how these positions will be staffed in the future since the great majority of incoming junior officers prefer the "substantive" fields. More officers than ever before have been detailed to USIA and AID; yet, the number is relatively small, and these two large functional areas, for all practical purposes, are outside of the career system.

About 58 percent of FSOs see themselves as area specialists, and their numbers are well distributed throughout the five geographic regions. The number of FSOs serving in Europe has declined substantially since 1962, with proportionate increases in Africa and Latin America. The proportion serving in Washington has also increased substantially. The educational level of FSOs is extremely high, with educational resources concentrated in a small number of fields.

CHAPTER 5

SOCIAL ORIGINS

AND CHARACTERISTICS

....

PROBABLY no other professional group in the United States has as strong and persistent an image of being closely tied to particular social and regional origins as the FSO corps.

The idea that diplomatic careers are the preserve of the sons of the upper classes in the northeastern United States, mostly graduates of the Ivy League colleges, has its roots, of course, in historical fact. Warren Ilchman states that before the Rogers Act of 1924 combined the Diplomatic and Consular Services, the diplomats had very definite feelings of "social superiority" over the consuls. "The man who entered the Diplomatic Service, with very few exceptions, had private means of support. Flowing from this were a host of social prejudices."[1]

Since the wage scale was inadequate, private means were necessary. Doubtless an important attraction for men of private means to enter the Diplomatic Service was the cultural affinity of upper class Americans, particularly those on the eastern seaboard, for Europe. The profession of diplomacy had been developed and established in Europe, and Europe was the world center of diplomacy. American diplomats were inclined to feel that the world of the consul was "pedestrian." "While the diplomat did not avoid routine, he lived in a much more prestigious and exciting world.

[1] Ilchman, *Professional Diplomacy in the United States, 1779-1939* (Chicago: Chicago University Press, 1961), p. 167.

He met the 'best people' in each capital and was part of the social life of the *Corps Diplomatique*. Even in dreary Central American posts, he was still an honored part of the European colony."[2] Of the men who entered the Diplomatic Service between 1914 and 1922, Ilchman reports, more than half were born in the nine northeastern states. More than 70 percent attended residential private secondary schools, compared to almost the same percentage of consuls who attended public schools. A greater percentage of the diplomats had college degrees (85 percent to 69), and there was a "vast difference" in the colleges attended: "Harvard, Yale, and Princeton provided 63.8 percent of all diplomats, 32.4 percent attending the first alone."[3]

The process that Ilchman has called the "democratization" of the Foreign Service definitely began with the merger brought about by the Rogers Act, and the beginnings of salaries and allowances that made it possible for men without private income to contemplate diplomatic careers.

The reality has changed substantially, but the image of the diplomat as the effete easterner has persisted, for several probable reasons. Certainly one is social distance. The doctor and the lawyer are familiar figures to virtually every American, but the diplomat is not. The widespread antipathy for many decades in the American heartland toward foreign involvements undoubtedly has helped perpetuate the striped pants stereotype.

The elitist ideology of the FSO corps contributes to the perpetuation of the upper class image of the Service. Even though the goal since the Rogers Act has been an aristocracy of talent instead of birth, this has not entirely gotten through to the public, since the nature of the talent is not easily demonstrable as with the doctor and the lawyer;

[2] *Ibid.*, pp. 151-52.   [3] *Ibid.*, pp. 164, 170-71.

172

Social Origins and Characteristics

thereby credence has been given to the image of a privileged caste. And, even though the reality behind the image has changed, the issue of the "representativeness" of the FSO corps is alive today.

My purpose in this chapter is to examine the reality of the social origins and characteristics of FSOs (as determined in the 1966 "Survey of the Diplomatic Profession"—SDP) in comparison, where comparable data are available, to other groups—graduating college seniors, military leaders, civilian federal executives, business leaders, and the total U.S. population.[4]

Place of Birth

Table 19 shows that despite the changes brought about by the Rogers Act and subsequent measures, the FSO corps is not nearly as representative of the regional breakdown of American population as civilian federal executives. Although the percentage born in the northeast declined from

[4] Data on military leaders in this chapter is drawn from Morris Janowitz, *The Professional Soldier* (Glencoe: The Free Press, 1960), data on civilian federal executives and career Civil Service executives is taken from W. Lloyd Warner *et al.*, *The American Federal Executive* (New Haven: Yale University Press, 1963). The material on business leaders is cited here as it appears in *The American Federal Executive* and *The Professional Soldier*; it actually originated in earlier studies by Warner and Abegglen, about 1952. The data on graduating college seniors comes from major surveys conducted by the National Opinion Research Center (NORC) in 1961 and 1962. At the request of the Herter Committee, NORC obtained data on interest in foreign affairs careers in its 1962 follow-up survey of graduating college seniors. The "NORC Foreign Service" group used in this chapter consists of 327 graduating college seniors who expressed definite interest in foreign affairs careers. The "NORC Total Sample" group consists of a representative sub-sample of 3,397 cases created by NORC for purposes of comparison. See National Opinion Research Center, "College Graduates and Foreign Affairs," Survey No. 452, The University of Chicago, May 1962 (mimeog.) and Frances Fielder and Godfrey Harris, *The Quest for Foreign Affairs Officers—Their Recruitment and Selection*, Foreign Affairs Personnel Study No. 6 (New York: Carnegie Endowment for International Peace, 1966). The last named source makes extensive presentations of NORC survey results.

53 percent before the Rogers Act to 43 or 44 percent in later periods, this is still far above the actual population. The FSO corps is underrepresented in the midwest, southwest, and the south, with the largest gap in the south. The military has a similar pattern, except that its concentration is in the south. Using Janowitz' 1950 sample of military leaders, it can be seen that only about half the proportion of military officers, as compared to FSOs, come from the northeast in contrast to considerably more than double the proportion from the south.[5]

Table 20 compares the urban and rural backgrounds of FSOs, as reported in the SDP, with those of military, government, and business leaders. The comparisons should be taken only as rough indications, not only because of the widely varying times of the surveys, but also because the SDP question was phrased differently than for the other groups. Rather than place of birth, it asked for a designation of the subject's hometown during pre-high school years (thus allowing for a response of "changed too frequently to say"). However, some corroboration of the marked difference of the FSO pattern compared to all the others is obtained from the 1961-62 survey of graduating college seniors, by the National Opinion Research Center (NORC). The urban-rural breakdown of seniors interested in foreign service careers is almost identical to that of the FSOs as reported in the SDP. Of course, the strongly urban background of FSOs is not surprising, given the high percentage born in the northeast and the image of urbanity and worldliness associated with a diplomatic career.

Father's Occupation and Income

The backgrounds of FSOs may still be largely concentrated in urban northeastern settings, but entrance is cer-

[5] Janowitz, *Professional Soldier*, p. 88.

Social Origins and Characteristics

TABLE 19
Comparison of Region of Birth of FSOs and Civilian Federal Executives, to Total U.S. Population, Selected Points in Time

Region	U.S. population (U.S. Census Data) (percent) Average 1910	1930-40	1960	Percent of 1959 civilian federal executives[6]	Percent of 1925-46 Foreign Service Officers[7]	Percent of 1961-64 Foreign Service Officers[7]
Northeast	28	30	27	30	43	44
Midwest	33	31	29	35	25	23
South	22	23	21	19	13	12
Southwest	9	7	8	6	3	4
Mountain	3	2	3	5	3	3
Pacific	5	7	12	5	8	11
Overseas	—	—	—	—	5	3
Totals	100	100	100	100	100	100

TABLE 20
Comparison of Urban and Rural Backgrounds, Percentages of Selected Groups[8]

	1966 FSOs	1959 Govt. Exec.	Military Leaders—1950 Army	Navy	Air Force	1950 U.S. Census
Urban	82	66	34	44	30	64
Farm and rural	12	34	66	56	70	36
Frequent change	6	—	—	—	—	—
Totals	100	100	100	100	100	100

tainly not restricted to the sons of the affluent or even of the middle class. Perhaps the most telling proof of "democratization" is the striking pattern of family income, shown in Table 21 in comparison to the foreign service group in the NORC survey.

[6] Data from Warner, *American Federal Executive*, p. 43.

[7] Data developed by C. R. McKibbin, Department of Political Science, Drake University. Percentages are taken of total numbers of officers entering the Service during the periods indicated.

[8] Source of data on government executives is Warner, *American Federal Executive*, p. 333; on military leaders from Janowitz, *Professional Soldier*, p. 87.

The Professional Group

TABLE 21

Family Income (percent)[9]

	NORC Foreign Service	SDP lateral entrants	SDP exam. entrants	Total SDP
Less than $5,000	17.0	45.7	29.5	35.4
5,000 to 7,499	23.5	24.1	22.1	22.8
7,500 to 9,999	12.7	12.7	12.2	12.5
10,000 to 14,999	13.6	8.5	17.6	14.3
15,000 to 19,000	8.6	3.8	2.9	3.2
20,000 and over	13.3	2.4	12.2	8.7
Not sure	11.4	2.8	3.8	3.1
Totals	100	100	100	100
Number	(327)	(212)	(375)	(587)

The heavy concentration of the SDP respondents in the lower end of the income spectrum shows how decisive the shift has been since the pre-Rogers Act days when a man had to have some wealth to undertake a diplomatic career. Clearly the diplomatic profession, like other professions, has become an avenue of upward mobility for those from lower socio-economic strata, particularly in the case of lateral entrants. Using different categories, Janowitz shows a similar trend for Army officers.

Despite the definite trend toward opening up the military and Foreign Service elites to all social strata, neither appears to be as open as business leadership, as shown in Table 23. The Warner and Abegglen survey of business leaders shows greater percentages of sons from two lower income groups—white collar and workingmen—than either

[9] The FSOs were asked in the SDP to estimate "family income" during the years of their later upbringing, i.e., the high school years. On the average, the FSOs are nearly a generation older than the NORC college seniors; for many of them the years of "later upbringing" would have been the Depression years. It was not possible to adjust the FSO "family income" estimates to 1962 dollars. For all these reasons, the data on the two groups obviously are not directly comparable. However, at least roughly the figures suggest similarity, and in any event support the major point, that neither the bulk of FSOs nor of aspirants to foreign affairs careers come from the more affluent levels of society.

176

Social Origins and Characteristics

TABLE 22
Army Officers, 1910-50:
Trends in Social Origin (percent)[10]

	1910-20	1935	1950
Upper	26	8	3
Upper middle	66	68	47
Lower middle	8	23	45
Upper lower	0	1	4
Lower lower	0	0	1
Totals	100	100	100
Number	(38)	(49)	(140)

TABLE 23
Military, Business, and Foreign Service:
Father's Occupation (percent)[11]

	Military leaders, 1950	Business leaders, 1952	Foreign Service, SDP, 1966
Small business	—	18	23
Large business	—	8	6
Total Business	30	26	29
Professional and managerial	44	29	39
Farmer	10	9	4
White collar	11	19	11
Worker	5	15	11
Other	—	2	6
Totals	100	100	100
Number	(362)	(8,300)	(587)

the military or the Foreign Service. The latter, however, shows 11 percent from a working-class background, compared to only 5 percent of the military officers. In keeping with the heavily urban background of FSOs, only 4 percent list their father's occupation as farmer. Lateral entrants show a much greater percentage than examination entrants from the "small business" background, and a slightly

[10] Adapted from Janowitz, *Professional Soldier*, Table 13, p. 90.
[11] Data on military and business leaders taken from *ibid.*, p. 93.

177

greater percentage from a working-class background. To account for the very large percentages of lateral entrants at the low end of the income spectrum, "small business" for the most part must have been very small.

In part, the large percentage of military officers whose fathers' occupations were in the "professional and managerial" category is accounted for by self-recruitment—many of the fathers were professional soldiers. Janowitz shows that the percentage of military leaders whose fathers were professional soldiers has been fairly high, although not nearly so pronounced as in the case of the German army, for instance. The proportion has varied over time, as follows: 1910, 7 percent; 1920, 10 percent; 1935, 23 percent; 1950, 11 percent; West Point graduating class of 1960, 25 percent.[12] The dip in the 1950 sample is "a consequence of rapid growth and the wartime recruitment of officer personnel from civilian society." Indicative of a future trend toward increasing self-recruitment is the high percentage of the West Point class whose fathers were professional soldiers.

Occupational inheritance is much lower in the diplomatic profession than in the military or medical professions, where it has been estimated that 20 percent of medical students are the sons of doctors.[13] Only 2 percent of SDP respondents listed their father's occupation as diplomat. The fact that examination entrants are more than twice as likely as lateral entrants to have fathers who were professional diplomats suggests the likelihood that, as in the case of the military, recent expansion of the diplomatic corps has caused the degree of occupational inheritance to decline. Strong support among SDP respondents for the idea of a son entering

[12] *Ibid.*, pp. 95-96.
[13] Natalie Rogoff, "The Decision to Study Medicine," in *The Student Physician* (Cambridge: Harvard University Press, 1957), p. 112.

Social Origins and Characteristics

a diplomatic career (discussed in the next chapter) indicates that occupational inheritance may increase in the future. Among SDP respondents who indicated their fathers were professional men, the breakdown among professions was as follows:

Profession	Percent
Diplomat	5
Military officer	7
Doctor	10
Lawyer	12
Clergyman	7
Missionary	2
Engineer	16
College professor	8
School teacher	7
Other	26
Total	100

Parent's Education

Table 24 compares the SDP sample and the NORC college seniors by level of education of fathers and mothers. The distribution is remarkably close in the two samples, whether the educational level of fathers or of mothers is compared. The most striking result is the extraordinarily

TABLE 24

Parent's Education, NORC and SDP Samples (percent)

	Father		Mother	
	NORC Foreign Service	SDP FSOs	NORC Foreign Service	SDP FSOs
8th grade or less	15.5	19.0	9.3	12.6
Some high school	12.3	10.6	14.9	11.6
High school graduate plus some college	33.2	28.9	43.7	48.3
College graduate	19.6	20.7	27.6	23.6
Graduate or professional school	19.3	20.8	4.7	3.9
Totals	99.9	100	100	100
Number	(316)	(585)	(323)	(586)

179

high educational level of mothers, higher than fathers in both groups if professional education is excluded.

The northeast has remained even more disproportionate as a place of education for FSOs than as a birthplace. Although the proportion of FSOs attending college in the northeast has declined over the years, it is still more than twice the proportion of population in the northeast.

TABLE 25

Last Place of Formal Education of FSOs (percent)[14]

Region	1925-46 FSOs	1960 U.S. census	1961-64 FSOs
Northeast	69	27	59
Midwest	13	29	13
South	6	21	5
Southwest	2	8	4
Mountain	1	3	3
Pacific	9	12	16
Totals	100	100	100

Still, the figures in Table 25 are not surprising, given the fact that 44 percent of the FSOs were born in the northeast, and other considerations such as the prevalence of highly regarded graduate schools in the northeast and the traditions some of them have of providing candidates for the Foreign Service. Obviously young men from the midwest, south, and southwest leave their home regions to attend schools in the northeast, possibly because they believe the schools in that region will prepare them better for a Foreign Service career.

Writing of the period up to 1939, Ilchman points to the continued importance to the democratized Foreign Service of Harvard, Princeton, and Yale, which provided 63.8 percent of the members of the old Diplomatic Service. He re-

[14] Data on FSOs from C. R. McKibbin, Department of Political Science, Drake University. Census data show percentages of U.S. population living in the regions.

180

Social Origins and Characteristics

ports that these three schools sent 36 percent of FSO recruits in 1926-30, 40 percent in 1931-35, and 26 percent in 1936-39. State universities provided 25 percent in 1936-39, up from the 9 percent to the Diplomatic Service.[15]

The big three of the Ivy League are still very important recruitment sources for the Foreign Service, but proportionately less so than before World War II. In a five-year period, 1957 to 1962, Harvard, Princeton, and Yale provided only 15 percent of the newcomers to the FSO corps. Table 26 compares the top 10 universities for the FSO corps during this period to the top 10 for the Civil Service in 1959.

TABLE 26

Top 10 Universities for the
Foreign Service and the Civil Service[16]

Civil Service, 1959		Foreign Service, 1957-62	
George Washington	3	Harvard	6
City College of N.Y.	6	California	12
California	8	Princeton	17
Ohio State	10	Yale	21
Minnesota	12	Georgetown	24
Illinois	14	Stanford	26
Washington	16	Dartmouth	28
Wisconsin	17	Columbia	30
MIT	19	Michigan	32
Michigan	21	Minnesota	34

Of the 926 FSOs who entered between 1957 and 1962, 325 came from the 10 universities in the table. Another 26 schools provided 215 officers, and the remaining 383 officers came from a broad range of 169 schools. Only three schools,

15 Ilchman, *Professional Diplomacy*, p. 236.
16 Figures on the Civil Service are from Warner, *et al, American Federal Executive*, p. 372; on the Foreign Service from the Department of State *News Letter* (Jan. 1964) , p. 24. The percentages are cumulative vertically; for example, Harvard provided 6 percent of the FSOs, California 6 percent, and Princeton 5 percent, for a total for these three universities of 17 percent.

The Professional Group

all of them state universities, appear in both lists in Table 26.

A final indication of the importance of Harvard, Princeton, and Yale is that of the 72 degrees held by the officers in the top two grades of the Foreign Service in 1966—the seven Career Ambassadors and 52 career Ministers—30 were taken at these three schools.

Religious Affiliations

Data on religious affiliations are not easy to obtain for comparative purposes.[17] Unfortunately no trend data on religious affiliations of FSOs exist, but it is possible to compare the SDP sample to NORC's college seniors and to military leaders.

TABLE 27

Religious Affiliations: FSOs, Military
Officers, NORC Survey

	NORC "Foreign Service"	Total NORC Sample	SDP Foreign Service Officers 1966	Army 1950	Navy 1950	Air Force 1950	West Point Class of 1961
Protestant	64.8	60.5	68.7	89	90	84	64
Roman Catholic	23.1	25.1	17.8	11	10	16	29
Jewish	3.4	8.2	6.2	—	—	—	2
Other	2.8	3.0	1.7	—	—	—	3
None	5.9	3.3	5.6	—	—	—	2
Totals	100	100	100	100	100	100	100
Number	(327)	(3,397)	(585)	(166)	(205)	(106)	(731)

Janowitz observes that the military elite historically has been overwhelmingly Protestant, but a trend toward greater representation is evident in the West Point class of 1961. If

[17] For example, Warner, *American Federal Executive*, p. 617, reports that they could not ask about religion, politics, and race in their survey for fear of endangering the size of the response.

[18] Data on the military officers is taken from Janowitz, *Professional Soldier*, pp. 98-99.

Social Origins and Characteristics

earlier data on FSOs were available, it is likely that a similar trend from a strongly Anglo-Saxon Protestant group to a more nearly representative one would be evident. As it is, Catholics are still slightly underrepresented in the Service. The NORC data are interesting, in that less than half the proportion of Jews appears in the "Foreign Service" group as in the total sample. The proportion of Jews actually in the Foreign Service is considerably higher, but is largely composed of lateral entrants.

Political Orientations

The comparison of political orientations of FSOs with those of military officers offers a marked contrast. Nearly 75 percent of FSOs are on the liberal side, choosing either "somewhat liberal" or "liberal" in self-rating their political orientations, while Army and Navy officers show very nearly that percentage on the conservative side, with Air Force officers at about 60 percent.

There are no significant variations among SDP subgroups on this question, with liberal sentiment well distributed by grades and method of entry. Janowitz shows

TABLE 28

Political Orientations: FSOs, Military
Officers, NORC Survey (percent)

	NORC "Foreign Service" N=327	NORC total sample N=3,397	SDP, Foreign Service Officers N=585	Military Officers, 1954[19]		
				Army N—211	Navy N—208	Air Force N—157
Conservative	4.6	6.0	2.4	25.1	23.0	14.7
Somewhat conservative	20.4	28.0	14.0	44.5	45.2	46.5
Somewhat liberal	39.5	36.6	42.4	21.3	18.3	31.8
Liberal	21.0	11.2	32.3	5.3	6.3	3.2
Neither (or no answer)	14.5	18.2	8.9	3.8	7.2	3.8
Totals	100	100	100	100	100	100

[19] Data on military officers from *ibid.*, p. 237.

183

that the most highly ranked military officers show conservative tendencies to a more pronounced degree than the next rank group.

The FSOs also come out as considerably more liberal than the college seniors, either those choosing a "foreign service" career or the total NORC sample. An indication that a diplomatic career has some appeal to those with a liberal political orientation is that the "foreign service" college seniors show up as slightly more liberal than the total NORC sample.

At least part of the difference between the NORC and FSO groups may be accounted for by a difference in the wording of the question. NORC used the word "very" in conjunction with "conservative" and "liberal," which may have caused a tendency to stay near the middle. Note that the largest percentage of any of the groups at an outside position is the nearly one-third of FSOs who regard themselves as "liberal."

Another difference in the wording of the questions was that the military officers did not have the option of choosing "neither liberal nor conservative" as did the NORC and SDP groups. Thus the comparisons should be taken only as roughly indicative; yet the differences are so pronounced that the lack of uniformity in wording is overshadowed. Certainly "conservative" and "liberal" are gross labels, but they do reflect basic orientations, if not specific political content.

Race and Representativeness

It was unnecessary to ask for an identification of race in the SDP, since the answer was already known. It is mainly on racial grounds that the issue of the representativeness of the Foreign Service is alive today.[20]

20 It is also alive in regard to women, but the reason that women are very much underrepresented in the FSO corps is widely understood and accepted. Because of the semi-nomadic existence of FSOs, it is virtually

Social Origins and Characteristics

For a long time the Foreign Service has been able to resist the imposition of geographic quotas. Before the Rogers Act the Consular Service had such quotas, but the Diplomatic Service did not. Repeatedly, as early as 1900, geographic quotas have been proposed, most recently by the Wriston Committee in 1954. By gradually improving its geographical representation, and by such devices as making its written and oral examinations available to candidates throughout the country instead of only in Washington, the Department of State has succeeded in avoiding quotas.

The Service has not succeeded, however, in appointing anything near a representative number of Negroes. Ilchman comments that few Negroes applied and few were appointed in the years up to 1939. There were two Negroes in the FSO corps in 1935, he states, and eight in 1942.[21] In 1967 there were 20 Negroes in the FSO corps, only a little more than one-half of one percent.

The problem was explored fairly thoroughly at the time of the existence of the Herter Committee in a series of meetings with Negro leaders and educators. The conclusion was that no systematic social bias existed, but that young Negroes, especially those from the southern Negro colleges, were culturally disadvantaged in competing with white students in the Foreign Service examination process. A much smaller proportion of Negro applicants than white applicants passed the examinations. Negro students from the first-rate northern universities were not applying for the examination in any appreciable number, either because they were not interested or because they suspected bias.

---

impossible for a woman to have a career as an FSO and also be married, a problem that is not true of most professional groups. This tends to depress the number of women recruited through the basic examination process, since the heavy investment in the officer in recruitment and training is very likely to be lost when early in her career she resigns to get married.

21 Ilchman, *Professional Diplomacy*, p. 235.

The Professional Group

One result of these meetings was development of a "foreign affairs scholars program" financed mainly by the Ford Foundation.[22] For each of several years 40 students from minority groups were selected during their junior years to come to Washington as paid interns in State, USIA, and AID. During their senior years, approximately 25 of the 40 were awarded $4,000 scholarships for a year of study in university programs especially useful to those contemplating foreign affairs careers. The students were not obligated to enter government employment, but were expected to take the FSO examination.

It is too early to know what specific effect the program will have on the proportion of Negroes in diplomatic service (the program was terminated in 1967), but undoubtedly the proportion will increase over time. Far from being biased, the State Department can be said to be eager to have qualified young Negro candidates. Ironically, progress may be slow because of the marked increase in mobility in very recent years of the well-educated young Negro college graduates and the fact that the salaries in the lower grades of the Foreign Service are not competitive with those offered by industry.

Conclusion

In summary, it is clear that in terms of social origins and characteristics, the FSO corps maintains certain elements of distinctiveness in comparison to other groups, and yet it has moved steadily on the path of becoming more socially representative of American society at large.

There continues to be a strong northeastern regional flavor in terms of birth and education; urban backgrounds are pronounced as are liberal political orientations. Jews

[22] *Washington Post*, Jan. 19, 1964, p. B4. The *Post* story said there were 39 Negroes in the Foreign Service in 1964, but this figure included FSRs and political appointees, as well as FSOs.

are well represented in the Service and Catholics are slightly underrepresented. Negroes are seriously underrepresented, but this is not a problem peculiar to the FSO corps and there are remedial efforts underway. FSOs are likely to have come from a middle or lower income stratum.

It seems clear that the regional flavor is the product of lingering traditions, proximity, and the character of the educational institutions in the northeast, rather than of any systematic bias. For example, it is perhaps significant that the west is overrepresented, in terms of formal education at least, although not to the same degree as the northeast. This suggests that the insularity of the American heartland in respect to the international character of diplomacy is still an operative factor, though a diminishing one.

Ilchman was satisfied that the Service had become democratized in the period up to 1939. In regard to the continued high incidence of the alumni of Harvard, Princeton, and Yale in recruitment into the Service, Ilchman pointed out that any attempt to restrict their entry "would be contrary to democratic presuppositions."[23] That reliance has decreased in the intervening time, and we have the overwhelming evidence of the family income background to support the democratization thesis. Clearly the Service has become an avenue of upward mobility, a fact nonetheless important if the avenue for lower income groups and Jews has been largely the unorthodox one of lateral entry.

The political orientations of FSOs clearly are not the product of social class, although regional overtones may have some significance. One suspects that in the main the liberal leanings of FSOs are the product of individual intellectual commitment, of a kind that would tend to make persons interested in the Foreign Service in the first place and would be reinforced in a diplomatic career with its

[23] Ilchman, *Professional Diplomacy*, pp. 236-37.

emphasis on cross-cultural skill and political accommodation.

The distinctive elements aside, FSOs are very much like other important groups in American society in becoming progressively less castelike. The conclusion in the Warner study seems apropos, that "our society, although much like what it has been in past generations, is more flexible than it was; more men and their families are in social motion."[24]

[24] Warner, *American Federal Executive*, p. 22.

CHAPTER 6

CHARACTERISTICS, NORMS,

ATTITUDES

....

THE CONCERN of this chapter is to describe some of the characteristics of FSOs, the norms and values that influence their behavior, and the attitudes of officers on a number of subjects. Stereotypes abound about the FSO corps, as is the case with every distinctive group. Like many stereotypes, they are dangerous, in that at best they are half-truths, and may convince many observers that there is no need to probe deeper. My purpose in this chapter is to probe more deeply.

Because any attempt to discuss the behavior of a group necessarily consists of generalizations, of extrapolation from sets of individual behavior to group behavior, it is obvious that there will always be exceptions, whether the generalizations have praiseworthy or pejorative connotations. One must deal in trends, in tendencies, in general qualities, in order to try to understand how FSOs as a group view themselves and their work. In doing so, it is clear that none of the observations represents a rigid mold for the behavior of all officers.

Personality Orientations

A good foundation is to review briefly the work of behavioral scientist Regis Walther who studied groups of FSOs in 1962 in comparison to other occupational groups by use of a survey instrument Walther developed, called

The Professional Group

the "Job Analysis and Interest Measurement" (JAIM).[1] The JAIM is a self-administered questionnaire containing some 125 multiple choice items having to do with attitudes, interests, beliefs, and preferences. The responses can be organized into 22 different scales measuring behavioral style in such areas as orientations, work content preferences, interpersonal behavior, formal organizational behavior, information processing behavior, and success criteria. The objective of JAIM is to measure the "personal qualities of the worker" (as differentiated from his skills and knowledge) that have "an influence on success or failure in a job." Walther explains part of the theoretical rationale for JAIM as follows:

> In order to function adequately, it is necessary for each individual to organize his experience. The nature of this organization gives rise to characteristic types of performance, conscious and unconscious, in various life situations. These behavioral styles are determined, in part, by the innate characteristics of the individual; by his experience with what works and with what does not work for him; and by the social standards and values to which he has been exposed.[2]

Walther compared groups of brand new FSO recruits to other groups of similar age, such as USIA recruits, Peace Corps volunteers, Civil Service management interns, and junior research engineers. He compared senior FSOs to junior FSOs, and he compared officers independently identified as high performers with those identified as low performers. He reported the results for FSOs in general:

[1] Walther, *Orientations and Behavioral Styles of Foreign Service Officers*, Foreign Affairs Personnel Study No. 5 (New York: Carnegie Endowment for International Peace, 1965).
[2] *Ibid.*, p. 3.

190

Characteristics, Norms, Attitudes

Compared with other occupational groups, the FSOs report that they like the kind of work that includes interpretation of data and the influencing of other people. Their style for analyzing information tends to be impressionistic and intuitive rather than formal, methodical, and statistical. Their preferred style for working with a formal organization is to do the work themselves rather than to work through a hierarchy. They greatly value personal intellectual achievement and place a moderate value on formal status, social service, and the approval of others.[3]

As an example of the comparisons between groups, Walther reported that "USIA officers are much more concerned about the opinions of other people; the junior FSOs value resourceful accomplishment. The USIA officers are more sympathetic and accommodating and value social service; the junior FSOs are more self-assertive and aggressive and value formal status."[4] The junior FSOs are very different from the Peace Corps volunteers and the research engineers and very much like the management interns. Junior FSOs and senior FSOs are very much alike, except that the latter identify more with authority and show willingness to fit into an authoritative structure. At the same time, they are more self-assertive and exert more personal leadership than the junior officers.

In comparing high and low performers within the FSO corps, Walther found that the high performers exhibit most of the same characteristics of the general group of FSOs, cited above, but to a more pronounced degree, ex-

3 *Ibid.*, p. 43.
4 *Ibid.*, pp. 10-11. As an example of the statistical reliability of the differences between the two groups, most of them were statistically significant at the .1 percent level, meaning that the differences could occur as the result of chance less than one time out of one hundred.

191

cept that they are much less concerned with social service than they are with formal status and resourceful accomplishment as success criteria. By comparison, the low performers are more concerned with social service and approval from others, with working in a hierarchical structure rather than an autonomous situation, and with a systematic-methodical approach to information in contrast to the empirical-intuitive approach of the high performers.[5]

The Young Officers

A useful concept for attempting to understand the norms, values, and attitudes of a distinctive group is *socialization*, meaning in general the process by which individual members of that group selectively come to learn "correct" behavior as sanctioned by the group. It is the process by which they learn the norms, values, and attitudes—hence the behavioral styles—which in large measure form the culture of the group.

The starting place is to look at what newcomers bring to the group. Our attention here is on the main source of recruitment, the orthodox method of the basic entrance examination. Lateral entrants will be considered later.

Walther's data provide us with an image of the personality orientations of young officers. It is possible to step back further and examine some personality characteristics of the population of college seniors interested in foreign service careers by means of the National Opinion Research Center (NORC) 1961-62 surveys cited in the last chapter. In terms of what students consider to be of major importance in their jobs, Frances Fielder and Godfrey Harris report NORC data showing that those interested in a Foreign

[5] Walther, *Orientations*, p. 34.

Service life differed from all other graduates in the following ways.[6] They were:

(a) much more likely to pick a career which involves "getting away from the city or area" in which they grew up.

(b) more likely to value opportunities "to work with people rather than things."

(c) more likely than all other graduates to consider as important "opportunities to be helpful to others or useful in society."

(d) more likely to seek the "chance to exercise leadership."

(e) less likely than all other graduates to value "making a lot of money."

(f) less likely to be attracted by "opportunities for moderate but steady progress rather than the chance of extreme success or failure."

In choosing self-descriptive adjectives, students interested in foreign service differed from all other graduates in the following ways:

(a) more likely to see themselves as cultured, intellectual, sophisticated, and idealistic, and less likely to be "middle-brow."

(b) more likely to be outgoing and talkative, and less likely to be cautious and quiet.

(c) more likely to see themselves as dominant, impetuous, and rebellious and less likely to be cooperative, obliging, fun-loving, and methodical.

[6] Frances Fielder and Godfrey Harris, *The Quest for Foreign Affairs Officers—Their Recruitment and Selection*, Foreign Affairs Personnel Study No. 6 (New York: Carnegie Endowment for International Peace, 1966) , pp. 15-16.

193

The Professional Group

A number of factors suggest that self-selection and strong career motivation are characteristic of those who pursue their interests and eventually enter the Foreign Service as junior officers. These factors include: the very small percentage in the NORC survey of those interested in a Foreign Service life, the view of Fielder and Harris that the interest does not seem very much related to the Department of State's formal recruitment effort, and the difficulty of the examination and the fact that long delays can occur between the time an applicant begins the process and the time he is actually appointed.

Both the Walther and the Fielder-Harris studies hold that the oral examining panels tend to select from among those who have passed the written examination "young people they consider most like the successful officers already in the system."[7] This, of course, is not surprising. As Theodore Caplow points out, any functioning hierarchy will "evaluate the candidate as a potential in-group member, and will therefore give special attention to his congeniality in the broadest sense," including "his ability to conform to the habits and standards of his elders."[8]

Passing the basic examination process has a profound impact on the young applicant, so much so that one hears it referred to as a "puberty rite" by critics of the corps. The fact that so few pass out of so many applicants heightens the impression that one is joining a very select company.[9]

[7] Walther, *Orientations*, p. 71. The quotation is from Frances Fielder and Godfrey Harris, *The Quest for Foreign Affairs Officers—Their Recruitment and Selection*, Foreign Affairs Personnel Study No. 6 (New York: Carnegie Endowment for International Peace, 1966), 60.

[8] Caplow, *The Sociology of Work* (Minneapolis: University of Minnesota Press, 1954), p. 71.

[9] For example, in calendar year 1964 only 198 persons were certified for appointment as FSOs, out of 10,957 who applied. Only 1,184 passed the written examination, and of these only 280 passed the oral test. See U. S. Department of State, "Department of State Manpower," Fiscal Year 1966 Statistical Report by the Management Reports Staff.

Characteristics, Norms, Attitudes

As in the case of all recognized professional groups, the new members feel that they are embarking on a lifelong career, an occurrence, as Caplow points out, usually marked by "great expense, great ceremony, and the taking of oaths."[10]

Entering the corps via the basic examination is the Foreign Service equivalent of graduating from the military academies. The young FSO is brought into the Service in a "class" of 20 to 80 other officers much as the military academies produce a graduating class: "Since graduation from an academy means entrance into a group which disperses very gradually—the officer is always associated with a particular graduating class—academy education means acquiring lifetime colleagues and the necessity of accommodating to them."[11] The importance of his class is not so pronounced for the FSO, but for many years afterward he will know where his classmates are serving and how well they have fared in the promotion process compared to himself. The entering group *does* constitute a "class" in the basic orientation course which all must take at the Foreign Service Institute. Indoctrination is perhaps too strong a word for what happens in this course, but socialization is not. Within a very short time, the newcomer, who might have been quite vague about the details of the career, has picked up much of the language, the concerns, the ambitions. Terms like "mainstream" and "substantive work" quickly become permanent additions to his vocabulary, and he becomes concerned about such matters as lateral entry and the promotion system.

The entire process yields a rich source of talent. FSOs themselves believe this. An SDP question asked officers to

10 Caplow, *Sociology of Work*, p. 106.
11 Morris Janowitz, *The Professional Soldier* (Glencoe: The Free Press, 1960), p. 127.

195

The Professional Group

evaluate the quality of junior recruits to the FSO corps in recent years, and the results were highly favorable.

TABLE 29

Quality of Junior FSO Recruits

Evaluation	Number	Percent
Poor	1	0.2
Average	21	3.6
Mixed—some poor, some brilliant	112	19.1
Generally very good	388	66.1
Outstanding	65	11.0
Totals	587	100

Interestingly enough, the more highly-ranked an officer, the more likely he is to have a very positive impression of the quality of recent entrants. Only 70 percent of the officers at levels 5 and 6 chose "generally very good" or "outstanding," compared to 85 percent of officers at levels 1 and 2 and 100 percent of the Career Ambassadors and Career Ministers. Also, a highly favorable impression of recent entrants is slightly more prevalent among lateral entrants compared to examination entrants.

The author's impression, based on frequent opportunities to observe incoming groups of junior officers in recent years, is that they fall in the "generally very good" to "outstanding" range. The Walther portrait of junior officers rings true, as does much of the image presented by NORC. Almost all the junior officers observed appear to be highly intelligent and articulate. Many appear to have good leadership potential. They are quite career conscious, understandably, or they might have chosen the Peace Corps instead of the FSO corps. There is an impression of vitality, of restrained excitement at being chosen to be among the select few to embark on a great adventure. As a result, the new officers are eager to learn and ready to adapt.

196

Characteristics, Norms, Attitudes

Career Motivations

One question in the SDP asked officers their opinion of the main attraction for the thousands of young persons who take the basic Foreign Service examination every year. The largest percentage of respondents (46.2 percent) chose the "desire to participate in the making of American foreign policy" as their answer. About a quarter (26.2 percent) saw the status and prestige of being an FSO as the main attraction, and 16 percent chose the "desire to live and work in foreign countries."

There probably is a certain vague idealism and romantic expectation among young applicants regarding "making foreign policy." One officer commented in his SDP response that it was a "traumatic experience" among younger officers "when we found out that international realities (a jungle world) did not conform to our idealistic teachings (university courses)."

When officers were asked *their own* reasons for taking the basic examination, 50 percent responded, "the desire to participate in the making of foreign policy" (with 20 percent choosing the status and prestige of the FSO corps, and 20 percent the desire to live and work abroad).

Certainly over time any romanticism about making foreign policy turns into a much more modest notion, but one that is nevertheless real for many FSOs. They rarely *make* foreign policy, but in their assessment of the local situation, in negotiating with foreign representatives, in reports sent back to Washington, in advice given to high-ranking officials, FSOs have frequent opportunities to *influence* foreign policy decisions.

The attraction of "making foreign policy" is not inconsistent with the point made in Chapter 3 about the general dislike FSOs have for formal policy-planning. As Walther's data show, the FSO's style is the empirical and intuitive

197

The Professional Group

one associated with observing, reporting, reacting, and attempting to predict consequences. The FSO is predisposed to this, and there is a need for this style in his career experience of serving in different foreign countries and attempting to keep his finger on the pulse of political events. The systematic and methodical approach associated with planning is largely alien to him. Janowitz draws the contrast to the professional soldier in this way: "Yet, because of professional background training and immediate responsibilities, diplomats and politicians place much less emphasis on explicit and formal planning procedures."[12]

More light is shed on career motivations in SDP questions as to whether FSOs would encourage interest in the FSO corps on the part of a son or daughter and reasons for that encouragement. More than 90 percent of the officers responding (579) said they would passively or actively support a son's interest in the Service, but the figure drops to 60 percent in the case of a daughter. The reasons for the support provide some indirect evidence on the officers' own career motivations

TABLE 30
Reasons for Supporting Career Interest
in the FSO Corps

Reasons	Number of responses	Composite score	1st place votes	2nd place votes
Relatively good remuneration and degree of financial security	359	764	6	37
Social status and prestige of the diplomatic profession compared to alternative occupations	365	878	20	33
Relatively good opportunity for FSOs to make an important contribution to the public service	503	2,205	293	138
Relatively good opportunity to continue personal intellectual growth and development	506	2,098	185	249
Relatively good opportunity to enjoy life	415	1,110	30	54

[12] Janowitz, *Professional Soldier*, p. 274.

198

The question was open-ended in the sense that officers could choose more than one reason, but if so they were to rank-order them. The composite scores were achieved by awarding five points for a first place vote, four points for second place, and so on. Among the five reasons, two clearly stand out as highly important in the minds of FSOs—the opportunity for public service and the opportunity for personal growth. Public service received 293 first-place votes.

The idea of public service should not be confused with "social service" in the Walther study, on which FSOs did not score as highly as Peace Corps volunteers and other groups. Social service implies a direct helping relationship to other individuals, whereas the FSO deals as much or more in ideas and abstractions in his public service roles of observer, reporter, negotiator, advisor. His idea of public service is more likely to be connected with "participation in the making of foreign policy" than with direct help to individuals.

When dealing with self-image, one cannot expect complete objectivity. Yet there is no reason to doubt that many FSOs genuinely see themselves as dedicated and self-sacrificing. FSO Glen H. Fisher writes of this sentiment: "The Foreign Service Officer realizes that he may never achieve the salaries of some of his college classmates who have gone into other professions or business, and he may have to face certain stress situations abroad which are indeed 'foreign' to friends at home."[13]

A strong emphasis on public service as a career motivation is probably typical of career services, if not of the general government employment. Janowitz makes the case for a strong public service tradition as the self-image for at least "a substantial minority" of military officers, in contrast to

[13] Fisher, "The Foreign Service Officer," *The Annals of the American Academy of Political and Social Science*, Vol. 368 (Nov. 1966), 75.

The Professional Group

the widespread notion that they are simply finding a secure home in the military.[14] In contrast, a major study of the public service found that only eight percent of a sample of government employees saw "opportunity to be of service" as a reason to become a federal civil servant, and this is a considerably larger percentage than in the general public. Three-fourths of the government employees cited "security and fringe benefits" as the reason. Only among the more highy educated persons outside of government, and among Federal executives and scientists, did public service receive as high as 16 percent of the choices.[15]

Pride and Prestige

The fact that the prestige associated with being an FSO is not rated as highly as public service as a motivating force for entering the career should not be taken to mean that this is an unimportant factor. Myron Lieberman states its importance trenchantly: "The influence of occupational status on the practitioner is both pervasive and fundamental. It affects who will enter the occupation and what specializations within it they will seek. It affects the quantity and quality of the work that is done, the job satisfaction of the practitioner, and the dress, manners, outlook, and moral ideas of the practitioner."[16]

It is clear that FSOs take strong pride in their service. This emerges in SDP reactions to statements comparing the British and American foreign services. Historically the British service has had a high reputation; as noted in Chapter 2, it formed the model for development of the American service. Yet nearly 67 percent of FSOs disagreed with the state-

[14] Janowitz, *Professional Soldier*, Chapter 6, p. 107 and Chapter 11.
[15] Franklin P. Kilpatrick, Milton C. Cummings, Jr., and M. Kent Jennings, *The Image of the Federal Service* (Washington: The Brookings Institution, 1964), pp. 224-34.
[16] Myron Lieberman, *Education as a Profession* (Englewood Cliffs: Prentice-Hall, 1956), p. 445.

ment that the British officer is generally a more competent representative of his government because of the longer tradition of diplomatic professionalism. Almost the same percentage of FSOs agreed with the statement that American FSOs are as well qualified or better than any diplomats in the world, including the British. This should not be read as denigration of Her Majesty's Diplomatic Service, which maintains a high reputation, but more as an indication of the strength of the confidence and pride FSOs have in their own service.

In another question, FSOs were asked to react to the following statement: "The FSO corps has steadily increased in competence and is today probably the best diplomatic corps in the world." The response was less bullish but still very positive—48.4 percent agreed; 16.3 disagreed, and 35.3 were not sure.

On all three of the foregoing questions there is a definite correlation with seniority. The more senior an officer, the more likely he is to take pronounced pride in the Service. The pride in the Service shows clearly in the responses to an SDP question on how officers would identify their occupation when introduced to a stranger at a party during home leave in the United States.

Officers overwhelmingly prefer the words "Foreign Service" to "State Department" or "government" or any other

TABLE 31

Occupational Identification

Response	Number	Percent
I'm in the Foreign Service.	173	29.6
I work for the State Department.	71	12.1
I'm a Foreign Service Officer.	288	49.2
I work for the government.	5	0.8
I'm in the diplomatic service.	40	6.9
Other	8	1.4
Totals	585	100

201

words for occupational self-identification. Almost half chose "Foreign Service Officer" and almost 30 percent chose "Foreign Service" for identification purposes.

Apparently the general public's attitude toward the professional diplomat is somewhat ambivalent, which FSOs sense. On the one hand, FSOs are prone to lament the lack of understanding and the reflexive criticism they often encounter. George Kennan sees these "popular attitudes" as a major occupational hazard: "The achievements of diplomacy are hard for the public to discern. The position of the diplomatist, on the other hand, is such that he constitutes a ready target for blame when things go wrong. The popular concept of the social habits of diplomacy and of the nature of diplomatic life continues to arouse jealousies and resentments."[17] On the other hand, more than 60 percent of respondents disagreed with the statement that "the general public estimation of the professional diplomatic corps has declined since the end of World War II" (less than 20 percent agreed, and 21 percent were not sure).

The majority is probably right, at least in the sense that the general public attaches very high prestige to the diplomatic profession, although its ranking in one set of surveys declined slightly from 1947 to 1963. In 1963 the National Opinion Research Center duplicated a 1947 study of the prestige accorded 90 occupations by a national sample of the adult population.[18] The occupations ranged from U.S. Supreme Court Justice at the top, to shoeshiner in 90th place. The major conclusion is that "there have been no substantial changes in occupational prestige in the United States" over a long period of time.

[17] Kennan, "Diplomacy as a Profession," *Foreign Service Journal*, May 1961, p. 24.

[18] Robert W. Hodge, Paul M. Siegel, and Peter H. Rossi, "Occupational Prestige in the United States, 1925-63," *The American Journal of Sociology*, Vol. LXX, No. 3 (Nov. 1964), 286-302.

The occupation of "diplomat in the U.S. foreign service" declined slightly from an NORC score of 92 in 1947 to 89 in 1963, dropping from a 4.5 ranking among the 90 occupations to 11th place.[19] In 1947 the only occupations rated higher were Supreme Court Justice, physician, state governor, and a tie at 4.5 with "Cabinet member in the federal government." This is impressive company. By 1963 such occupations as scientist, government scientist, college professor, and U.S. Representative in Congress had moved ahead. Chemist and lawyer were tied at 11th place with diplomat. However, the researchers pointed out that "changes of one or two points in the NORC score of an occupation could hardly be adequate for establishing a real change in prestige or even the direction of change in prestige (if any)."

Except for the somewhat vague grouping of "government scientists," this extraordinarily high prestige rating of the diplomat appears to be unique among groups of government employees (as differentiated from the highly rated political positions such as Cabinet member, Congressman, etc.), even among career services. Apparently the prestige of the military officer is not particularly high, and the Kilpatrick study was generated by concern for the relatively low prestige of government service in general.[20]

FSOs are certainly not unaware of their high prestige rating; it helps offset the burden of misunderstanding and criticism they feel they are bearing. The high prestige is

[19] The NORC score is a composite a weighting of the possible responses—excellent, good, average, below average, poor.

[20] Janowitz, *Professional Soldier*, pp. 226-28, discusses the apparent "relatively low" prestige of military officers and their own belief that "they are not adequately recognized." In the 1963 NORC study, "Captain in the regular army" received a low ranking of 27.5, but this is not a fair comparison, since captain is a relatively low rank. Presumably an occupational designation of "military officer" would be more comparable to "diplomat." For a discussion of how the FSOs rate the professionalism of the military, see the next chapter.

The Professional Group

very apparent when they are serving abroad, as well as at home, if not so much in Washington then certainly in home communities when officers are on leave. The sensing of high prestige has an important bearing on the behavior of FSOs. One must live up to the image and maintain it, and this reinforces notions of correct conduct, of sanctions for those who do not, and the stake one has in the career.

Status and Ambition

Elements of formal status, many of them unique in character, are important in the diplomatic career, and doubtless much of the prestige of the career is derived from them. As implied in the earlier discussion of young officers, one achieves a measure of status merely by entering the FSO corps. FSOs receive presidential commissions for appointment at every grade, not only upon initial entry. Thus promotion lists must be confirmed every year by the Senate. The Herter Committee contemplated recommending the abandonment of commissions for the junior grades, but this touched a sensitive nerve.

Some of the unique elements of formal status available to the FSO are inherent in long-standing customs of diplomacy, sanctioned by international law, such as diplomatic immunity. Two important status symbols assured to the FSO are the diplomatic passport and having one's name on the diplomatic list. A source of irritation to many FSOs is the fact that these privileges must be widely (although unevenly) shared with many non-FSOs, the employees of other agencies as well as some FSRs and Staff corps personnel, thereby, it is feared, debasing their currency.[21] The diplomatic passport usually guarantees the holder quick

[21] Not only must the privileges be shared, but at many of the larger U. S. embassies the diplomatic list has become so big that even FSOs might not automatically appear on it, particularly the younger officers.

entry to a foreign country, even in difficult circumstances, and freedom from customs inspection. Being on the diplomatic list can be important because in many cases the host country may limit the granting of duty-free import privileges to those on the list. This is a deep-seated irritation, for example, to Staff corps personnel who thus may not be able to bring an automobile into the country because of a prohibitive duty.

The official status of the FSO at his post abroad provides access to three communities—composed of other Americans residing or traveling abroad, host nationals, and the multinational diplomatic community. In the case of the last two, being on the diplomatic list can be crucial. In many countries even young officers are able to move freely within the political, military, cultural, and other elites of the host society. In case of need, the FSO *is* the United States Government to the nonofficial American abroad. In his article on the FSO "subculture" Glen Fisher writes that the diplomatic "community reflects a pattern of living and working which has grown out of many years' experience as diplomats have represented their governments in foreign countries, have learned and practiced the conventions of international diplomacy, and have shared the common experiences and problems which diplomats face regardless of nationality."[22] The status level of the FSO in respect to these communities is largely determined by his rank and diplomatic or consular title, and, as discussed in Chapter 4, by the kind of work he does. These factors are also highly important status determinants within the FSO culture, but to these one must add a third and crucial factor—the general reputation of an officer among his colleagues for sheer competence. The pecking order is clear as to rank, title, and function, moving from the low-ranking titles such as

[22] Fisher, "Foreign Service Officer," p. 75.

Vice Consul and Second Secretary on up to the high-ranking titles such as Consul General, Counselor, Minister, and, of course, the pinnacle—Ambassador. A Counselor for Political Affairs within an embassy has much more status than a Counselor for Administrative Affairs. For a younger officer a prized assignment is "principal officer" in a smaller post, even if it is a two-man consulate. One hears FSOs speak of getting their "own post" much as naval officers speak of getting their "own ship."

It is hardly possible to exaggerate the status of an Ambassador.[23] Fisher's description is so apt that it is worth quoting at length:

> Foreign Service society has a definite social structure. At the top is the career Ambassador and his wife. This is so by formal rank, and informally so, as this position implies recognition of the top qualities of the Service, the Ambassador's years of experience with exposure to the great variety of contingencies one must meet in the Service, and his repeated endorsements by the promotion system. He has direct responsibility for all official Americans in his country. The prestige of the United States rests on his shoulders at all times; he is the personal representative of the President of the United States. Both the social ethics of FSO society and the necessity for a clear chain of command require loyalty and deference to the Ambassador. Once an FSO is named Ambassador, his social role changes as his status affects his personal relationships with other officials. The casual and easy friendship is not so easily established, and his previous

[23] Still another ranking of occupations, an older one, shows "U. S. Ambassador to a foreign country," second only to "Supreme Court Justice" (and ahead of cabinet member, senator, and governor of a state). See Mapheus Smith, "An Empirical Scale of Prestige Status of Occupations," *American Sociological Review*, Vol. 8, No. 2 (Apr. 1943), 185-92. The lowest ranked occupation in the Smith survey was "prostitute"; FSOs are fond of referring to diplomacy as the "second oldest profession."

friendships are handled more carefully. He is "Mr. Ambassador" at his post and retains a right to the title thereafter.[24]

In many countries a high standard of living goes along with the status, and in fact is part of it. Often it is of a nature—elegant residence, staff of servants, chauffeured limousine, use of an air attaché's plane, and so on—that a man quite literally would have to be a millionaire to emulate at home.

It is small wonder, then, that many FSOs are ambitious to become an ambassador. This, of course, is not just a matter of status and emoluments, but of the substance which they symbolize, the influence and leverage which becoming an Ambassador affords the individual as a professional. With approximately 85 out of 118 ambassadorships held by career officers, as distinct from political appointees, the prize is by no means an unreal and remote possibility for the competent, careful officer. Roughly, the FSO has three times the chance of becoming an ambassador that a military officer has of achieving flag rank.[25] Asked in the SDP if young entering FSOs "normally should aspire to become an Ambassador," 72.3 percent answered in the affirmative. Only 14.4 percent said "no" and 13.3 percent were not sure. A slightly greater percentage of examination officers than lateral entrants (75 percent to 67 percent) answered "yes."

Following this question, officers were asked to rate their own chances of achieving the ambition. Enough realism enters the picture here to make one wonder if the strong endorsement of the ambition is not perhaps dysfunctional.

[24] Fisher, "Foreign Service Officer," p. 79.

[25] Janowitz shows (*Professional Soldier*, p. 67) that .8 percent of Army officers are generals and the same percentage of Naval officers are admirals, which compares to 2.4 percent of FSOs serving as ambassadors.

The Professional Group

TABLE 32
Self-rating of Possibility of Becoming an Ambassador

Rating	Number	Percent
No possibility	119	20.2
Barely possible	149	25.3
Possible	182	31.0
A good chance	100	17.0
Very likely	20	3.4
I am serving or have already served as an ambassador	18	3.1
Totals	588	100

More than 45 percent of the respondents said it was not possible or only barely possible that they would become an ambassador. Only 120 officers were quite optimistic (those choosing "good chance" or "very likely" for their response). Yet if one extrapolated the 20 percent SDP sample, it would mean that about 600 officers in the total corps would see themselves as being in a good position to compete for approximately 85 ambassadorships.

Only 33 percent of the examination entrants in the total sample ruled themselves out ("no possibility" or "barely possible"), compared to 70 percent of the lateral entrants. Political officers were the most optimistic among the functional specialists (excluding program directors), with 28 percent choosing "good chance" or "very likely" compared to about 20 percent for the total sample. Among the area specialists, the Arabists stand out as very optimistic, with 48 percent choosing either of these same two responses, followed by African specialists (33 percent) and Atlantic Affairs specialists (27 percent).

In sum, prestige and status are potent factors in the FSO career. A young, former FSO in an interview explained one reason for his resignation: "The trouble with most FSOs is that they are too concerned about *being* something or *becoming* something—being a DCM or becoming an

Ambassador—and not concerned enough with *doing* anything." This is certainly exaggerated, but it does point up a danger: Prestige and status are so potent in the FSO career that they often can become ends in themselves.

Elitism

Prestige and status are closely related to the elitist ideology of the FSO corps. This ideology manifests itself in a number of ways, in the issue of the representativeness of the Service, as discussed in the last chapter, and in attitudes on the character of the profession, its role, and its future, as discussed in the next chapter.

Elitism is manifested in the essentially defensive posture of most FSOs in regard to the Service. If one is a member of an elite group there is a strong tendency toward having a stake in protecting the eliteness of that group. This is done in a number of ways, by replenishing the group with new members who conform to the elite standards, by maintaining that conformance internally, by avoiding control by outsiders of a kind that could significantly affect the eliteness of the group, and by avoiding to the maximum extent possible incursions by outsiders.

The last is seen, for example, in the attitudes of FSOs on the extent to which career officers should occupy the top jobs in diplomacy. An SDP question asked officers to indicate the approximate percentage of career officers they felt should hold the ambassadorships and deputy chief of mission positions.

The response for the DCM position is as close to consensus as anything in the SDP, with almost 90 percent of all respondents saying that *all* deputy chiefs of mission should be career officers. This is probably related to the fact that, with a certain air of realism, the great majority of FSOs subscribe to the view that not all ambassadors can be career

The Professional Group

TABLE 33

Percentage of Career Officers
Who Should Hold Top Positions

	Ambassador		DCM	
	No.	Percent	No.	Percent
60 percent	14	2.4	0	0.0
70	88	15.2	0	0.0
80	200	34.5	5	0.9
90	209	36.0	51	8.9
100	32	5.5	514	89.2
Not sure	37	6.4	6	1.0
Totals	580	100	576	100

officers, although respondents would prefer a larger proportion than is actually the case. If an ambassador is not a career man, the strong belief is, then a professional should be right behind him.

On Being a Success

If the main ambition is to become an ambassador, it is instructive to examine how FSOs think one should go about attaining it. An SDP question asked officers to rate 16 attributes or experiences "in terms of importance or usefulness to attaining the top ranks of the Foreign Service and possibly becoming an Ambassador." They were asked to make their ratings according to the real world of what it takes to be a "success," not the ideal of what should be. In evaluating the 16 elements of the question, the responses tended to form into three groups.[26] Four qualities or ex-

26 In Table 34 a graphic method of portraying the results is achieved by assigning a numerical value to each response. A response of "possibly negative" has a value of 1, and a response of "crucial" is 5. By totaling the numerical values of all the responses to each of the 16 subparts to the question, it was possible to obtain a total numerical value for each subpart. For example, total numerical value of subpart A ("Area Specialization") is 1,843; this can be ranged against a scale that shows all possible responses in which, if all respondents chose "possibly negative," the total score would be 580, and if all respondents chose "crucial" the total score would be 2,900. The actual total of 1,843

periences fell toward the low side of the scale, as unimportant to success in the FSO corps: (d) other agency experience; (e) several tours in administration; (g) entry at the bottom; (j) extensive preservice work. Six other qualities or experiences fell toward the high end of the scale, as important to success in the FSO corps: (b) extensive Washington experience; (c) concentration on political work; (h) managerial experience; (m) winning respect of colleagues; (n) mastering a foreign language; and (p) good political connections. The remaining six qualities (a, f, i, k, l, o) were roughly in the middle band of "useful," but perhaps not essential.

It takes a rather high percentage of the vote toward the polar extremes to place one of the 16 subparts in either the "unimportant" or "important" groups. For example, more than two-thirds of all responses were either "negative" or "not important" for "several tours in administrative work." Conversely, nearly 80 percent of all responses were either "important" or "crucial" for "winning respect of colleagues in the corps."

At the margins, this division into three groups becomes a little arbitrary. For example, "senior training" and "a good basic understanding of economics" are only a shade away from being in the "important" group. Another way to form a rough impression in looking at the graph is to use the "useful" line as a divider with six of the bars on the negative side and 10 on the positive side.

For subgroup variations, the more senior an officer, the more likely he is to think that weighing each assignment

---

for "Area Specialization" falls somewhere between these poles, since it is the total of all the actual responses. The average number of respondents (580) was used as the basis for constructing the scale. For further understanding of the responses, the low and high percentages are shown on the left and right sides of the scale, respectively.

carefully (i) is not important, that preservice experience (j) is important, that understanding economics is important, (o), and that political connections (p) are not important. If an officer entered laterally, he is more likely than examination entry officers to think that the following are important: political work (c); managerial experience (h); a graduate degree (k); and experience in all major fields of FSO work (l).

On the question of entry at the bottom (g), there was little variation, with lateral entry officers only slightly more inclined than examination officers to see this as important. This response may seem curious, since there is such strong emphasis in the corps on entry at the bottom and resistance to lateral entry. The explanation probably is that respondents here are simply being realistic and responding, as they were asked to do, in terms of past and present reality, not in terms of what should be or what would normally be the case. In point of fact, as we shall see in detail in Chapter 8, quite a few lateral entrants have been very successful in the Service. Yet, more than twice the proportion of lateral entrants than examination entrants virtually rule themselves out in respect to the main ambition within the Service.

Table 34 offers interesting indices of change. If the same question had been asked 20 years ago, it is very likely that two of the items now in the "important" range would have been ranked very low—"extensive experience in Washington" and "managerial experience." Economic knowledge probably would have been ranked lower than now, and several items would have puzzled the respondents as hardly applicable to them—assignment to another agency, administrative work, and senior training.

The item with the highest score—"winning respect of colleagues in the corps"—is indeed critical to success. Ear-

Characteristics, Norms, Attitudes

TABLE 34
On Being a Success in the FSO Corps

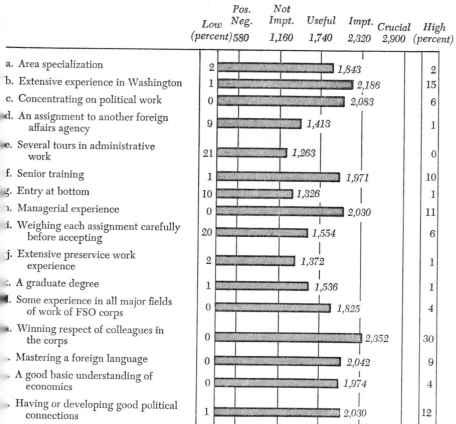

	Low (percent) 580	Pos. Neg. 1,160	Not Impt. 1,740	Useful 2,320	Impt. Crucial 2,900	High (percent)
a. Area specialization	2			1,843		2
b. Extensive experience in Washington	1			2,186		15
c. Concentrating on political work	0			2,083		6
d. An assignment to another foreign affairs agency	9		1,413			1
e. Several tours in administrative work	21		1,263			0
f. Senior training	1			1,971		10
g. Entry at bottom	10		1,326			1
h. Managerial experience	0			2,030		11
i. Weighing each assignment carefully before accepting	20		1,554			6
j. Extensive preservice work experience	2		1,372			1
k. A graduate degree	1		1,536			1
l. Some experience in all major fields of work of FSO corps	0			1,825		4
m. Winning respect of colleagues in the corps	0			2,352		30
n. Mastering a foreign language	0			2,042		9
o. A good basic understanding of economics	0			1,974		4
p. Having or developing good political connections	1			2,030		12

lier it was mentioned that one of the major elements of
status is the reputation of an officer among his colleagues.
The FSO corps is like virtually all professional groups in
that it is at the same time strongly collegial and strongly
individualistic. The individualism is inherent in developing one's own professional qualifications, in making choices
that advance one's own career, in taking pride in one's own
accomplishments, and it is reinforced in the semi-nomadic

213

life style the FSO must carry on. Yet equally strong is the collegial and fraternal character of the group. It is one's colleagues who sit on the assignment and promotion panels that are crucial to one's career advancement. George Kennan sees one of the great rewards of a diplomatic career precisely in its fraternalism: "One looks for these rewards, first of all, in the understanding and respect brought to one's work by one's own colleagues—in the sheer professional comradeship they afford. This is true of many professions: it is to the colleague, not to the outsider or the client, that one looks for real appreciation."[27] Kennan goes on to draw the behavioral implications, the obligation on the individual officer to help create "the collegial atmosphere," to "recognize a responsibility for the morale of those around him, just as he has to draw on them for his own morale."

Causes of Concern

Some insights into the mood and temper of the FSO corps can be gained by examining what it is that worries officers. An SDP question arrayed nine items and asked respondents to indicate the extent to which they had been concerned about them. The same sort of presentation is used for Table 35 as was used for Table 34, with total scores for each of the nine items ranged against a scale based on total possible responses, and percentages for the low and high choices shown.

The two things that FSOs clearly worry about the least among the nine possibilities are selection-out and whether they have chosen the right career; note the very large percentages for both that chose "never" as a response. The two about which most concern is felt are the only two among the nine that are not personal in nature—the gen-

[27] Kennan, "Diplomacy as a Profession," p. 24.

Characteristics, Norms, Attitudes

eral condition of the corps and how the State Department is managed; a very high percentage of officers are "frequently" concerned about these two.

One tentative interpretation of these results is that while personal morale seems reasonably good ("very little" concern about the wisdom of having chosen a Foreign Service career) there is widespread recognition that problems beset the Service. These results and others in the SDP that will be reviewed in the next chapter indicate clearly that there is widespread understanding of the role challenge which both the FSO corps and the Department of State face in regard to the total management of foreign affairs. A significant point which will occupy our attention in detail in Chapter 7 is that the last two items in Table 34 correlate strongly with seniority: the junior officers are very much more worried than senior officers about inadequate challenge in their work and whether or not they have chosen the right career.

TABLE 35

Extent of FSO Concern over Nine Selected Items

	Low (percent)	Never 580	Very Little 1,160	Some- times 1,740	Frequent- ly 2,320	High (percent)
1. How well you are accepted and respected by colleagues in FSO corps	4			1,617		17
2. Possible adverse effects of overseas life on one or more family members	13			1,578		21
3. General condition of the FSO corps	2			1,864		40
4. Possibility of selection-out	50		964			3
5. How well you are able to live up to demands of your job	7			1,573		17
6. How the State Department is managed	1				1,984	51
7. How soon you will get promoted	2			1,631		24
8. Less challenge in your work than you had expected or hoped for	16			1,460		16
9. Whether or not the FSO corps is the right career for you	30		1,259			10

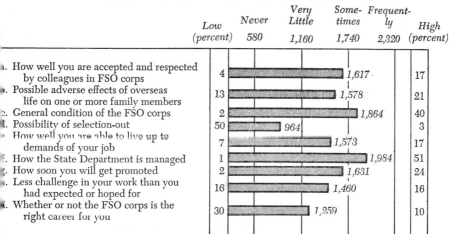

215

The Professional Group

Prescribed Behavior

There does not exist a generally accepted, fully articulated code of ethics, of prescribed behavior, for the professional diplomat.[28] One reason certainly is that much of the prescribed behavior is obvious and pervasive, either in the long-standing mores of the profession or in the public service standards of modern-day America. Included would be such concepts as honor, integrity, loyalty, and good moral character. That such qualities are widely distributed among FSOs is assured by the weight of tradition and by such devices as the security clearance investigation and the self-disciplining processes of the Service.

In an effort to achieve some idea of what FSOs think about at least some values and modes of behavior, an SDP question was phrased thus:

> Every professional group tends to develop its own code of ethics—its values, ideals, prescribed behavior. How would you rate the following styles of behavior in terms of their propriety and importance for the professional diplomat?

The results are shown in Table 36 with percentages for the four possible choices reading across for each of the 10 styles of behavior rated.

The most strongly held mores, those with close to or more than 90 percent of the respondents citing as usually imperative or always imperative, are (a) placing the good of the Service over one's personal good; (c) readiness for worldwide service; (g) following political decisions even if

[28] In attempting to follow up on a remark by Secretary of State Dean Rusk, that the Foreign Service should have a "Hippocratic Oath," the Committee on Career Principles of the American Foreign Service Association tried in 1966 to develop a code of ethics, but the project was not completed.

FSO Evaluations of Behavioral Styles

	Irrelevant or unimportant to the professional diplomat	Completely optional—this behavior depends entirely on the situation	Usually imperative—most officers should act this way most of the time	Imperative—an FSO should always act this way
a. Placing the "good of the service" over one's own personal good	0.9	8.5	61.0	29.6
b. Not being completely frank in negotiations if it helps win one's point	8.5	78.7	10.6	2.2
c. Readiness to serve anywhere in the world in any job at the discretion of the Secretary of State	0.9	10.1	61.3	27.7
d. Acting rationally and avoiding any display of emotion	1.0	21.7	55.7	21.6
e. Taking whatever steps one can to strengthen the professional group	5.4	23.9	45.7	25.0
f. Entertaining regularly as part of the job	1.2	40.9	48.2	9.7
g. Following political decisions fully even when one personally disagrees	0.0	5.0	43.5	51.5
h. Maintaining proper dress and manners	0.9	9.9	50.9	38.5
i. Advocating positions which may be unpopular but which one feels to be important	1.4	17.9	46.7	34.0
j. Avoiding the use of political influence for one's own career	9.6	32.9	27.2	30.3

one personally disagrees; (h) and maintaining proper dress and manners.

Three others are also strongly endorsed, in the 70 to 80 percent range: (d) acting rationally and avoiding emotional display; (e) helping to strengthen the professional group; (i) and advocating unpopular positions which one feels to be important.

Again, the sense of service, of dedication and self-sacrifice, comes through strongly in the responses to a, c, g, and i. One officer said: "In a crisis, every citizen might be a patriot—an FSO must be a conscious patriot all his career. Not a flagrant type, just a quiet dedication—something like a priestly vocation."

On the question of carrying out political decisions with which one personally disagrees, one officer wrote: "If the officer feels the political decision is positively harmful to U.S. interests in a *crucial* way, he should squawk loud and long, but in the final analysis, as a professional, he is bound to carry out the President's orders." The difficulty of the possible dilemma involved is expressed in the comment of another officer: "I feel that in extreme cases one should resign if one disagrees with political decisions."

To capture something of the flavor of the strong emphasis on honesty and integrity, following is a sampling of written comments generated by the SDP question on prescribed behavior:

FSO-3: "Unquestioned personal honesty."

FSO-6: "Total personal honesty and integrity."

FSO-3: "Utter integrity! An FSO must be completely reliable at home and abroad. Any FSO who lacks integrity should be selected-out."

FSO-5: "Complete honesty in communications with colleagues and superiors."

218

FSO-6: "In-service honesty, i.e., avoiding moralisms or debating-type arguments in reports and internal correspondence or discussions."

The item about "not being completely frank in negotiations if it helps win one's point" elicited a number of comments, illustrating some of the inner subtleties of diplomacy. The high moral premium placed on honesty comes through again, but so does a certain touch of operational realism.

FSO-3: "It is of absolute importance that an FSO *not* be dishonest in negotiations even if it helps him win his point."

Career Minister: "Frankness is the best diplomacy in general, but one cannot afford to disclose his hand completely when dealing with others who are not frank. Deception, however, is almost never wise."

FSO-4: "We work with a limited number of people abroad. 'Slipperiness' in negotiations determines future negotiations re the individuals involved."

FSO-2: "We are often advocates, and no advocate makes his opponent's case for him. It is a well-established principle that the only permissible lie a diplomat may tell another diplomat is 'I don't know.' It is permissible because disbelief in it is permissible."

Other qualities—discretion, ethical behavior, fairness— emerge in the written comments:

FSO-5: "Keeping personal opinions, such as the wisdom of U.S. policy or the legitimacy of the Ambassador's parents, if not to oneself at least in the official family. This is a serious failing, especially among junior officers."

FSO-1: "Invariable courtesy and fairness toward local employees who have much influence in their countries

219

The Professional Group

on the reputation of the United States for whom they work."

FSO-3: "Fairness to subordinates and peers, candor with superiors."

FSO-3: "Ethical behavior in one's personal, family, and financial affairs; willingness to recognize talent at all levels of advancement."

Several officers stressed the importance of a wide-ranging interest in the world and in the specific country of assignment. An FSO-4 stated the point this way: "Taking pains to learn the language of the country, travel to far interior places and making contact with all classes of people, showing a genuine interest in their ways, traditions, and culture; becoming articulate about their art, music, and literature; having at least one or two intimate friends among them—and advising the American colony in this direction."

Another officer, an FSO-2, questioned whether many officers could "remain in the service for the full-life career" in the absence of a "wide ranging, even electric interest in all sorts of aspects of the world."

The strong endorsement of "maintaining proper dress and manners" in Table 36, and the moderately strong acceptance of "entertaining regularly as part of the job" are indicative of another area of important behavioral influence—the etiquette and prescribed sociability of Foreign Service life. Janowitz' description of the social code of the military system is very applicable to the Foreign Service in most particulars. After pointing out that entrance into the system assures the officer of essential social acceptance, Janowitz comments: "The essence of the social code is not its exclusiveness, but its pervasiveness."[29]

For the Foreign Service Officer and his wife serving abroad, the social code is indeed omnipresent. In the minds

[29] Janowitz, *Professional Soldier*, Chapter 10.

of many, protocol is virtually synonymous with diplomacy. FSO Glen Fisher, however, makes the point that the social code goes far beyond the formalities of protocol:

> Some of the customs and conventions of the diplomatic community are formalized in practices of protocol, in use of diplomatic titles, in formats for official correspondence, and the like. Much more of it is less formal, and represents skills, attitudes, values, and styles of living and dealing with other people which have grown out of the diplomat's cumulative experience over many years and generations of diplomatic personnel.[30]

Some idea of the pervasiveness of the social code emerges here and there in a handbook put out by the Office of the Deputy Under Secretary of State for Administration in 1964. An interesting compilation of ideas and techniques that have worked well for various U.S. Ambassadors, the handbook is mainly concerned with managerial and task-oriented ideas, but it deals with social conduct as well. The vignettes are anonymous and in the first person as contributed by various chiefs of mission.[31]

> When my wife and I are giving a large party, I expect members of the mission to arrive a few minutes ahead of time and to remain, unless permission is obtained, until the official closing hour. If there is a receiving line, several officers and their wives are responsible for greeting incoming guests, introducing them to enough other people in the party that they have someone to talk to.
>
> ....
>
> I let each officer know that I expect him to assume primary responsibility for certain areas of our overall

[30] Fisher, "Foreign Service Officer," p. 76.
[31] U.S. Department of State, *This Worked for Me . . .* , 1964.

representational needs. This includes areas which the Embassy assigns him and others he himself proposes. I also impress on him the fact that representing the United States in the Foreign Service is a 24-hour-day, 7-days-a-week job.

....

The wives of our officers have welcomed the direction of their energies into constructive channels in the community. My wife works actively with them, encourages them "to do something extracurricular," and gives suggestions and guidance in this regard.

The Processes of the Service

The administrative processes of the Foreign Service have a profound influence on behavior in the dual and related sense of serving as generalized instruments of control and sanction for the group as a whole and in providing constraints and guidelines for individual behavior.

The major processes are arrayed in Table 37, which shows the responses of officers to two SDP questions. The

TABLE 37

Evaluation of Administrative Processes of the Service*

	Don't know	*Definitely needs improving*	*Acceptably done*	*Very well done*	*Must be done by FSOs*	
					Yes	*No*
a. Recruitment at Junior Officer level	14.1	13.5	51.2	21.2	66.6	33.4
b. Recruitment for lateral entry	24.5	53.3	21.7	0.5	73.5	26.5
c. Training	3.4	31.1	58.1	7.4	25.8	74.2
d. Assignment	1.4	46.1	50.5	2.0	75.3	24.7
e. Promotion	0.9	33.1	58.7	7.3	80.5	19.5
f. Selection-out	23.1	40.4	34.6	1.9	79.0	21.0
g. Inspection	7.3	19.5	55.8	17.4	85.1	14.9

* Read percentages across for each of the two parts of the table.

222

main body of the table deals with an evaluation of how well the seven functions are being performed. On the righthand side are responses to the question of whether or not each function should be performed by FSOs or by groups in which FSOs form a majority.

Officers gave two of the functions—recruitment at the junior officer level and inspection—very high marks, with more than 70 percent at the "acceptably done" or "very well done" levels. Two other functions, training and promotion, score nearly as highly. Opinion was pretty well divided on whether assignment procedures need definite improvement or are acceptably done; the remaining two functions, recruitment for lateral entry and selection-out, received preponderantly negative votes. About the only marked variation among subgroups was that examination entry officers were generally more favorable about the assignment process than the lateral entrants (58 percent choosing "acceptably done," to 38 percent of the lateral entrants) .

The two negative votes, on lateral entry and selection-out, are difficult to interpret. Other SDP data (as we shall see in Chapter 7) strongly suggest that more should be read into the negative votes than merely the view that two processes are not well-handled. In a broad sense, the data suggest the not unrelated ideas that there should be less lateral entry and more selection-out.

On the queston of whether the processes should be managed by FSOs or groups in which FSOs form a majority, respondents were very clear that they should be so managed in six out of seven cases, offering some confirmation of the observation that a strong tendency toward self-government is a marked characteristic of career systems. The exception was training, in which the ratio was nearly reversed. By slight margins, examination entry officers voted more strongly than lateral entrants that the functions should be managed by FSOs, again with the sole exception of training.

This configuration suggests that training stands apart from the other administrative processes as not vital to the self-discipline and control of the FSO corps. In the military, "career officers look upon training as a primary responsibility, accepted without question."[32] This is definitely not the case in the Foreign Service. In comparative rankings of three professional groups (discussed in detail in Chapter 7), FSOs rated themselves the lowest on two indices of professionalism: "a relatively set pattern of preparatory education," and "a belief that members should stay abreast of new knowledge relevant to the profession, often involving formal training." There has been increasing interest in training over the years, but in the main it is still largely incidental to the career. Quite appropriate to FSOs is Herbert Kaufman's comment on the U.S. Forest Service: "On-the-job training is unquestionably the largest single element in the Service training armory."[33]

Recruitment, whether at the bottom or laterally, and selection-out are obvious control mechanisms in determining who is qualified to enter the profession and who is not qualified to remain in it. The control and disciplining functions of the Inspection Corps are obvious in its title. This body of approximately 20 senior FSOs makes on-site inspections at overseas posts, rendering an important administrative service in terms of the standards of conduct of the corps, helping to give those standards form and substance and to propagate them. The inspectors evaluate the performance of every officer at the post, and these evaluations, along with the efficiency reports turned in annually

[32] John W. Masland and Lawrence J. Radway, *Soldiers and Scholars* (Princeton: Princeton University Press, 1957) , p. 53.
[33] Kaufman, *The Forest Ranger: A Study in Administrative Behavior* (Baltimore: The Johns Hopkins Press, 1960) , p. 171.

by supervisors, form the basis for the judgments of the promotion panels.

The assignment and promotion processes have a crucial impact on the behavior and career progress of the FSO. In a previous work, the author described these processes in detail.[34] The importance of the assignment process was stated as follows: "For the FSO, the question of his next assignment can be vital. He may feel that it will affect, for good or bad, the future course of his career, his wife's disposition, the health and education of his children, whether or not he can save money, and a host of other personal considerations."

Assignments and promotions are the administrative lifeblood of the corps and are very much interrelated. In both cases, "winning the respect of colleagues in the corps" is critical to the individual officer, producing in turn intense pressure on the individual to live up to what he perceives to be the norms of his colleagues. An officer's reputation among his colleagues, often passed by word of mouth, is more important in making assignments than is the formal, written record on his performance. The formal record is more important in the promotion process, but it, too, is an expression of the officer's reputation, although written in artful language that takes experience to master and even more experience to interpret. Because rated officers are able to see most of the efficiency reports written by their supervisors, a negative report is more likely to consist of damning by faint praise than outright criticism [35]

[34] John E. Harr, *The Development of Careers in the Foreign Service*, Foreign Affairs Personnel Study No. 3 (New York: Carnegie Endowment for International Peace, 1965), Chapter 2, "The Assignment Process" and Chapter 3, "The Promotion System."

[35] There has been a long-standing controversy over whether efficiency reports should be seen by rated officers—how and when they should be seen, and to what extent they should be seen. The latest compromise is that the main body of the rating is to be shown to the em-

The Professional Group

Since certain functional fields and types of assignments are likely to result in faster promotions, these are avidly sought. In turn, faster promotions are likely to place one in an excellent competitive position for the more choice assignments. There is thus very powerful circular reinforcement for staying in the "mainstream." This, of course, is not an arbitrary business, but a reflection of what is considered to be important work, the "substantive" work of the FSO corps as discussed in Chapter 4; it is the work that attracted officers—most of the examination entrants, at least—to the FSO corps in the first place.

One can hardly fault the system for rewarding what its members regard as the most important work, but a major problem is the slowness of this kind of system to respond to new needs. For example, with respect to the role challenge to the FSO corps to manage all operations in foreign affairs, it would make sense for many officers to obtain operational experience in the newer programs such as information and development assistance. Assignment panels have tried to find good officers for assignment to other agencies and the precepts to the promotion panels have stressed for years that such duty should be rewarded. Progress has been very slow, though accelerating in recent years. Many officers still fear that such assignments will not be considered in the "mainstream" and that supervisors in the other agencies will not be sufficiently skilled in the artful language of the FSO promotion system.

Table 36 shows that "readiness to serve anywhere in the world in any job" is a strongly held norm of the Foreign Service. It is regarded as bad form for an officer to be excessively petulant and choosy about an assignment that is pretty much set, which is why "weighing each assignment

ployee, but a "Development Appraisal Report" attached to the main report is not to be shown to him.

carefully before accepting" was not rated very highly in Table 34 as leading to success. However, few officers allow themselves to become the helpless pawns of the assignment process. Although an officer cannot control his exact assignments, he can do a great deal to precondition their general nature. The result was summarized by the author as follows: "In summary, the ideal of world-wide commitment does have operational significance. It is misleading only if it conjures up an image of a selfless group of men who silently go their appointed ways. The correct image is one of a group of men who are highly vocal about their assignments, but who are generally willing to deliver when the chips are down."[36]

The importance of the promotion system to the Service as a regulatory and governing process, and its impact on individual members, can scarcely be exaggerated. Promotion panels for each grade level of the Service are convened each fall amid considerable pomp and ceremony. Half or more of the senior officers comprising the panels are brought to Washington from their overseas posts for the two or three months of deliberations.[37] The product of their labors is the promotion list of some 600 to 700 names which will go from the White House to the Senate for approval the following spring. In Glen Fisher's words: "For the FSO community, the annual announcement of the promotion list —like an early spring rite—is the formal reinforcement of the social structure." Those promoted are "understandably jubilant," and they are likely to receive letters of congratulation from friends from all corners of the world. For those who hoped to be promoted but who are not, it is a "time for sober reappraisal," and "the threat of still not

---

[36] Harr, *Development of Careers*, p. 52.

[37] FSOs comprise a majority of each promotion panel, but also included are public members and a USIA member, as well as observers from other agencies.

227

being on the list next year helps keep performance high."[38]

As Caplow points out, "The official ideology of any hierarchy includes the insistence that all promotions are determined by merit and achievement." Competence and the type of work performed are certainly major factors in determining who gets promoted. Probably even more important is an image of general suitability for an FSO career. In Caplow's words: "The most important selective elements, however, are those which have to do with the workings of the hierarchical system itself. Thus, the elders are inclined to select those who are like themselves in general appearance, and who, in addition, have demonstrated specific ability to conform to hierarchical expectations, to render personal service to their sponsors, to conduct themselves prudently in internecine conflicts, and to maintain the interests of the group against all outsiders."[39] The net effect is to bring to the fore persons who have carefully shaped themselves to conform to group norms: "Such persons will be extremely conservative, will hesitate to take unprecedented actions, and will, in general, reserve their heaviest condemnation for those who violate the fraternity rules of their own group."

In Arthur Schlesinger's view, the FSO promotion system "was in effect a conspiracy of the conventional against the unconventional." His vivid, though perhaps overstated, idea of the result is: "At times it almost looked as if the Service inducted a collection of spirited young Americans at the age of twenty-five and transmuted them in twenty years into bland and homologous denizens of a conservative men's club."[40]

In an SDP comment an FSO-2 cited what he believed to

[38] Fisher, "Foreign Service Officer," pp. 80-81.
[39] Caplow, *Sociology of Work*, pp. 71-72.
[40] Arthur Schlesinger, Jr., *A Thousand Days: John F. Kennedy in the White House* (Boston: Houghton Mifflin, 1965), pp. 411, 415.

be the area "of most importance and costly weakness" to the Service:

The premium put on getting along well with one's colleagues—particularly one's superiors—rather than on effective performance; the inhibiting influence of the fact that errors of commission are much more dangerous to an individual than errors of omission.

Thus many FSOs are deeply ambivalent about "the system." In intimate conversation many officers will bitterly criticize the system and its pressures for conformity. Yet virtually all will agree that some such system is essential. There have been frequent minor tamperings with the workings of the system, but no widespread sentiment for radically altering its character.

Conformity

The pressure of the administrative processes of the Service provides at least partial explanation for the graphic picture of conformity presented by Chris Argyris in a study provocatively entitled *Some Causes of Organizational Ineffectiveness within the Department of State.*[41]

Argyris spent a week with each of three groups of 20 senior officers in a residential seminar setting in which the intent was to stimulate relatively open conversation among the officers about themselves, their careers, the "system," and their interpersonal relationships and styles. The officers represented the cream of the Service; included were a number of ambassadors, ambassadors-to-be, and DCMs.

The Argyris study is intent on describing and at least partially explaining the "living system" of the State Department and the Foreign Service. Argyris characterized the "liv-

[41] Published as "Occasional Paper Number 2," by the Center for International Systems Research of the Department of State (Washington, D.C.: GPO, 1967).

229

ing system" as containing "norms that inhibit open confrontation of difficult issues and penalize people who take risks. I intend to show that the living system rewards certain types of interpersonal styles, helps to create a perception of the Foreign Service as being a rather closed club, induces a degree of blindness on the part of the members concerning their impact on each other and 'outsiders,' and generates an intricate network of organizational defenses that makes the members believe that changing it may be very difficult if not impossible."

Four norms were set forth by Argyris who drew liberally on the tape-recorded quotations of the officers involved in the seminars:

1. Withdrawal from interpersonal difficulties and conflict
2. Minimum interpersonal openness, leveling, and trust
3. Mistrust of others' aggressiveness and fighting
4. Withdrawal from aggressiveness and fighting

In addition, Argyris delineated several values widely held by members of the Foreign Service:

1. The substantive side of the organization is paramount.
2. To be rational is to be effective; to be emotional is to be ineffective.
3. Effective leaders direct, oversee, control the efforts of their subordinates.

The rest of the study deals with some effects of these norms and values—the development of interpersonal styles to cope with them, success and failure in the living system, development of a high degree of conformity, ineffectiveness of groups. Argyris concluded:

We have a powerful circular loop, a process within the Foreign Service culture that tends to reinforce the participants to minimize interpersonal threat by minimizing risk-taking, being open and being forthright, as well as minimizing their feelings of responsibility and their willingness to confront conflict openly. This, in turn, tends to reinforce those who have decided to withdraw, play it safe, not make waves, and to do so both in their behavior and in their writing. Under these conditions people soon learn the survival quotient of "checking with everyone," of developing policies that upset no one, of establishing policies in such a way that the superior takes the responsibility for them.

He further concluded:

This network of interconnected coercive processes creates a tight system with the ability to make individuals behave according to the system's demands. All participants now will experience the system as all-powerful and unchangeable. Although they may dislike the system, they will tend to feel a sense of helplessness and resignation about changing it.

Argyris took pains to point out that the analysis was only partial, that it focused on the pathology rather than the strengths, that much of the behavior is characteristic of large organizations in general, that change for the better is possible if extremely difficult, and that he was not simply being critical of FSOs. Several times he underscored his high regard for officers as individuals whom he saw as much the victims of as the contributors to their own living system.

One of the most interesting features of the Argyris study is the fact that it was published by the Department of State itself, in a rare exhibition of candor among large organizations. In his foreword Deputy Under Secretary for Administration William J. Crockett wrote that the decision to publish the study "was not taken lightly." Among reasons for publishing the study, Crockett stated that "being honest and open about the problems dealt with in this study offers the best beginning for dealing with them effectively and constructively." Argyris recommended a long-range program to change the "living system," which would start with the top executives of the State Department and build on the ACORD program.[42]

Conclusion / A Model of Socialization

In this chapter I have tried to describe some of the characteristics, attitudes, and behavior of FSOs and some of the causative influences. The picture that emerges is one of a sophisticated, status-conscious, highly intelligent, ambitious, and dedicated group, one that is simultaneously awarded high prestige and much criticism from the larger society. Organizationally and professionally the group is conservative and slow to change, and individual members are under strong influence to conform to group norms.

Out of the many aspects of behavior examined in this chapter, a model of the socialization process within a group of this kind can be delineated. The steps are:

1. *Self-selection.* Because of the difficulty of entering the professional group, it is chiefly persons who are highly motivated and who sense that their own interests and values are congruent with those of the group who are likely to persist; such persons are predisposed to adapt readily.

2. *Formal selection.* Those entrusted with selecting newcomers to the group generally take care to search for qualities that are prized within the group; in large measure, they tend to reproduce themselves. This provides added insur-

[42] The work of Argyris leading to his provocative report was one of the precursors of the ACORD (organizational development) program conceived and launched later by Crockett and his staff aide, Richard W. Barrett.

ance that the newcomers will fit in well and will adapt readily.

3. *Indoctrination.* In formal training and in less formal interaction with veteran group members, newcomers quickly become aware of what is expected of them in terms of social and professional conduct.

4. *Weeding-out.* There is a strong tendency for the separation of members who are not suited to the group, either by the individual's own choice or by formal group action. Although this can happen throughout the career, there is a tendency for separation to occur in the early years when neither the group nor the individual has invested too much in the association.

5. *Reinforcement in the career experience.* Throughout years of work experience and exposure to the group's culture, the individual's assimilation of group norms becomes progressively deeper.

6. *Increasing stake in the career.* At some point, usually in the mid-career years, the member's investment in the career and in the group reaches the stage at which any possibility of separation is severely threatening. As the individual's mobility decreases and his dependence on the group increases, his tendency to conform to group norms becomes pronounced.

7. *The influence of status and prestige.* As the individual rises in the career, achieving higher status and greater prestige, his self-esteem and welfare become inextricably bound up with the welfare of the group.

8. *The influence of esprit de corps and professional mystique.* Progressively, shared experience and initiation into the mysteries of the profession tend to separate the individual member from the outside world and increase his identification with the group.

9. *Organizational pressures.* In frequent contrast to the "free" professions, the organizational context of a career system tends to generate additional pressures that work toward group cohesiveness, as in more direct constraints and sanctions (a promotion system) and the proximity of perceived rival groups (the "administrators").

10. *Paternalism in the senior ranks.* By the time the individual achieves "success" as generally recognized within the group, usually in his senior years, he is no longer under pressure to conform, but is now one of those who is exerting pressure. He is a "success," he has reaped honors, and he can retire at any time with a handsome annuity; consequently, he feels freer in expressing himself. But he is now a product of the socialization process: he is a leader, he is influential, and he tends to take direct responsibility for the welfare of the group.

This model, of course, is essentially neutral; it merely describes what is likely to happen in a career system such as the FSO system. Whether the processes involved are functional or dysfunctional, in the case of a particular career system or for particular individuals, is another question. Some members of the group may at times see the processes as sinister and manipulative; others will see them as quite natural and supportive of their own interests.

CHAPTER 7

CHANGE AND THE PROFESSION

....

A MAJOR FOCUS of the SDP, one that elicited much written commentary from respondents, dealt with the state of the profession of diplomacy largely in terms of changes that have occurred or could occur. My purpose in this chapter is to review the survey results in this area and examine opinion on several key issues that emerge from the data, with respect to the future state of the profession. Further, I will explore a remarkable ferment and efforts toward change that have developed recently within the Service.

Past Change

An SDP question on past changes was phrased as follows:

There has been a great deal of discussion about changes in the ways that the United States conducts its foreign affairs in recent decades. How would you evaluate the following changes that have occurred? Make your evaluations in terms of your view of the general value or utility of the change, not in regard to how well it may have been accomplished.

Officers evaluated the eight changes shown in Table 38 on a five-point scale ranging from "bad" to "very much needed." As in past tables, results are shown in a bar graph representing composite scores achieved by totaling the point values (from 1 to 5) awarded to each possible response.

The Professional Group

Percentages of officers choosing the lowest and highest responses for each item are shown in the margins.

TABLE 38
Evaluation of Recent Change

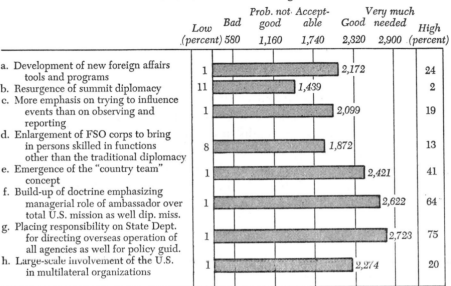

	Low (percent)	Bad 580	Prob. not good 1,160	Accept-able 1,740	Good 2,320	Very much needed 2,900	High (percent)
a. Development of new foreign affairs tools and programs	1				2,172		24
b. Resurgence of summit diplomacy	11		1,439				2
c. More emphasis on trying to influence events than on observing and reporting	1				2,099		19
d. Enlargement of FSO corps to bring in persons skilled in functions other than the traditional diplomacy	8			1,872			13
e. Emergence of the "country team" concept	1				2,421		41
f. Build-up of doctrine emphasizing managerial role of ambassador over total U.S. mission as well dip. miss.	1				2,622		64
g. Placing responsibility on State Dept. for directing overseas operation of all agencies as well for policy guid.	1					2,723	75
h. Large-scale involvement of the U.S. in multilateral organizations	1			2,274			20

In evaluating the past changes listed, FSOs responded extremely favorably, with a near-negative vote only for summit diplomacy. Four changes are in the acceptable-to-good range: new foreign affairs tools and programs; more emphasis on influencing events than on observing and reporting; enlargement of the Service to bring in new persons in functions other than the traditional ones; and large-scale involvement of the U.S. in multilateral organizations.

There is strong endorsement for three other changes, which are related, in that they have to do with increased management responsibility and authority for the State Department and the FSO corps in all overseas operations. These three, all falling in the "good" to "very much needed" range, are: emergence of the "country team" concept, build-up of doctrine emphasizing the managerial role of the Ambassador over the total U.S. Mission, as well as his diplomatic role; and placing responsibility on State for directing the overseas operations of all agencies, as well as for its policy guidance role. In all three cases, extremely high percentages of respondents chose the highest possible response. Note in particular the overwhelming 75 percent citing as "very much needed" the placing of responsibility on State for the direction of all overseas operations, which was the purpose of NSAM 341 of March 1966 discussed in Chapter 3.

Of the three high choices, the least enthusiasm is shown for the "country team" concept, probably because in the minds of some this still retains a connotation of "decision by committee," although it is often not the case in practice.

There was little variation among subgroups, except that in the case of three of the items (d, e, f) lateral entrants came out somewhat more strongly in favor of the changes than did examination entrants.

Altogether, the attitudes of FSOs on significant past changes strikes a strong positive note, in marked contrast to the gloomy views expressed during the Wriston period and more recently by senior retired FSOs.

Present and Future Change

Another SDP question asked FSOs to evaluate 10 more recent change efforts, most of them currently being attempted or seriously contemplated. The evaluation was to be in terms of the effect of the change efforts "on the professionalism and competence of the FSO corps."

Table 39 employs a different method of presentation to provide a visual profile of where opinion is concentrated—toward the negative or positive ends of the spectrum. The

237

The Professional Group

TABLE 39

Evaluation of Possible Changes

	Don't know	Bad	Prob. not good	Accept-able	Good	Very much needed	Doesn't go far enough

a. The Hays Bill

b. Integration of more than 700 USIA career officers

c. Increasing use of FSRS to fill special needs

d. A planning-programming-budgeting system for the foreign affairs community

e. Greater use of systems and computers

f. Extending National Policy Paper effort to more countries

g. More emphasis on training at each career stage

h. Cutback in the number of U.S. agencies and their personnel operating abroad

i. Maintaining a consistent volume of lateral entry every year

j. Removing some consular and administrative jobs from the FSO corps to the Staff corps

238

percentage response to each possible response for each of the ten items in the question is shown vertically on a scale of 0 to 50 percent. A line connecting these percentages then completes the profile. The sum of the seven percentages for each item is 100 percent.

A quick glance at the profiles indicates that three—the Hays Bill, USIA integration, and a consistent volume of lateral entry (a, b, i)—are toward the negative end, in the "bad" to "probably not good" range.[1] In particular, opinion is negative on the Hays Bill and USIA integration, with about 60 percent of respondents choosing either of the two negative responses. These results correlate inversely with grade level; the more junior an officer is, the more likely he is to oppose the Hays Bill and USIA integration. More than 70 percent of the officers at levels 5 and 6 chose either of the two negative responses, compared to about 45 percent of officers at levels 1 and 2. These tendencies hold when examined by method of entry as well; that is, when lateral entrants are screened out (they tend to be less negative on these issues than examination entrants as a whole), the junior examination entrants are still considerably more negative than the more senior examination entrants. A similar pattern holds for lateral entry (i).

There is strong support for two of the changes, cutting back the number of agencies and their personnel abroad, and removing some consular and administrative jobs from the FSO corps. In both cases, more than 80 percent of respondents chose one of the last three responses (good, very much needed, doesn't go far enough), with "very much needed" drawing the largest percentage. There are no significant subgroup variations on the cutback of other agencies, but in the case of removing some administrative

[1] It should be noted that officers filled out the SDP questionnaires in May and June 1966 before the demise of the Hays Bill and the USIA integration plan, as described in Chapter 2.

The Professional Group

and consular jobs from the FSO corps, the lateral entrants are considerably less supportive than the examination entrants, in particular the junior officers. As the analysis in Chapter 4 would indicate, this is understandable; most junior officers are not interested in administrative and consular work, and therefore would be just as happy to see jobs in these fields removed from the corps. On the other hand, many lateral entrants, in particular the more recent entrants, are located in these two functional fields, and probably can imagine themselves going along with the jobs.

A third item—"more emphasis on training at each career stage" (g) —receives almost as strong an endorsement as the two leading items. This offers some confirmation of the observation in the last chapter, that training, historically never a critical element in the FSO's career, is generating greater interest.

The remaining four changes (c, d, e, f) all show flatter curves, indicating rather divided opinion, but in general, moderate support. The planning-programming-budgeting system and extending National Policy Papers are seen with slightly more favor than the other two. Three of these four (d, e, f) are in a somewhat esoteric or technical realm; thus, they are the items that receive significant percentages in the "don't know" column.

Taken together, Tables 38 and 39 present an interesting pattern. FSOs were positive about past changes, including some changes on which sentiment was largely negative when they were taking place. They were particularly enthusiastic about three changes that tend to strengthen their hand in control of foreign affairs. In regard to possible new changes, FSOs are extremely negative on two (the Hays Bill and USIA integration) intended by their sponsors to help make improved management and control a reality. And, of the three changes FSOs strongly support, two are essentially

240

negative in character—cutting back other agency operations abroad and eliminating administrative and consular jobs. The pattern suggests that at least some FSOs favor greater control because they see it as a means of paring down operations and returning to a more elitist concept in terms of the makeup of the corps.

Agents of Change

Additional insight into the attitudes of FSOs on change was gained by an SDP question which asked officers to register their opinion of the locus of pressure for change in the past, and to indicate their preference for the main source of change in the future. In both cases, respondents were asked to designate two sources of change.

Officers have a clear picture of who the main agents of change of the FSO corps have been in the past. Table 40 shows that more than half of the respondents cite "special

TABLE 40
Identification of Change Agents, Past and Future

	Change agents in past		Should be change agents in future	
	1st choice (no.=581)	2nd choice (no.=569)	1st choice (no.=574)	2nd choice (no.=554)
a. The Congress	6.0	10.9	2.9	10.5
b. Senior policy officials of the Department	5.2	7.2	51.4	22.2
c. Senior administrative officials of the Department	25.3	39.0	5.6	16.9
d. Senior Career FSOs	1.7	1.9	18.6	22.9
e. Special study groups such as the Herter Committee and the Wriston Committee	53.2	29.7	9.4	15.0
f. The White House	6.4	8.8	9.2	10.1
g. The Bureau of the Budget	0.2	1.1	0.4	0.2
h. Other (write-in)	1.2	0.7	1.1	0.9
i. None—don't believe change has been or should be great enough to specify an agent of change	0.9	0.7	1.4	1.3
Totals	100	100	100	100
No Answer	7	19	14	34

241

study groups" and a fourth cite "senior administrative officials" for the first choice. These two loom large for second choice, as well with almost 30 percent and almost 40 percent, respectively. Particularly since the idea of "change" is used in the question in a very general sense, with no specific changes identified, these results seem quite objective and on the mark. The White House, as originator of the Kennedy letter and NSAM 341, so favored in Table 38, might have been selected by more officers had major types of change been identified in the question.

Clearly officers would like to shift the locus of change in the future. There is a strong call for leadership from within the Department of State, with 51.4 percent choosing "senior policy officials" and 18.6 percent choosing "senior career FSOs." The White House and special study groups each receive nearly 10 percent of the vote. The preferences are quite scattered for second choice in future change agent roles.

In summary, the results suggest that officers know who was responsible for change in the past. They want two other groups to take the lead in future change, two groups seen as deficient in this regard in the past. The fact that these two groups are identified as desirable change agents in the future, and that few officers chose the option of saying that change should not be great enough to specify agents of change, does not necessarily add up to a ringing endorsement of change itself. Probably the more correct interpretation, for the majority of officers, would be: "*If* there is to be change in the future, we want policy officials and senior career officers to take the lead."

The State of the Profession

Three SDP questions were aimed at gaining some assessment of how FSOs view the state of the profession today,

Change and the Profession

one question dealing with the core skills of the profession, another with a comparative ranking of three professional groups, and the third seeking opinion on the basic definition of the diplomatic profession today.

Two of the questions were fairly complicated. In the first (Table 41), officers were asked to rank 11 functions in order of descending importance in terms of their opinion of the relative extent to which each function is or should be toward the core of the diplomatic profession. The 11 functions in Table 41 are shown in rank-order according

TABLE 41
Rank-ordering of Diplomatic Functions

Functions in rank order	Total weighted score	Number of 1st place votes	Number of 2nd place votes
1. Managing and coordinating a variety of programs designed to advance U.S. interests in the host country.	5,477	260	96
2. Conducting negotiations with representatives of foreign governments.	5,328	164	142
3. Reporting on significant events and trends in the host country.	5,057	61	155
4. Influencing citizens of the host country to understand and support U.S. policies.	4,321	41	69
5. Developing formal statements of U.S. policy to guide the activities of our missions in specific countries.	3,718	32	55
6. Protecting the rights and safety of American citizens in foreign countries.	3,642	10	21
7. Briefing Congressmen and other visitors on the situation in the host country.	2,316	0	3
8. Persuading citizens of the host country to undertake ways of improving their own society.	2,277	2	20
9. Explaining U.S. policies whenever possible to American citizens.	2,114	0	8
10. Representing the United States on major cermonial occasions.	1,765	0	3
11. Issuing visas to foreign nationals for immigration or travel to the U.S.	1,590	1	1

243

to the composite responses of all officers participating in the survey (that is, the table shows the functions in order according to the results, not in the order in which they appeared in the original question).

The "total weighted score" was achieved by awarding 11 points to a function when an officer ranked it first, 10 points when he ranked a function second, and so on down to one point when a function was ranked 11th, and then totaling all the points so awarded for each function. To give a further indication of the voting pattern, the number of first and second place votes that each function received is also shown.

Rank-ordering of this kind is always difficult; yet the results here seem to form a fairly clearcut pattern. The first three functions—management, negotiating, and reporting—are strongly endorsed as central to the diplomatic profession today, each with more than 5,000 points and each with substantial numbers of first and second place votes. The pattern of response to the first two, with the total scores being so close, suggests that the view is widespread in the FSO corps that the highly successful performer in U.S. foreign affairs today must be both manager and diplomat.

The next three functions—influencing host country citizens to support U.S. policies, formal policy guidance, and protection of American rights and safety—clearly form a second echelon of highly important functions. There is quite a drop to the next five functions, with a decline of more than 1,300 points on the weighted score from 6 to 7.

In all cases, the lower rankings should not necessarily be interpreted as meaning that officers think the functions are unimportant; the more likely explanation in at least some cases is that others should perform the functions or

Change and the Profession

that there is insufficient opportunity for FSOs to perform them.

The top-ranking of management as a core skill in the modern profession of diplomacy is interesting and highly significant. Fully 45 percent of respondents (260 officers) awarded it first place, compared to 28 percent and 11 percent of the first place votes, respectively, for negotiating and reporting. This 1-2-3 order for these functions holds for every subgroup in the survey, but the *degree* to which management is ranked highly varied in an interesting way. The choice of management as the top function correlates directly with seniority: the more senior an officer, the more likely he was to choose management. However, in contrast to a frequent occurrence in other SDP responses, this correlation is not due to the preponderance of lateral entrants at the senior grades. It is the senior examination entrants, not the lateral entrants, who vote most strongly for management as the top function in modern diplomacy. This striking pattern is shown in Table 42. There is thus no confusion in this case of management with administration. In fact, only 37 percent of the administrative officers rank management as first, compared to more than 60 percent for such esoteric groups as the Arabic and eastern European specialists.

TABLE 42

Percentages by Which FSO Subgroups Choose
Management as Top Diplomatic Function

Time of entry	Method of entry	
	lateral	examination
Pre-1954	43.6	54.4
1954 to 1958	38.1	46.1
Post-1958	33.3	35.2

The second major question dealing with the state of the profession today asked officers to compare three profes-

245

The Professional Group

sional groups—medical, diplomatic, and military (career officers) —in terms of 13 criteria of professionalism.[2] Respondents were asked to rate each of the three professions in terms of the extent to which it fulfills each criterion, on a 1 to 5 scale (1 meaning lacking in the particular criterion and 5 meaning very nearly or completely fulfilling the criterion).

The results of these ratings are shown in Table 43. The 13 criteria are listed in the lefthand column and opposite each is the total numerical score achieved for each of the three professional groups. The scores were arrived at simply by totalling the numerical value of the ratings from all questionnaires turned in. Using the first criterion of a "self-conscious sense of professionalism" as an example, if all respondents rated the medical profession as nearly devoid of this criterion (a 1 rating), the total score would have been 580; if all respondents had rated it as completely fulfilling the criterion (a 5 rating), the total score would have been 2,900. The actual result is a score of 2,812, meaning of course that the medical profession was rated extremely high on this criterion by all or nearly all respondents.

The grand total of all the scores at the bottom gives some idea of the over-all comparative ranking. As might be expected, medicine is seen as having the attributes and characteristics of professionalism to a marked degree, outdistancing the other two groups numerically by a large margin. The diplomatic and military professions are ranked very closely, with the military having a slightly larger point total.

[2] The list of 13 indices of professionalism was developed by the author, incorporating his own ideas, suggestions by Professor Mosher, and ideas gleaned from the literature in the sociology of the professions. In regard to the last named source, a particular debt of gratitude is owed to Myron Lieberman's excellent compilation of the characteristics of professional groups, many of which appear or are reflected in the 13 indices of Table 43. See Myron Lieberman, *Education as a Profession* (Englewood Cliffs: Prentice-Hall, 1956), pp. 2-8.

Change and the Profession

TABLE 43

Comparative Ranking of Three Professional Groups

Criteria	Medical	Diplomatic	Military
a. A self-conscious sense of professionalism—members feel strongly that they are professional men	2,812	2,268	2,588
b. Provides a unique, definitive, and essential social service	2,725	2,264	2,249
c. Has an articulated, professionally approved code of ethics	2,663	1,883	2,236
d. A high degree of self-government and internal control within constraints imposed by society	2,370	1,821	2,234
e. Has a professional association which concerns itself with research into the substance of the profession—the development of new knowledge	2,455	1,308	1,901
f. An emphasis on intellectual techniques in performing its service	2,146	2,356	1,575
g. Entry at a relatively young age based on rigorous selection, and long-term career commitment	2,552	2,247	2,255
h. A relatively set pattern of preparatory education, largely controlled by the professional group itself	2,796	1,281	1,993
i. A belief that members should constantly strive to stay abreast of new knowledge relevant to the profession, often involving formal training	2,488	2,108	2,282
j. A broad range of autonomy for both the individual practitioner and the professional group as a whole	2,477	1,488	1,286
k. An acceptance by the practitioner of broad personal responsibility for judgment made and acts performed within the scope of professional autonomy	2,573	2,023	1,815
l. An emphasis on the service to be rendered, rather than the economic gain to the practitioner	1,691	2,506	2,361
m. Success in resisting the breakdown of professional autonomy as organizational or bureaucratic constraints grow stronger	2,344	1,379	1,851
Totals	32,092	24,932	26,626

247

The underlined numbers are the high scores for each criterion. At a glance it can be seen that the over-all high score of the medical profession is the result of its being ranked the highest of the three groups on 11 of the 13 criteria. Respondents fault the doctors only on use of "intellectual techniques" and the question of "economic gain versus service." It is these same two criteria on which the diplomatic profession receives the highest ranking, quite consistent with Table 30.

A median score, meaning a professional group fulfills a criterion to an average extent, is 1,742; therefore, any score appreciably below this means the group is seen as considerably lacking in the criterion. With this as an index, FSOs see their profession as considerably lacking in regard to the character of their professional association (e), a relatively set pattern of preparatory education (h), autonomy (j), and success in resisting bureaucratic and organizational constraints (m). Not all of these should be seen as normative judgments. For example, relative lack of autonomy is simply a fact of life for professions wholly within the government as are diplomacy and the military.

While the military profession is not ranked highest on any criterion, it is ranked lowest on only four (b, f, j, k), so that it comes out with a higher total score than diplomacy, which is ranked lowest on eight of the 13 criteria.

Altogether, the results seem to be the product of realistic appraisal. The doctors certainly would not like their low ranking on the "economic gain versus service" index, but this is undoubtedly a general public relations problem the medical profession faces. One might feel that the FSOs are overdramatizing their problem of organizational and bureaucratic constraints (the last of the 13 items in Table 43), but there can be no doubt that the view is strongly and widely held within the corps.

The value of the rankings along indices of professionalism

is less to state definitively whether or not a given occupational group is a profession, which by itself would be a rather empty exercise, and more to see where the strong and weak points of the group are. It would be fascinating to administer the same question to a sample of doctors and military officers, and indeed to other professional groups. It would also be highly instructive to administer the question to the same group at different points in time to see if the tendencies are toward or away from professionalism.

The third major SDP question in this area posed three viewpoints on the present status of the profession of diplomacy. As Table 44 shows, one viewpoint holds that diplomacy is no longer a profession, another that it is a profession that has basically changed, and the third that it has not basically changed as a profession. The respondents rejected the first and divided on the other two, going about two to one in favor the "new diplomacy" over a more traditional view of the profession. The "new diplomacy" paragraph in the question is a paraphrase of language in the Herter Report, as cited in Chapter 1.

Support for the "new diplomacy" view of the profession correlates by seniority: 45 percent of officers at grade levels 5 and 6 chose this concept, compared to 61 percent at 3 and 4, 69 percent at 1 and 2, and 75 percent at the Career Ambassador and Career Minister levels. In terms of length of service, the correlation holds for examination entrants, but is reversed for lateral entrants: the more recently an officer entered the Service laterally, the more likely he is to support the "new diplomacy" concept. Among functional groups, political officers and consular officers show the least support for the "new diplomacy" concept at about 55 percent; the groups that are highly supportive are the program directors (80 percent), administrative officers (72 percent), and economic officers (65 percent).

There were more write-in comments on this question than

The Professional Group

TABLE 44
Evaluation of Present Character of the Diplomatic Profession

	Number	Percent
Diplomacy no longer a profession: It is no longer possible to consider diplomacy a profession in the same sense that law and medicine are professions because the situation has changed so much that one cannot say with any precision what the profession is or does. Instead of "diplomacy" one can only speak of "foreign affairs" which is something much broader and is no more a profession than is the general public service.	24	4.1
Diplomacy a profession, but basically changed: Diplomacy is a profession today, but it has changed basically; it has become the "new diplomacy." It is no longer useful to think of foreign affairs as a single professional field. Rather, it is a broad spectrum into which a number of professions, some of the orthodox domestic variety, and other peculiar to foreign affairs, must be fitted and modified. This places a premium on the capacity to coordinate activities. Each foreign affairs profession is part of the profession of the new diplomacy, and the highest form of it is the capability for leadership and direction of the varied fields.	350	60.2
Diplomacy not basically changed as a profession: Diplomacy is a profession today, and it has not changed basically. It is true that there are a great many functions and specialties in foreign affairs today, but diplomacy is not to be confused with these nor with management of the varied functions. Diplomacy involves the conduct of formal relationships among sovereign states and is characterized chiefly by the historic functions of representation, negotiation, and reporting. Some may regard diplomacy as one specialty among many in foreign affairs today, but if so it is first among many and it is the only one which may truly be classed as a profession.	181	31.2
Other: If none of the above fits nearly enough your point of view, take as much space as you need to write in your own definition and description of the profession of diplomacy as you see it today. Use the back cover if you need more space.	26	4.5
Totals	581	100
No answer	7	

on any other, indicating that the management challenge to the Foreign Service is a lively issue within the corps. A frequent theme in these comments was that the truth of the matter lies somewhere between the two views of the profession, or is a combination of the two—that the true professional today must be able to perform well in both managerial and traditional roles. An FSO-3 wrote: "Today's diplomatic leader must practice the art as described in choice 3 at the same time he acts as coordinator in choice 2, i.e., the manager must be a diplomat-manager and the diplomat must know how to manage."

An FSO-6 expressed the point as follows:

The classic functions of diplomacy remain as important as ever, indeed they have grown in importance because the "manager" of the "new" diplomacy should be *rigorously* trained as a political generalist. Number 2 above is unacceptable because the diplomat must be more than a manager—he should aspire to statesmanlike qualities. Number 3 is unacceptable because the old-style diplomat must learn modern methods of getting things done if he is in fact to function in the "old style."

An FSO-1 wrote:

Both 2 and 3 are partially correct. It may be a matter of semantics, but I do *not* think diplomacy is "coordination." Modern diplomacy disposes of many new tools and for them to be effective they obviously must be coordinated. But that is management, not diplomacy. It would also follow, though, that a good modern diplomat must also be a good manager.

There were several comments that seemed reasoned and positive in the sense of attempting a synthesis of the traditional arts of the diplomat and modern management needs. A good example is the comment of an FSO-3:

My view lies between 2 and 3. I do believe that diplomacy is or should be a profession involving the conduct of formal relations between sovereigns. I agree that the traditional functions of negotiation, representation, and reporting continue to be the core functions of diplomacy. However, these functions can no longer be adequately performed without effective coordination and direction of the non-traditional functions of a modern embassy. Diplomacy has moved from the chamber music to the symphonic scale and although the basic purpose remains the same, leadership and direction have become essential to its achievement.

A larger number of written comments illustrate what might be labeled a yes-but syndrome—agreeing that management is now important, but emphasizing some kind of qualification. Most of the qualifications fall into one of two categories: a fear that management is being overemphasized and hence is dangerous, and the view that the essentials of the profession have not changed and that thorough training in them will produce the best diplomat-manager.

The qualifications are stated in language ranging from moderate to extreme. A moderate view was expressed by a Career Minister:

> I agree that diplomacy has become the "new diplomacy" which embodies new fields of professionalism and puts a premium on the capability for leadership and direction of the varied fields. This concept can exaggerate the role of the coordinator, however, if it fails to include recognition of the qualities required for the practice of traditional diplomacy, which remains the mission's most important substantive responsibility.

Other officers express the fear that the emphasis on "leadership and direction" is a "dangerous oversimplification"; that "foreign affairs is not a factory," and that diplomacy "cannot be run like General Motors." An FSO-6 stated this view:

> Scientific management is important and necessary, and it is high time the Department got a healthy dose of it. It is a great mistake, however, to consider it the mystical panacea for every foreign affairs problem. It is hard to document, but there are many indications of a colossal naivete among the administrators with regard to the complexity of the traditional functions of reporting and negotiation. With justification, career diplomats are wary of the wild-eyed managers who appear all too willing to apply their mystical concepts to every and all situations.

On the theme that the essence of the profession has not changed despite new management needs, one FSO-6 wrote:

> The basic aim of diplomacy is to get a foreign country to act or not to act in accordance with our interests in a given situation. It takes more U.S. representatives to do this today, but the essentials remain the same in spite of foreign assistance, intelligence agents, public relations people and the like.

An FSO-2 made a similar point in holding that the style rather than the nature of the profession has changed:

> New techniques and skills have been introduced. But such facts as the inability of any single diplomat to master all the required knowledge, and the consequent dependence on specialists who may or may not appreciate the complexities involved in the objective, changes the style of diplomacy rather than the objective or the essential nature of diplomacy itself.

Among those who rejected the idea of a "new diplomacy," there was bitter criticism of management. An FSO-6 complained that "the Department of State hierarchy appears more interested in the gimmicks and paraphernalia of 'better management' than in advancing the cause of professionalism in what remains of a diplomatic service." An FSO-2 was even more bitter:

> Why spend years learning the ropes, gaining experience, know-how and the justified confidence that one has become expert in the *making and carrying out of U.S. foreign policy* only to find that what is now desired is a *Coordinator* of various domestic programs, technical in nature, operating overseas, and that talent from outside will be called in just as the hopeful FSO has reached the point where his "way of life" should be utilized for the benefit of the U.S. Why spend years in Paramaribo or Dhahran or learning three languages, on "the way up," if that concept is no longer valid, as it seems no longer to be.

An Elite or a Profession?

The elitist concept was a prominent source of concern in the written SDP comments. Some officers make the case that it is more correct to see the FSO corps as an elite group than as a professional group; these officers discussed the qualities of elitism, and several expressed a liberal view of where and how they can be obtained. Others see elitism and professionalism as inextricably bound together; a weakening of one results in a weakening of the other. There is also a view that the management role and elitism are not mutually exclusive.

An FSO-2 expressed "doubt that diplomacy ever warranted the status of a profession," and went on to discuss the "skills, talents and personality traits" needed. Another FSO-2 said that the status of diplomacy as a profession is less important than the "standards of excellence, dedication,

254

experience, and availability to serve under any and all conditions." He went on to point out that "the Foreign Service has no monopoly" on these qualities: "We need a Foreign Service corps primarily so we can staff a variety of jobs globally at any time, and it will be effective to the degree it is staffed with people of ability, has a pervading sense of dedication, and is run on merit defined as service to the U.S. interest."

An FSO-6 sees a need for "a quality of mind, attitude, personal behavior, a certain judgment, a way of approaching and handling problems that strike one as professional." He holds that these qualities "are not confined to FSOs and are not their specific preserve; rather, they can be found in the military and among other agencies in foreign affairs." A similar liberal view of elitism is stated by an FSO-2, but he cites the value of a career system in developing the needed qualities: "These qualities are not immutable (or inscrutable to outsiders) à la Harold Nicolson or other old fogies on the theme of traditional diplomacy. Nevertheless, they must be learned, experience from the bottom is the best teacher, and we take needless risks whenever we shortcut the regular admission process."

A Career Minister saw the failure to adhere to the "career principle" as the chink in the armor of professionalism and elitism: "A sense of professionalism is very difficult to develop when it is apparent to FSOs that persons with no previous experience in the Foreign Service can perform the top jobs with satisfaction to the Administration." He went on to discuss a problem that FSOs have in defending the elitist concept: the "extreme difficulty of identifying and defining professionalism in the Foreign Service," which consists of many "subtle and unmeasurable" qualities.

The weakening of professionalism by the dilution of the elite quality of the corps was expressed by an FSO-4 as follows: "No 'old-line' FSO I know could agree that the FSO corps as now constituted could be dignified with the term 'profession,' given the variety of technical, administrative, and consular officers now in the FSO corps." An FSO-5 criticized "an anachronistic trend toward dilettanteism" in the profession:

> The military would hardly think of appointing a member of the State Department as a Lieutenant Colonel and sending him to Viet Nam. Colleges hardly base their academic faculty recruitment on the basis of "equal opportunity" rather than academic excellence. I doubt whether technicians in the Public Health Service are sent out as doctors. Yet we do all these things—bring in poorly qualified outsiders, convert Civil Service personnel whose value lies in Washington-based competence. All become "instant diplomats"—and the results go far beyond a question of morale.

An FSO-6 passionately defended elitism:

> A man skilled in foreign languages, representation, negotiation and the like is still worth ten to a hundred times as much as AID technicians who are unable to communicate with foreigners, peace corps types who want to change a world which has resisted change for centuries, and press agents who attempt to peddle our civilization like soap.

A rare example of snobbism was provided by another young officer:

> In a reaction against alleged previous domination by "Ivy League" types, the Foreign Service has, in my opinion, swung too far in favor of seeking to be representative at the sacrifice of its elite quality. Quite frankly, I feel that the recruiting system is presently weighted in favor

of the *Midwesterner* and the graduates of the land-grant colleges. The fact that the newly-appointed officers are still predominantly from the West Coast and Ivy League colleges only confirms the fact that this educational background constitutes the best preparation for the Foreign Service. There are, however, a number of Midwesterners taken into the Service for reasons (partially) of geographic representation. These individuals are often inferior in intellect, ability, and the sophistication required of a diplomat.

Another officer, an FSO-2, takes the pessimistic view of professionalism lost through the damaging of the elitist character of the corps: "I am convinced that the changes made in the Service went far beyond what was necessary or desirable, and in the process destroyed the career as an 'elite' service based on merit."

Some comments seemed to strike in the direction of finding an accommodation between elitism, the traditional skills of diplomacy, and the management role. In effect, this amounts to a view that a relatively elite group should be maintained which, while already practicing the traditional role, would also take on the management role. An FSO-3 who believes that "leadership and direction" is the most important function of the professional diplomat warns against "reorganization plans" designed to transform the Foreign Service "from a profession (i.e., an elite corps of professional diplomats) to something broader which will be no more a profession (or an elite corps) than is the general public service."

An FSO-5 who also agrees with the emphasis on management in the "new diplomacy" concept, states:

I want to make it clear that I do *not* (most emphatically) believe that the FSO corps should be expanded to em-

257

brace all the new functions. I believe the corps and profession are distinct under this definition. The corps should provide the coordinators of all the activities, and the specialists in representation, reporting, and negotiation in the "core" activities.

A junior officer states his belief in the following way:

Leadership and direction of the varied fields involved in foreign affairs is the highest form of the diplomatic profession, but a clear line of demarcation must be drawn between this broadened generalist competence of the diplomatic corps and the highly specialized competence which must prevail in the various other fields.

Another junior officer expresses ideas in a similar direction:

I recognize the need for a foreign affairs career (or careers) that includes many competent medium-level specialists—but somehow a system should be devised (either *within* or *outside and above*) the broad career which would permit persons of special ability and motivation to rise at a rate commensurate with capacity while acquiring high competence in the "core" rather than the specialized skills.

An indication that there may be substantial support for the idea of a managerial elite as the answer to the role problem of the FSO corps is found in the responses to another SDP question. Officers were asked to respond to the following statement: "The real role of the FSO corps is to develop a managerial class to supervise all programs and functions in U.S. foreign affairs." The pattern of responses was as follows: agree, 36.6 percent; disagree, 52.9 percent; not sure, 10.5 percent. This is a strong and specific statement, and the fact that more than a third of respondents support it is surprising. That more do not support it should

Change and the Profession

not be viewed as inconsistent with the high premium placed on management in Tables 41 and 44, given the fairly radical character of the statement.

That even such a concept as this would still be meant to incorporate the traditional diplomatic role is indicated by reactions to another SDP statement: "The historic functions of diplomacy—representation, reporting, negotiating—are as important today if not more important than ever before." The responses showed very strong support: agree, 84.9 percent; disagree, 10.8 percent; not sure, 4.3 percent.

Some idea of the strength of elitist sentiment can be gleaned from another SDP question which asked officers to register their preference for one of four alternative models for the future state of the FSO corps. Opinion was well divided among the four possible models, as shown in Table 45, with the fourth alternative—one calling for a smaller corps but also having more officers at a high professional level in all major functions—drawing the most interest to

TABLE 45

Preferences for Future State of FSO Corps

Preference	No.	Percent
1. It should expand to encompass more persons at a professional level who serve abroad in making a career of service in one or more major programs in U.S. foreign affairs.	111	19.0
2. It should stay roughly as it is now in terms of size and functions.	124	21.3
3. It should contract in size to become a smaller and more elite corps of professionals practicing the core skills of diplomacy.	108	18.5
4. It should contract in size but also include more officers at a high professional level in all of the major functions of foreign affairs.	200	34.3
5. Not sure.	40	6.9
Totals	583	100
No answer	5	

259

the level of more than one-third of the total responses. A more purely elitist model in a traditional sense (No. 3) does considerably less well, drawing less than 20 percent of the vote.

There is a marked difference of opinion among examination and lateral entry officers. More of the latter favor the first two models (56 to 32 percent), while a greater proportion of examination officers than lateral entrants (60 to 39 percent) favor the last two models, both of which call for a smaller FSO corps. Particularly strong in this direction are the younger examination entrants (those who entered since 1958) whose support for the last two models approaches 70 percent.

Lateral Entry

Closely related to concern for the elite character of the FSO corps is the controversial question of lateral entry. Any significant change in the size and character of the FSO corps must almost surely involve the lateral entry question. If the corps is to be made smaller and more "elite," one suspects it would be largely lateral entrants who would be dropped, perhaps in some intensification of the trend in this direction over the past few years, which was discussed in Chapter 4. If the corps is to be enlarged to encompass newer functions, this can be done only through lateral entry in the manner of the USIA integration plan.

We have already seen the strongly negative Service opinion on USIA integration. Other SDP references to lateral entry (such as asking officers to evaluate how well lateral entry recruitment is performed along with a number of other administrative functions) brought forth a liberal sprinkling of short written notes on the margins of questionnaires turned in: "too well done," "should be *no* lateral entry," "too much lateral entry," and so on.

Change and the Profession

An SDP question asked officers to react to the following statement: "The professional competence of the FSO corps has been weakened by too much lateral entry." The responses: agree, 48.8 percent; disagree, 38.2; not sure, 13.0. Not surprisingly, there is a radical division of opinion on the question between lateral entrants and examination entrants, with 64 percent of the latter agreeing with the statement compared to 21 percent of the former. A tendency noted elsewhere in SDP responses for lateral entrants to increasingly reflect the attitudes of examination entrants the longer they are in the Service is present again. The greater the longevity of the lateral entrant, the less likely he is to disagree with the statement.

The dislike of lateral entry is based on at least two considerations which, taken together, approximate what is referred to in the Service as the "career principle." One of these is the fear that too much lateral entry will inflate the upper ranks of the Service and do injustice to junior examination entrants by depressing their promotion rate and siphoning away key assignments. An FSO-3 expressed this viewpoint: "It is my opinion that opportunities for promotion up the ladder from the junior levels have become progressively worse due largely to the great influx of lateral entrants," causing the loss of much of the "self-discipline and dedication" of the corps.

The second consideration is that too much lateral entry will dilute the quality of the corps. An FSO-5 puts it this way: "As long as massive injections of personnel are made at above the junior officer level, the foreign service will not be a profession and the quality of its performance will suffer."

For some, the dislike of lateral entry is related to the dislike of administrators. Not only are most lateral entrants administrative specialists, but the administrators are seen

261

The Professional Group

as responsible for lateral entry. An FSO-2 points to "the source of many of our troubles" as the domination of the Service by men "whose whole background consisted of administrative experience of the housekeeping type." The result:

> Having no conception of what diplomacy calls for (having themselves no substantive experience and often no experience abroad at all), they have turned the Foreign Service career into one where there are still many individually brilliant officers, but one whose general level is mediocre because it includes so many mediocrities eased into the Service on spurious grounds (along with some good lateral entrants) and at the same time buries the others in a general atmosphere of stifling frustration.

The fact that viewpoints on lateral entry very often are exaggerated, to the level that the problem begins to take on some of the aspects of a myth, only illustrates how strongly held the norms are.

As the analysis in Chapter 4 indicated, the lateral entry population is dwindling as retirement, selection-out, and conversion take their toll, while lateral intake since 1961 has been at a low level of approximately 20 to 30 persons per year. Although a significant number of lateral entrants have been highly successful in the corps, the majority paved the way for more rapid advancement of examination entrants by occupying most of the low-status jobs. As we have seen, the average age per grade of lateral entrants is much higher than that of examination entrants.

In view of the prevailing attitudes, the socialization process for the lateral entrant, though different in important respects from the socialization of examination entrants as discussed in the last chapter, is every bit as pronounced and probably more severe. The lateral entrant faces a number

of handicaps. He is a "loner," not entering as a member of
a group as junior officers do. Often he has not undergone
much pre-conditioning for a change that may come to him
relatively late in life. The heavy odds are that he will be
coming in to work in one of the lower-status functional
fields, since lateral entry normally is resorted to for the purpose of adding specialized skills not in adequate supply
within the corps; these are the fields the examination entrants have shied away from.

The lateral entrant is made to feel somewhat humble by
being accepted for entry into the corps. There is no positive
recruitment program, merely a capability for examining applicants and a readiness to accept a certain number each
year in line with shortages in the specialized fields. There is
no careful watching of eligible persons to spot and tap the
talented ones in the manner, let us say, of a major business
or industrial firm going out of its way to find talent. There
is no publicity about lateral entry opportunities. The Reserve or Civil Service officer interested in the FSO corps
(one must be employed by the government for three years
to be eligible for lateral entry) must take it upon himself
to find out how, when, and where to apply. The process is
rather impersonal; he is likely to receive a cold response or
be delayed for months. He has little knowledge of what is
in store for him and no idea of what his chances are.

After acceptance the lateral entrant, like an immigrant,
may feel that he is in an unreceptive atmosphere. And,
again like an immigrant, he may feel that in order to suc-
ceed he must become purer than the pure and abler than
the able, which is why lateral entrants do not form a cohesive group within the Service, or represent a force for
change, although their opinions for the most part, as we
have seen in various SDP responses, tend to be somewhat
more liberal on matters affecting the character and makeup

The Professional Group

of the Service than those of examination entrants. As long as lateral entrants remain in the low-status fields they are without power; when they move to the high-status fields, they become in important respects virtually indistinguishable from examination entrants of the same vintage.

It is against this background that the fears of lateral entry seem exaggerated. In point of fact, the influx of lateral entrants over the years has changed the mores of the FSO corps very little.

Room at the Top

Among considerations of change, concern has developed recently over the shape of the corps. The idea has grown that the upper middle levels of the Service have become swollen, thereby inhibiting the more rapid advancement of able younger officers.

Junior officers in particular, as we shall see shortly, do not like what they see above them; they are apt to place the blame on lateral entry, especially the Wriston program. The Director General of the Foreign Service, in a recent article in the State Department *News Letter*, pointed out that the shape of the Service no longer resembles a neat pyramid, but is one in which "the middle bulges." "It is plain that we need to begin to think more creatively about ways and means of reshaping the 'pyramid' of Foreign Service Officers towards congruency with the 'pyramid' of the Service's needs."[3]

Some see a related problem in the "corridor corps," the appellation given to the officers, many of them senior in grade, who are visualized as roaming the corridors of the State Department in search of a meaningful assignment. In an SDP comment, a Career Minister touched on both prob-

[3] John Steeves, "Letter from the Director General," Department of State *News Letter* (Nov. 1966), pp. 1, 62.

264

lems in terming as "a thorny question" the "fact that there are not enough top jobs for the talented, experienced senior officers." "The present tendency to bring people along rapidly without working out a system to solve the problem of what to do about the overburdened top structure of the pyramid is serious."

Actually, as Janowitz points out, a diamond shape is "a typical manifestation of organizations which have grown more complex," in place of the classic organizational pyramid, due to the explosion in knowledge and increased specialization.[4] There is a journeyman level in the specialized fields in the military where it is honorable to retire as a Colonel. It is not particularly honorable to retire as an FSO-3, a grade which is comparable in rank and pay to that of Colonel. The Herter Committee addressed itself to the problem of the lack of a journeyman level in the FSO system. If one accepts a need for such a level, the idea that entering FSOs should all aspire to Ambassador becomes dysfunctional.

Although the actual extent of need for personnel at the upper middle levels is not clear, the corridor corps is probably more the product of the phenomenon of "topping out" than of actual overstaffing at these levels. The physical rigors of FSO life and the internal psychological rigors of the system are such that it is not uncommon for officers to experience an appreciable loss of vitality and momentum at, say, age 50, a tendency doubtless encouraged for some by the realization that no matter what they do they will not make Ambassador. It is a malaise that attacks lateral and examination entrants alike, one that will continue to exist in some measure at least if there is *understaffing* at the upper middle levels. George Kennan described the phe-

[4] Morris Janowitz, *The Professional Soldier* (Glencoe: The Free Press, 1960), p. 66.

nomenon graphically: "It seems to me that I have seen, over the decades, an unduly high percentage of older men in this Service who prematurely lost physical and intellectual tone, who became, at best, empty bundles of good manners and, at worst, rousing stuffed shirts."[5]

The concern over swollen ranks at the upper middle levels is based in part in the strong sentiment for a smaller, more elite, streamlined corps. There is a widespread feeling that the Service has become too impersonal, too mechanistic. This is manifested, for example, in the dislike of management technology in general and computers in particular. Although unease about computerization is fairly widespread it is pronounced in the Foreign Service. In two recent magazine articles, William Attwood and Stewart Alsop touched on this nerve. Attwood called for a "de-computerization of personnel," and Alsop opined: "An FSO can hardly be blamed for being cautious if his professional competence is constantly being measured by computers."[6] These are strange notions; one wonders where the authors ever came across them. To anyone who knows anything about the real state of computer technology in the Department of State, the thoughts expressed by Attwood and Alsop are ludicrous. Far from being over-computerized, the Department lacks, for example, a personnel data base adequate to tell with some degree of certainty whether and to what extent it is overstaffed at the upper middle levels of the FSO corps. It is for reasons such as this that attempts were made to develop a manpower utilization system.

[5] Kennan, "Diplomacy as a Profession," *Foreign Service Journal*, May 1961, p. 25.
[6] Attwood, "The Labyrinth in Foggy Bottom," *Atlantic Monthly*, Feb. 1967, p. 50; Alsop, "Let the Poor Old Foreign Service Alone," *Saturday Evening Post*, Mar. 11, 1967, p. 14.

Change and the Profession

Ferment Within the Ranks

Over the past several years there has been unprecedented ferment within the FSO corps. Previous agitation has usually been defensive in character, as at the time of the Wriston program, but much of the current ferment is apparently concerned with positive change. It is most evident at the junior level, includes a remarkable group effort at the mid-career level, with signs of response and scattered individual efforts at the senior level. The ferment is all the more remarkable when one considers the pressures for conformity discussed earlier, and recognizes that in a corps which is scattered all over the world, natural organizational inertia is compounded, and it is difficult to organize for change. What happens must usually happen in Washington, where larger numbers of officers are to be found in one place and there is proximity to the seat of power.

Unrest in the junior ranks began to coalesce in 1965 in the Junior Foreign Service Officer Club (JFSOC), an organization created in the late 1950s for social purposes. All officers, of course, may belong to the American Foreign Service Association (AFSA), but because of their low rank, junior officers have little influence in the Association. Over a period of time this had the effect of converting the JFSOC from a social club into a focal point for junior officer grievances and impulses for change. Until late 1966 there were perhaps not more than 10 to 12 activists, but the informal communication network among junior officers serving in Washington is good, since the officers have much in common and each officer has friendships stemming from entrance class associations.

The ferment among junior officers began with classic economic grievances, and gradually escalated into a concern about job and career satisfaction, reaching more recently a

267

plane of intellectual and philosophical consideration of the character and direction of the Foreign Service as a whole. The economic grievances were centered on the unhappy plight of the junior officer while he is serving in Washington. All FSOs find it a difficult adjustment to come to Washington for a two- to four-year assignment after living abroad. The reason is that while serving abroad they receive a variety of allowances in addition to their base pay, the principal one being a housing allowance which in effect covers their rent and utilities (whether in the form of actual rent payments or of living in government-provided housing). Because of their semi-nomadic existence, not many FSOs own a home in Washington, so that when they are assigned to the Department they find themselves casting about in a high-rent market without benefit of allowance.

After the Federal pay raise of 1965, the base pay of an FSO-8 was $6,269; an FSO-7 received $7,262. At this level, a return to Washington meant a cut of 25 percent or more in net income. This situation was exacerbated for the junior officers in 1965 when they began to observe that other young men of similar age and educational background, both in industry and in the Federal Government, were moving ahead much faster and earning considerably more. The comparison focused on the management interns in the Civil Service system who, as we saw in the Walther study cited in Chapter 6, are in many respects comparable to the young FSOs. In the General Schedule (GS) of the Civil Service, a management intern (MI) will start at GS-7 (same base pay in 1965 as FSO-8) or at GS-9 (base pay in 1965 of $7,479). However, the MI moves ahead much faster than the FSO. Fielder and Harris described the situation as follows:

> Advancement in the MI program is almost meteoric, compared to that for FSOs serving in the Department of State.

268

Change and the Profession

In effect, the FSO can expect to reach the rank of Class 2 after 21.7 years; his counterpart in the domestic agency program will reach a nearly equivalent GS-15 after only 8.7 years. Preliminary studies from one agency indicate that the Management Intern will be an average age of 37 when he reaches GS-15; the average FSO-2 in 1962 was 46 years old.[7]

Deputy Under Secretary for Administration Crockett asked his Management Planning Staff to study the problem. Its report stated that over the first 10 years of service, depending on his rate of advancement, the junior officer will have earned from $25,000 to $40,000 less than the Management Intern. The gap is almost entirely offset by the value of the allowances FSOs receive while serving abroad, and after 10 years or so the FSO's base pay begins to exceed that of his counterpart in the Civil Service. The immediate problem, therefore, was the plight of junior officers actually serving in Washington. As a temporary expedient, the report recommended the payment of a differential; as a long-term solution, it recommended speeding up the promotion rate at the junior grades. Crockett approved both recommendations, but the differential was never implemented because of lack of funds.

The reaction among many of the senior men of the Service was stiff; it was perhaps characterized by one senior officer who said that the problems of the junior officers serving in Washington were "a test of their commitment to the Foreign Service." This was an understandable attitude, but it underestimated the mobility of modern society. During this period, several junior officers resigned and took jobs

[7] Frances Fielder and Godfrey Harris, *The Quest for Foreign Affairs Officers—Their Recruitment and Selection*, Foreign Affairs Personnel Study No. 6 (New York: Carnegie Endowment for International Peace, 1966), 31.

in other government agencies and private firms in Washington at nearly double their salaries; so instead of evaporating, the junior officer protest grew stronger. Faster promotions have in fact become a reality. For example, in recent years approximately one-third of the officers at FSO-6 could expect to be promoted each year; in 1967, the ratio jumped to 50 percent.

Other problems were raised by the Board of Directors of JFSOC in two similar communications, a memorandum in February 1966 to the Director General of the Foreign Service and another memorandum in May 1966 to Crockett.[8] The board said the views were offered "not with the intent to lobby, but rather as an expression of concern about the institution to which we hope to devote our careers." The basic sentiment was "that a feeling of professional uneasiness and uncertainty is prevalent among junior FSOs which, justified or not, tends to lower morale and create a climate for resignation."

The communications raised questions about the resignation rate of junior officers and the number of lateral entrants and FSRs occupying jobs that normally went to FSOs. Questions were raised about the Hays Bill, not overtly negative in tone, but asking for information on what positions would be surrendered and acquired for State Department officers in an "integrated" service.

The JFSOC Board made it clear that the major worry was over the character of work officers would be performing in a Foreign Service career: "The greatest concern of junior FSOs is that many of their jobs do not provide a chance to develop the skills of leadership and executive ability required to reach senior-level positions." The conclusion was:

---

[8] The memorandum to Crockett, and his response, appear under the title "Junior Foreign Service Officers and the Personnel System," in the *Foreign Service Journal*, Aug. 1966.

Change and the Profession

"The world today offers a variety of interesting and challenging positions in international affairs, both within and outside the government. Job mobility has become an accepted practice. Since the Foreign Service is not financially competitive, even with other government agencies, it must make more challenging and responsible jobs available to junior FSOs."

The JFSOC Board expressed the belief that it was speaking for the majority of junior officers, and on the underutilization issue, at least, an SDP response indicates that they undoubtedly were. Officers were asked to reply to the statement, "The problem of young officers having more talent and intelligence than their jobs generally call for is getting worse, and something should be done about it." The responses: agree, 53.6 percent; disagree, 32.2; not sure, 14.2. Almost 70 percent of the officers at grade levels 5 and 6 agreed with the statement, compared to 44 percent of those at levels 1 and 2.

Crockett was able to provide reasonably satisfactory answers to most of the questions in the *Foreign Service Journal* dialogue. He spoke of the pressure to speed up promotions, claimed that the rate of "voluntary" resignations of junior officers was holding fast at a two percent level (see Chapter 4), pointed out that lateral entry was occurring at a very low rate, and made the case that "a great majority" of FSR appointments were to jobs not normally occupied by FSOs. On the Hays Bill, Crockett said it would not result in "integration" of either personnel or agencies; USIA officers converted to FSO status would remain USIA officers. He took issue with the juniors on the matter of the prestige of the FSO corps.

On the issue of more responsible jobs, however, Crockett was able to say little more than, "Concern about responsibilities has always troubled able, ambitious young people in all professions and businesses. There is no clearcut answer to the problem. We can only discuss it and give you our honest assurances of our agreement with your goals."

There followed several meetings between Crockett and delegates from JFSOC. Later in the year the circumstances surrounding the resignation of a very promising young officer caused Crockett to ask his Organizational Development Staff (ACORD) to hold a workshop to probe the problem. A group of 14 persons was assembled, half of them junior officers. Most of the others were senior officers, including one Career Minister, who were in charge of administrative and training activities relevant to the junior grades of the Service. The workshop was supposed to last only one day, but the level of participation was so high that the group convened on two additional occasions. The workshop identified 15 problems which the majority regarded as important, although not every member agreed that every problem was genuine. The list of problems is so revelatory of the ferment going on in the junior ranks that it is worth reproducing in full:

I. *Career Development*

 A. Growing dissatisfaction with the projected aspects of jobs in the Foreign Service at the mid-career and senior levels, in terms of responsibility and influence.

 B. Apparent lack of challenging jobs, especially in Washington.

 C. Assignment to jobs based more on seniority and less on competence.

 D. The number of able officers exceeds the number of challenging jobs to which they can aspire—underemployment.

E. Rapid promotion for better-than-average officers is limited.

F. There is frustration with career rewards, and temptation from outside the system plays on this frustration.

II. *Weakness of Foreign Service in Career Market*

A. The Foreign Service is decreasingly competitive in pay, responsibility and activity in foreign affairs.

B. The Foreign Service has failed to take advantage of modern organizational concepts and practices, specifically in the areas of developing managerial talent through training and assignment practices.

III. *Communication and Credibility Gaps in the Service*

A. There is a lack of realistic thinking and planning about what the Foreign Service should be like in 10-20 years, and the career and management implications.

B. The dichotomies between the older and younger generations, and between the new foreign affairs and old traditional functions has slowed progressive action in the Foreign Service.

C. Expected to be managers of the future, junior officers have little voice in determining future policy and programs in the Foreign Service.

IV. *System Restraints on Dissent, Creativity, and Individual Growth*

A. Fear of criticism and retaliation inhibits officers from voicing dissent or expressing non-conformist ideas.

B. The Foreign Service system reserves decisions for the highest levels and suppresses ideas from lower levels.

273

V. *The Appraisal System Neither Utilized Nor Trusted*

    A. There is a lack of counseling on the job, especially for junior officers.

    B. The "hidden" efficiency report discourages frankness, encourages mistrust, and negates the guidance value of entire system.

A few quotations from the tape-recorded first session of the workshop provide a further idea of the tenor of the discussions:

> "Resignations are not significant by their numbers, but *who* is resigning and *why* is the crucial issue."

> "Job mobility is there for the young officer. Career development and job aspects are the number one concern of junior officers."

> "Playing it safe is the surest way of advancement."

> "Officers are not challenged to their abilities and therefore personal growth, willingness to take the initiative and willingness to be different are not brought out."

> "Speaking out in any but a positive way is just not done in the Foreign Service."

> "Risk-taking needs guts. Junior officers are looking ahead while senior officers are reminiscing and looking back."

> "We are not developing managers."

More meetings with Crockett and his successor followed, and several junior officers participated in one meeting with Under Secretary Katzenbach. In January 1967 the JFSOC Board, to test whether or not it was representing junior officer viewpoints properly, called an open meeting. Approximately 50 junior officers attended and heard reports on the workshop and the meetings with Crockett.

The audience was highly responsive, eliminating concern that the viewpoints espoused by the activists were not representative of widespread opinion. More members were signed up for JFSOC, and committees on membership, data-gathering, junior officer problems, and foreign affairs management were established.

From the socialization model presented in the last chapter, one might extract the hypothesis that conformity and caution are more pronounced at the mid-career ranks of a career system than at the junior or senior ranks. The pattern of some SDP responses provides support for this hypothesis: on a number of questions that might reasonably be regarded as testing liberal versus conservative viewpoints on the FSO career system, the mid-career officers show up as more conservative than the juniors and seniors. The low incidence of the kind of ferment described in the junior ranks is another indicator. This does not necessarily mean that restiveness does not exist at the mid-career ranks, but only that it is likely to be more efficiently repressed.

However, one remarkable effort did occur in 1966 which went even further than the junior officer unrest, in the sense of diagnosing the basic problems of the Service with clarity and presenting a model for the future. Six mid-career officers engaged in an extended discussion of the problems of the Service and formulated their analysis and proposal in a memorandum to the Director General. Aside from rank, the six men had in common their location in Washington and experience in personnel operations, although none of them was an administrative officer. Their communication was printed in the November 1966 issue of the *Foreign Service Journal* under the title, "1966: Are We Obsolete?"

In the letter to the Director General, the six officers reported their starting point as consideration of what should happen if the Hays Bill failed. They said that this subject took them "considerably further afield," to the view that "the structure of the Foreign Service was, or should be, a reflection of its role in the foreign affairs community." They concluded that "the Foreign Service was bound legally and psychologically by the Acts of 1924 and 1946 to the conduct of foreign affairs at an essentially technical level."

By "technical level," the six authors meant the traditional functions of the FSO corps, a reference not calculated to endear them to many of the elders of the Service. The heart of the letter follows.

> Since 1946, however, the manner in which foreign affairs is conducted has changed with the development of new tools such as military, economic and technical assistance and persuasion techniques. These tools are in the hands of other agencies of the United States Government.
>
> We further concluded that this diminution of responsibility and authority was the principal cause for the disquiet with which Foreign Service officers contemplate their present role in foreign affairs.
>
> It was, then, a short step to the conclusion that in 1966 the proper role of the Foreign Service officer corps is the *direction* of foreign affairs without regard to agency boundaries, rather than the *conduct* of foreign affairs at the technical level. This conclusion seemed to us inescapable with the publication of FAMC 385 and with the advent of such powerful tools as PPBS and FAPS.[9]

The authors went on to say:

> We emphasize the revolutionary nature of this shift in focus because we do not wish to be accused of nostalgia for a past most of us never knew and which is, in any event, no longer pertinent. Rather, we have attempted to

[9] FAMC 385 is the unclassified State Department announcement of NSAM 341 of March 1966, discussed in Chapter 3.

look forward to a solution of the problems the Foreign Service will face in the future.

The letter concludes by expressing concern "lest the Department of State and the Foreign Service forfeit the opportunities for service implicit" in NSAM 341, and voicing the belief that "job satisfaction becomes a critical element" in attracting and retaining the best people in foreign affairs: "We believe that too many talented officers are being asked by the Foreign Service to perform tasks which do not afford these satisfactions. The fault lies with the present role of the Foreign Service. To fulfill the new role suggested above may require a new structure." The proposal made by the six officers argues some of the points in the letter at length and makes the following conclusion:

If the proper role of the Foreign Service officer corps is to provide creative direction in the multiagency field of foreign affairs, then the duties of Foreign Service officers should prepare them to play this one role—*instead of* the many roles the Foreign Service officer is now asked to fill. The Foreign Service officer must be recruited, assigned, trained and developed with the sole end of fitting him to serve in positions of executive responsibility requiring great creativity and rigorous analytical capabilities.

On this conclusion, the authors based their proposal for the addition of a "third track" to the Foreign Service system, one composed of officers capable of fulfilling the executive role in foreign affairs. Only officers in this track would be FSOs; all others would be in the FSS category. The other two tracks, presumably all their members being in the FSS category, would be composed of administrative support personnel, on the one hand, and officers engaged in the traditional and "technical" diplomatic functions on the other hand. No one would be allowed into the third track of executives who had not "demonstrated unusual competence in the technical functions of classic and modern diplomacy." The authors went on to recommend training for the third track in "the areas of economics, mathematics, and the management of large, complex organizations."

Thus after a pungent and telling diagnosis of the Foreign Service's present-day role problem, the six authors presented an essentially elitist solution, with their elite to be composed of executives or executive-diplomats, rather than those performing the traditional diplomatic functions.

Inevitably the junior and the mid-career movements began to link up. A JFSOC group has established a working relationship with "the six," as the authors of the letter and proposal to the Director General have come to be called. In a later article in the *Journal*, one of the activists among the junior officers, D. Bruce Jackson, commented:

> The proposed "third track" of foreign affairs executives would free the Service from its continuous oscillation between specialization and "broadening" and would provide an avenue for rational development of real foreign affairs leadership. On this part of the mid-career proposal, and on the initial statement of the crisis confronting the Foreign Service, I think there is enthusiastic agreement from junior officers.[10]

Jackson, however, rejects the three-track idea, as such, both on pragmatic grounds and because he thinks it overstates the case for executives: "The simple device of designating officers as either FSO-specialist or FSO-generalist would establish all the necessary distinctions without disrupting existing status symbols." What Jackson has in mind

[10] Jackson, "On Getting Into the Kitchen," *Foreign Service Journal*, Mar. 1967, p. 27.

is a synthesis of the executive and diplomatic tracks in the FSO-generalist concept:

> The Foreign Service actually has a unique chance to achieve the needed synthesis. It has a unique breadth of mandate—to run American foreign affairs, not merely to staff an agency; it has a unique tradition of eliteness—a chance to retain people who in any other agency would already have left to choose their own unorthodox outside paths upward; and it has a unique tradition of smallness —a chance to avoid the sluggish mediocrity which tends to be the result of the endlessly subdivided decision-making of the big bureaucracies.

There is no organized movement as yet among the senior officers, but there also seems to be no automatic and organized defense attempting to smother the ferment at the lower ranks. There are, in fact, signs of a response to the ferment, and numerous scattered examples of individual efforts of a progressive nature.

For example, an officer serving as a DCM was assigned to the Foreign Service Institute where he created the first executive development courses ever offered there. A highly respected senior officer, serving as Deputy Assistant Secretary in the Bureau of Cultural Affairs, almost single-handedly developed a programming system to cover the Department of State's cultural programs. Even the feared computer is being confronted by FSOs. Another highly respected senior officer took it upon himself to study computers, and produced an excellent account of what they are and how they might be used in foreign affairs.[11] In an editorial, the *Foreign Service Journal* stated: "If the State Department is

11 Fisher Howe, *The Computer and Foreign Affairs: Some First Thoughts,* Occasional Paper No. 1 of the Center for International Systems Research (Washington: Department of State, 1966).

going to exercise total leadership in the community of foreign affairs agencies, then—among other things—we must
lead in the computer revolution."[12]

There has been a definite effort to make the *Journal* more
of a forum for creativity and dissent, including publication
of the articles cited on the stirrings at the mid-career and
junior levels, and publication of an abridgement of the
Argyris study (discussed in Chapter 6) before its full appearance.[13]

A number of senior officers coming out of seminars such
as those led by Argyris are attempting to work directly on
problems of conformity, leadership, and group effectiveness, with the help of behavioral scientists serving as consultants. Many senior officers are facing with wisdom and
courage the very difficult and new role of the Country Director, which will be examined in the next chapter.

There have been efforts to improve the quality of the
American Foreign Service Association. A lateral entrant,
Lucius D. Battle, was elected president of the Association
in 1962. Then serving as Assistant Secretary of State for
Educational and Cultural Affairs, Battle became Ambassador to the United Arab Republic, to be followed by Assistant
Secretary for Near East and South Asian Affairs. His farewell address to the Association in September 1963 was an
impressively frank and open criticism of the past and a call
for leadership in the future:

> The Foreign Service, through the association, should
> anticipate where it is going and what its goals are and
> should always try to be one step ahead of the Department
> in anticipating where it ought to be going. That way, it
> can influence; it can guide. It must remove itself from

[12] *Foreign Service Journal*, Mar. 1967, p. 31.
[13] Chris Argyris, "Do You Recognize Yourself?" *Foreign Service Journal*, Jan. 1967, pp. 21-26.

the posture it has had in years behind us of opposing and following. It must lead.[14]

Carrying the point further, Battle quoted a memorandum he had written to the Association's Board:

> I have often wondered why we, as a Service, have feared to act progressively for so many years lest people would control us. In so doing, we have lost the opportunity to control other people, and the power and influence of the Service have been weakened thereby. I believe that we can handle our problems, and that our capacity as a Service to lead is greater than we have even been willing to test.

Further, Battle made a telling analysis of the Service's role problem and its failure to legitimize the new functions in foreign affairs:

> Serious challenges to our superiority have come not when we wished to expand our influence but rather when we viewed it too narrowly. The challenges have come not because our horizons were too vast but because we made them too restrictive. We declined in years past to face new realities in the fields of foreign relations— intelligence, information, economics, political-military relations—and to equip ourselves for these challenges in times when the inevitable importance of these fields was apparent to some of us. We declined to press upon ourselves and the Department of State the urgent need for facing these new areas of international policy. As a result, new agencies were created to do what we should have done but would not accept as legitimate.

[14] Battle's address is printed in full in the House Hays Bill Hearings: *Foreign Service Act Amendments of 1965*, Hearings before the Subcommittee on State Department Organization and Foreign Operations of the Committee on Foreign Affairs, 89th Cong., 1st Sess., May 19, 20, and 25, July 13-14, 1965, pp. 339-41.

The Professional Group

Although the Association did not follow Battle's advice during the period of the Hays Bill and USIA integration efforts, part of the blame must be attributed to the sponsors of these efforts for their failure to involve FSOs adequately in the development and planning of the ideas. Consequently the Hays Bill and the USIA integration plan were not well understood within the Service. The result was an almost instinctive negative reaction, as is evident in the SDP responses analyzed in this chapter.

However, the challenge posed by Battle ultimately did find a response in an action taken by the Board of the Association in the fall of 1966. Spurred by the ferment bubbling in the ranks, the board created a "Planning Committee" to study the association itself and recommend ways to make it a more effective and responsive instrument for the professional group. Former Ambassador E. Allan Lightner was named chairman of the committee, and the membership included several of the activists from the junior and mid-career ranks.

The Lightner Committee's report to the board called for the association to become "an organization with a serious intellectual base and an active—even combative—concern for the people at the heart of foreign affairs regardless of their agency affiliation." The report stated that "the Association now suffers the legacy of the past in which it represented exclusively the interests and views of the Foreign Service Officer Corps." It said the association should fully represent all professionals in foreign affairs, regardless of agency affiliation or personnel category. The report made a long series of recommendations designed to broaden the association and improve its professionalism, and stressed the importance of leadership and involvement of the professionals themselves in major change efforts.

The final recommendation of the Lightner Committee

urged the association "to give priority attention to studying its own structure to the end of insuring itself the dynamic and forceful leadership which will be required to implement the recommendations of this report." The activist groups must have read this very carefully, for they decided to leave nothing to chance. Out of the junior and mid-career groups, with the addition of a few senior officers, there coalesced a new "group of eighteen" which staged a remarkable coup in the summer of 1967 by taking over control of the association.

The group included men from AID and USIA, as well as State. Several of them were already members of the AFSA Board. The youngest members were 29 years of age; the average age of the group was 36. The senior members included a Country Director and an officer designated to be an Ambassador.

Normally the leadership of AFSA, which has more than 7,000 members from the various foreign affairs agencies, is selected without any political contests. By a typical inner-circle arrangement, a slate of officers is drawn up for nomination to an "electoral college" which is empowered to name the board and officers of the association. The slate is sent to the AFSA members so they may endorse it. The "group of eighteen" in effect formed a political party and sent their own ballot listing their names to the AFSA membership. Some of the eighteen were already on the regular AFSA slate; for the others, a write-in campaign was mounted.

Under the heading "*Un Peu de Zèle*," the ballot of the eighteen stated their platform, calling for more professionalism by AFSA, more influence on "decisions of major importance in the areas of administration and personnel," and "a new vision of the future of the foreign affairs community." The ballot said that if the eighteen were elected to

283

the electoral college, "they will select the officers and Board of Directors of AFSA for the coming two years from among themselves—thus assuring you at least an approximately direct election as well as a coherent program and active leadership for your Association." The ballot also said "the group would hope" that Ambassador Foy Kohler, then President of AFSA, would agree to serve another two-year term. Kohler, who had been Ambassador to the Soviet Union and was currently Deputy Under Secretary of State for Political Affairs, is very popular in the ranks and is something of a rarity in having held important posts in State, AID, and USIA during his career. The eighteen had held discussions with Kohler, and had found him to be a kindred spirit.

Kohler accepted a second term, and on September 28, 1967 the new leadership of AFSA was installed, with the new chairman 31-year-old Lannon Walker. In his luncheon address, Kohler said:

> When members of the group told me in early July of their "activist" plans, my reaction was that it was about time someone cared enough about the Association to make a run for office. It has seemed to me for some years past now that an ingredient too frequently absent from the affairs of both the Association and the Foreign Service Officer corps was a sense of passion, of caring deeply about matters of importance and daring to do something about them.

There still remained the problem of articulating more specifically what the ferment was all about. Some progress in this direction developed in the report of the Committee on Career Principles, a key committee of AFSA that normally operates under terms of reference which, if scrupulously followed, guarantee a conservative position. When this committee was reactivated early in 1967, the new chairman, Ambassador William Leonhart, took pains to include among its members some of the activists from the junior and mid-career levels, including two of the six authors of the radical memorandum and proposal to the director general. USIA, AID, and the FSR category in State were represented on the committee as well. Career Minister Outerbridge Horsey, serving as vice chairman of the committee, took the lead at the first meeting in proclaiming the terms of reference to be stuffy and in need of broadening. The representatives of the junior and mid-career levels of the FSO corps proposed that their number be augmented, and this was accepted.[15]

The result was that the "interim report" of the committee, delivered in November 1967, turned out to be extraordinarily progressive in character. It started out by broadly endorsing the reform efforts of the past:

> We have found, in preparing this report, that our discussions have led us to accept most of the broad principles and many of the specific proposals which characterized, among others, the Foreign Service Act of 1946, the program of Wristonization begun in the mid-1950s, the Herter Report of 1963 and the Hays Bill of 1965. They have also led us to a better awareness of the problems of shepherding proposed changes through the executive and legislative machinery—much less of gaining their acceptance by those affected.[16]

The report criticized the "closed nature of the foreign services" and the "guild-like structure" which has kept out "the newer methodologies in foreign affairs." As its basic

---

15 The author served as a member of this committee as a representative of the State Department FSR group.

16 The "interim report" appeared in full as a supplement to the *Foreign Service Journal*, Nov. 1967, pp. 30A-30D. The final report did

aim, the committee cited the wording of one of its earlier working papers:

The fundamental question to be considered is how the foreign affairs of the United States can best be organized and conducted consistent with NSAM 341 and various other directives related to the pre-eminent authority and responsibility of the Secretary of State. . . . (The Committee) believes that the psychological moment is at hand for a reexamination of the role of the Department of State and the Foreign Service in the over-all "foreign affairs community" and the structure and organization of the career service or services required to carry out that role.

The report called for improved research, contingency planning, "greater use of managerial tools," an interagency data base, "applications of programming techniques and information handling systems in foreign affairs." It stressed that the problems of rapid change involve "not the Foreign Service alone but the foreign affairs community."

Regarding the personnel issue, the report stated:

"The Foreign Service of the United States" remains the goal. . . . It has not yet been achieved. . . . The Committee generally and strongly favors the type of integration which would ultimately produce—from the several principal foreign services now extant—"The Foreign Service of the United States." . . . It believes the three principal foreign services should move more rapidly and energetically to eliminate superficial and artificial distinctions among the *de facto* career services and to achieve

---

not become available until late 1968 when this book was already in page proof. The final report, "Toward a Modern Diplomacy," was published as Part Two of the *Foreign Service Journal* of November 1968. An interesting document, it strongly projects the positive thrust of the interim report, but also displays clear strains of elitism.

the longer term goal of effective integration of the foreign services of the Department of State, AID and USIA.

Thus the report stops short of favoring the extension of the career personnel category—the FSO category—to officers of USIA and AID. It speaks somewhat vaguely in support of some sort of future "integration." It supports the idea of a separate career service for USIA, and states: "We *do not propose* a single service without distinctions between kinds of skills or levels of responsibility."

Conclusion

The over-all impression from the survey results reviewed in this chapter and the ferment within the ranks of the FSO corps is that the Foreign Service no longer has a problem of understanding the role challenge that it faces. The problem remaining, and it is an extremely difficult one, is whether the Department of State and the Foreign Service can adequately meet that challenge.

The overwhelming majority of officers welcome such measures as the Kennedy letter and NSAM 341, designed to strengthen the Department of State and the Foreign Service for a leadership role. Management of foreign affairs is ranked first as a function of the Service, and more than 60 percent of officers endorse the "new diplomacy" model as the correct one for the Service. After more than 20 years of defensiveness in the face of strong pressures for change, the voice of Lucius Battle calling for a positive approach is being joined by others, especially at the mid-career and junior ranks. The contrast to the conservative views of the older and retired officers, cited in Chapter 1, could hardly be more striking.

A graphic picture of the pressures for conformity and conservatism in the Foreign Service emerged in Chapter 6; and yet, the remarkable ferment described in this chapter has occurred and is occurring. The explanation for this is that the ferment has been a long time in the making, it has not been generated out of small considerations, and it represents widespread and growing sentiment within the Service. There seems to be recognition within the ranks that the challenge is a real one and that the FSO corps must meet it or take the risk of becoming a declining professional group.

One can point to the developments that have spurred the ferment—the activism of the Kennedy administration, the Kennedy letter, the dissolution of the OCB, the Herter Report, NSAM 341. Included in this list must be the change program mounted by Crockett during the period 1963-67. The reader will note the similarity between the thrust of the views now being espoused by the FSOs and the major change ideas and efforts of Crockett and *his* band of non-FSO activists, as described in Chapters 2 and 3. In this regard, there has been a misfortune in the time sequence of these developments. Crockett's major change efforts, the Hays Bill and the comprehensive programming system, and many of the related efforts have failed, due in some measure to the lingering conservatism of the FSOs and their frequent active and passive resistance. The shoe fits on the other foot, as well: Crockett and his men did not recognize and capitalize on the incipient ferment in the FSO ranks. Now that the Crockett thrust is gone, the new activism of the FSOs finds no financial and logistical support whatsoever in the bureaucracy, given the managerial void at the top of the State Department and the fact that Crockett's replacement dismantled those change efforts of his which did take some root. There is the added complication of the new malaise in U.S. foreign affairs in general, due to the Vietnam war, the balance of payments problem, and the strong pull for attention to domestic problems—all symptomized by the late 1967 White House instruction to all foreign affairs agencies to cut their overseas staffs across-the-board by 10 percent, an operation that came to be known as "the BALPA exercise" (from "balance of payments").

That the ferment will remain strong in the face of these problems is doubtful. Change requires organization, hard work, risk-taking. Already I have noted the yes-but syndrome and the fact that some of the tentative solutions proposed by the activists retain a flavor of elitism by ascription. Whether the ferment within the ranks will be vigorously focused on basic problems or will lose energy by addressing symptoms, details, and vagaries remains to be seen.

Yet the Foreign Service is clearly ready for change. This is certainly a necessary condition for both the Department of State and the FSO corps in meeting the role challenge discussed so frequently in this study. It is certainly not a sufficient condition. Discussion of what the other conditions might be is reserved for the concluding chapter. A useful prelude will be to examine at closer range the leaders within the Service and problems of coordination and leadership.

CHAPTER 8

COORDINATION AND LEADERSHIP

....

IN ESSENCE, the role challenge to the Department of State and the FSO corps has to do with coordination and leadership. The Department and the corps have been asked to exert greater managerial influence over the spectrum of foreign affairs policy formulation and operations, to bring about more effective coordination of diverse activities and programs. In preceding chapters, we have examined a number of factors that are broadly relevant to the challenge—the personnel system, the character and makeup of the FSO corps, managerial strategies within the Department, the norms and attitudes of FSOs. Here the purpose is to view at closer range some of the conditions and forces that affect the capability of FSOs to meet the challenge both in the field and in Washington, and then to examine those most directly concerned—the top-ranking officers in the Service.

The number of variables in examining coordination is potentially enormous; I shall by no means attempt to review them all. For example, the problems associated with the management of foreign policy crises are specifically excluded, for two reasons. The first is the high security classification normally attendant in a crisis situation. Only the tip of the iceberg is public, and by the time the crisis is desensitized, it is extremely difficult to track back all that really happened. Perhaps the best hope for research progress here will be in some kind of rigorous, internal case-study program, with the cases eventually being made public.

290

Coordination and Leadership

Deputy Under Secretary Crockett launched such a program in 1965, but it was cancelled because of lack of funds.

The other reason is that a crisis by definition is an abnormal situation, although some would hold the opposite is true in the Department of State. When a serious foreign affairs crisis occurs, decision-making escalates; the Secretary of State may in effect become the country desk officer for country X when it blows up. The barriers and inhibitions to coordination that exist in the absence of a crisis may readily be overcome in a crisis as the salience of the problem draws in higher-level officials and as time constraints mitigate against bureaucratic routine. My concern here is with the ongoing, day-to-day coordination and management which in large measure is intended to avoid crises.

I will first discuss some of the broad conditions that affect coordination in the field to provide a basis for comparison to the problems of the Country Director reorganization in Washington and the problems of coordination the Country Director faces. The extent to which these conditions inhibit or promote coordination is variable according to the particular situation; a condition that is severely dysfunctional in one situation may be less so in another. The problem of the manager or decision-maker is to recognize that the conditions exist, to assess their impact in the given situation, and to find ways to deal with them.

Coordination in the Field

U.S. Missions abroad vary a good deal in terms of major tasks and organizational complexity, reflecting the general character of U.S. relationships with the host country and the latter's importance on the world scene. Most of the missions can be crudely typed according to major task. For example, in most western European nations, the major function of U.S. missions is one of maintenance, of maintaining the normally sound relations between the U.S. and the host country through a broad variety of collaborative and representational efforts. In most iron curtain countries, the major function has been a formal representational one, usually under rigid constraints. In some countries, the dominant theme is counterinsurgency, as in Korea in the early 1950s and South Vietnam at present. In a great many developing nations, the major function of the U.S. mission is development assistance, with almost all elements of the mission involved in one way or another in attempting to help bring about modernization of the host society.

The internal complexity of missions is a function of their size and program mix. Obviously coordination is a much greater problem in New Delhi than in Copenhagen. This is not simply a division between the developed and underdeveloped countries. The U.S. embassy in London is a great deal more complicated than the U.S. embassy in Ouagadougou. But, by and large, it is in the developing nations that one finds the more complex program mix, with such operations present as military assistance, P.L. 480, the Peace Corps, the AID program, the larger USIA programs.

Because of his uniquely high status and authority, the ambassador can profoundly influence the character of coordination within the mission. All ambassadors are keenly interested in political events, and work to build personal relationships at the highest levels of the host society. Not all of them move beyond this to concern themselves with active management of a large enterprise. Much depends on the ambassador's attitudes toward the various programs nominally under his command and the extent of his interest in them, on whether his style is toward the authoritarian or permissive ends of the spectrum, on whether he is an innovator, how well he communicates, whether he reacts to events or moves positively to work on coordination and collaboration.

For example, in the Executive Review of Overseas Programs described in Chapter 3, the precise nature of ambassadorial review sessions in the field was left open in recognition of the fact that ambassadorial styles varied, but the guidance material clearly envisioned a series of group situations cutting across agency lines, much as did the program categories in the Comprehensive Country Programming System. Most ambassadors did in fact use the exercise as an opportunity to work on improved communication and creativity in group situations and to focus on intergroup problems. Several ambassadors, however, worked strictly on a one-to-one basis with the agency representative concerned. At least one ambassador worked all by himself, reviewing submissions, making decisions with no confrontation nor discussions, and sending them in to Washington.

The differing styles of two ambassadors whose careers were outwardly very similar offers another example. Both men, now retired, spent most of their 30 years of career service in the Near East, each serving as Ambassador to Near Eastern countries a number of times. One man's attitude toward the newer functions such as information and aid was Briggsian; he viewed the Country Team idea as an attempt to cut down his authority by running foreign affairs on a committee basis. His DCM carried the brunt of meetings and management. The Ambassador was aloof and almost inaccessible, but superb in terms of command of Near Eastern languages and close relationships at the top in the host society. The other man was open, energetic, and positive, highly accessible, and determined to make his Country Team an effective working group.

Within the constraints of policy and program decisions

made in Washington, the ambassador has virtually unlimited authority over the day-to-day conduct of his Mission. Ambassador Livingston Merchant expressed the point in this way in testimony to the Jackson Subcommittee: "I think you can only blame the individual ambassador if he does not run a tight, disciplined, and well-coordinated mission. I think the authority is there, all of the necessary authority is there."[1]

Although rarely does an ambassador actually select the chiefs of his key mission components, he can exercise a veto power on nominations for assignment to his mission. Much more sparingly used, but widely recognized, is the ambassador's power to cut short the tour of duty of a mission officer, of any agency, and send him packing. The ambassador can act as a filter in communications to and from Washington, and he can dispense certain rewards such as deciding who will be on the diplomatic list and who will attend what functions. Because most of the administrative support is provided by the Department of State, the ambassador can decide whether the atmosphere will be austere or liberal in terms of services and recreational facilities.

The key men in the mission are the DCM, the political and economic counselors, the AID mission chief, the public affairs officer (USIA), the senior military attaché, and the chiefs of the military assistance mission, the Peace Corps, and the CIA station, if these programs exist at the mission. In a country where the aid program is big and active, the AID Mission Chief can be a power unto himself and is easily the most important man in the mission, next to the ambassador, because of the large resources at his disposal.

There is no legal and traditional precedent for the DCM

[1] U. S. Congress, Jackson Subcommittee, "Administration of National Security," Part 7, 88th Cong., 2nd Sess., Feb. 27, 1964, p. 462.

position which gives the DCM anything like the authority possessed by the ambassador. The DCM depends for his authority on the support of his ambassador, his own personal effectiveness, and the fact that everyone knows he will be chargé d'affaires when the ambassador is absent. There are several styles for the DCM position, but the most prevalent one is that of alter ego to the ambassador. Ambassador Samuel Berger described this style to the Jackson Subcommittee:

> The administrative device to achieve this is to have the deputy present at all the ambassador's meetings; accompany the ambassador on every possible occasion, including his meetings with the foreign minister; be present when the ambassador receives callers; be present as often as possible at the ambassador's representational functions; have the deputy see all incoming and outgoing official ambassadorial correspondence; and have all work and papers within the embassy come to the ambassador through the deputy.[2]

In countries where there is a considerable number of subposts, as in Mexico where there are 13 Consulates General and Consulates, in addition to the Embassy, a supervising Consul General will be present in the mission to coordinate activities of the subposts. In many cases the Principal officers at the subposts will be running a miniature country team with other agency personnel present in the district—a branch public affairs officer, an AID man in charge of area activities, a deputy Peace Corps country representative.

The constraints on the time of the ambassador and the DCM, particularly if the latter serves as alter ego, can be severe, so much so in some cases that the two begin to pro-

2 *Ibid.*, Part 3, July 24, Sept. 18, 1963, p. 261.

vide a microcosmic reflection of the time problems of the Secretary and Under Secretary of State. When he first arrives at his post, the ambassador can spend weeks doing almost nothing but making formal calls and receiving callers. Thereafter, the representational demands are such that the ambassador and DCM often will find themselves busy seven nights a week. Ceremonial functions during the day and receiving official visitors from Washington can make great inroads on one's time.

The first duty of an ambassador is to nurture close relationships within the power structure of the host country. This takes time, and so does the daily cable traffic. Thus, even in the absence of a crisis situation, the ambassador and DCM may be hard put to find time for a positive coordinative role that goes much below the surface of program activities.

In Chapter 3 some of the administrative processes for program and policy formulation in Washington were described, particularly as they relate to the budgetary cycle and interagency decision-making. These place important limitations on the ambassador's decision-making authority. He has no direct control over the budgets of other agencies represented in his mission, and, in the absence of a programming system, he has no regularized means for involving himself in the goal-setting, program planning, and program execution of the various agencies.

This does not mean that the ambassador has no influence; as indicated, his authority on the local scene is very strong. It does mean that he has no way of exercising that influence systematically. A program may look different in actual operation in the field than it did in Washington, and ambassadorial influence can have a lot to do with local program variations. If he does not like an activity, an ambassador may exercise negative power by delaying its progress and raising the wisdom of the activity anew in communications to Washington. Or, if he takes particular interest in a program he can cut into the budgetary cycle at an early stage and exert some influence on the future shape of the program.

The point is, these interventions are at best sporadic. Ordinarily they must come at the initiative of the ambassador. For staff work, he usually must depend on the program personnel themselves. The net result is that the various agency programs are largely self-contained and semi-independent operations, working on their own cycles of goal-setting, planning, execution, and review.

In the absence of a comprehensive budget and any regular requirements for goal-setting and program planning and review, the major instruments of coordination are the meeting and the written communication.

The Country Team meeting is standard, though its frequency, composition, and style will vary from post to post. The ambassador may have other regular meetings. In addition, committees may grow up around particular program interests; for example, many posts have a youth committee for coordinating programs addressed to young leaders in the host society.

Telegrams to the Department frequently offer a point of coordination in the clearance process and in review and signing off by the ambassador. Most posts still engage in the custom of sending off a weekly round-up report to Washington (the "weeka") on all of significance that has happened in the host country. This frequently calls for a collaborative effort among the various sections of the Mission.

Although in the main the sections of the Mission can operate almost completely independently, there are frequent opportunities for collaboration and some interde-

297

pendencies. USIA will publicize the programs of AID and the Peace Corps. The Labor Attaché may devote several hours a week to assisting USIS in its media output to a labor audience. There are opportunities for mutually helpful information flow between USIS and the Political Section, between AID and the Economic Section, between the branch posts and the mission.

One device for improving coordination that is infrequently used is the assigning of one officer to two roles, as when the Counselor for Economic Affairs also serves as the AID Mission Chief or as Deputy Chief.

Each major agency operating in a mission abroad tends to have its own particular subculture, born out of characteristics of the parent agency and the nature of its programs, and out of differences in individual career experiences, career prospects, conditions of service, and patterns of tenure. Much of the flavor of the differences is visible to the eye in touring a mission. The embassy proper is a distinctive institution and its ambience is likely to have traces of elegance, from the great seal of the United States over the portals to the Marine Guards on duty to the dignified opulence of the Ambassador's office. Normally the atmosphere is sedate; officers are prone to wear vests and hardly anyone walks around in shirtsleeves. USIA very often will be in different quarters, as close to the heart of the capital city as possible, and the atmosphere is a busier one, with practically everybody in shirtsleeves. It is essentially an editorial office, with stacks of books and films on tables, a news ticker going, pictures all over the walls. Most often, AID will be in a different building, too, and the atmosphere usually will lack distinctiveness. It will be like the headquarters of any of a thousand business firms in the capital city, with local overtones such as faulty elevators and spartan furnishings. One is likely to see suntanned technicians, clad in sandals and khaki shorts, just in from a field project. As at USIA headquarters, local employees will be very much in evidence. The Peace Corps headquarters will be the most informal and unpretentious of all, since it is a Peace Corps norm to avoid visible signs of affluence as rigorously as political ties to the mission are avoided. Peace Corps staffers, for example, do not avail themselves of commissary privileges. When groups of volunteers are in town, the Peace Corps headquarters takes on something of the atmosphere of a college student union. In terms of dress, virtually anything goes.

These natural differences are reinforced by the relative independence of each agency's operations. For the individual agency staff member, the greater part of interaction, reinforcement, support, occurs within his own group.

Although group interaction on the job occurs for the most part in meetings, there is normally a good deal of social interaction after hours, stemming from the one thing all personnel have in common—their status as official representatives of the U.S. government in a foreign country. There are many shared problems in such areas as housing, schooling, marketing, and domestic staff. The degree of sociability varies with the situational context of the mission. There is much less social interaction in Paris, for example, than in the semi-primitive capital of a remote new African state, where the cohesive forces are strong and the mission group begins to take on some of the characteristics of an extended family.

As a positive force for improved coordination, sociability does not always overcome the negative force of the stereotypes that inevitably flow from differences in subcultures; in fact, under some conditions one can imagine proximity heightening the stereotypes. The FSOs might be seen as faintly superior and condescending in attitude, and as in-

299

terested mainly in reading newspapers and moving in limited circles. USIA people might be seen as engaged mainly in busywork with little sense of direction. FSOs might be resentful of AID people because they see them as having less sensitivity and understanding of the host society than they, but receiving higher salaries. Jealousies might arise over the differences in resources that the various agencies have at their command. Although most personnel are provided common administrative services by the Embassy Administrative Section, there are differences in perquisites stemming from the differences in regulations among the agencies, and these can cause rivalry and jealousy.

For the most part, the goals that govern work in the mission, whether articulated or not, are not of a nature that in themselves will force coordination and interaction. In part, this is a function of the fact that much of the goal-setting and program planning tends to be self-contained within each agency. Broad, generally understood goals for the mission as a whole tend to be at a high level of abstraction, and in such cases the U.S. margin of influence is likely to be minimal. The mission may be pressing for action to improve the investment climate in the host society, helping to eradicate rural violence, encouraging formation of a center-left coalition, or trying to improve understanding of U.S. involvement in Vietnam. If any of these states come to pass, it would be a rare case in which anyone could say with any degree of certainty that action by the U.S. mission was the specific cause. If it is difficult to take credit, it is also difficult to place blame if the desired state does not come to pass.

The result of the intangibility of most goals and the compartmentalized administration of agency programs is that opportunities for coordination and collaborative enterprise, in the absence of crisis situations, have low visibility. This is a point elaborated perceptively by Richard Walton,

Coordination and Leadership

Purdue University social scientist, after studying inter-agency coordination at a major U.S. mission abroad.[3] Walton points out that in this social system lack of coordination normally does not produce manifest problems, in contrast, say, to an industrial firm where faulty coordination will result in obvious breakdowns. So long as breakdowns do not occur, any level of coordination might be regarded as satisfactory.

Missions normally do not have staff and management research components of a kind that can discern opportunities for coordination, raise their visibility, and act as a catalyst to stimulate the activity. Only the ambassador and the DCM are in a position to take a broad view of mission activities, and I have already commented on their handicaps in terms of time constraints and lack of systematic tools. If there is a staff aide to the ambassador, he usually will be too overburdened with detail to perform the role of management analyst, even if he had the training and desire to do so.

A familiar theme in the literature in public administration is the set of problems often found in relationships between a home office and its field posts—lack of understanding, faulty communication, distrust, poor coordination. A normally bad situation is compounded in foreign affairs by remoteness and some of the other problems already discussed—the intangibility of goals, the multi-agency mix, and the lack of systematic tools. The feelings run worse from the field to Washington than vice versa. Operators in the field are prone to see Washington as a great bureaucratic sludge which is either unresponsive when something is wanted or bristling with bright ideas that no one needs. The lack of a systematic, meaningful dialogue between

[3] Walton's study was sponsored by Deputy Under Secretary Crockett's ACORD program, and the observations were made in Walton's mimeographed report.

301

The Professional Group

Washington and the field is a severe handicap to effective coordination. Repeated so often that it has become a cliché is the view that Washington should have a Country Team set-up like the field does.

The Country Director Reorganization

There was a fairly widespread assumption that a long step toward a Country Team arrangement in Washington had been taken when the Country Director reorganization occurred in the Department of State following the issuance of NSAM 341 in March 1966. In his message accompanying the NSAM, Secretary Rusk said:

> I look to the Country Directors to assume full responsibility, under their Assistant Secretaries, for all activities in the country or countries assigned to them, and to be single focal points in Washington to serve our Ambassadors. In a sense, we are applying the valuable experience that has been gained in the operations of Country Teams abroad to operations here in Washington.[4]

To provide a visual image of the change that occurred, Figures 1 and 2 show the "before" and "after" of the reorganization in the Bureau of Far Eastern Affairs, one of the five regional bureaus in the Department of State.[5] In the prior structure, the basic unit was the country desk officer—one man who concerned himself totally with a single foreign nation.[6] He and several other desk officers

[4] U.S. Department of State, *News Letter*, Mar. 1966, p. 3.

[5] Differences in names and grammar from 1962 to 1967 in the chart represent actual changes in State Department usage. Note that the name of the Bureau has been changed to "East Asian and Pacific Affairs."

[6] In the case of very small geographic units, some desk officers would be responsible for more than one. For a good description of the desk officer in action, see Robert E. Elder, *The Policy Machine: The Department of State and American Foreign Policy* (Syracuse: Syracuse University Press, 1960), Chapter 2.

Coordination and Leadership

would comprise an office representing one subpart of the region, reporting to a Deputy Office Director and an Office Director. The latter would in turn report to the Deputy

FIGURE 1
BUREAU OF FAR EASTERN AFFAIRS (FE)—1962

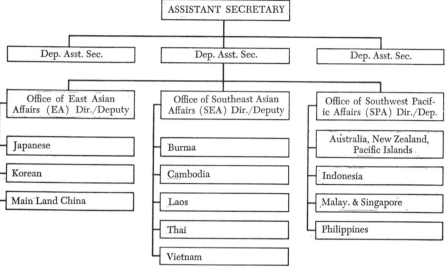

FIGURE 2
BUREAU OF EAST ASIAN AND PACIFIC AFFAIRS (EA)—1967

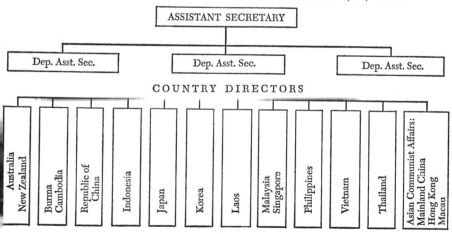

The Professional Group

Assistant Secretaries and the chief of the bureau, the Assistant Secretary.

The idea in the reorganization was to eliminate the Office Director and Deputy Office Director levels and to upgrade the country desk officer. In becoming country director, the desk officer would in effect be at the Office Director level. It was Secretary Rusk's long-cherished idea that this cutback in layering would result in better communication and more vigorous management on a country-by-country basis.

In 1962 there were 21 Office Directors in the five regional bureaus, counting only those pertaining to specific geographic units and not the functional or multilateral Office Directors of which each bureau has several. Today, there are 50 Country Directors. At the geographic director level, then, the five bureaus have moved from an average of about four officers each to 10. The 50 Country Directors are responsible for some 130 geographic entities, or an average of 2.6 each. It was not deemed practical to move entirely to a one man per country structure, given the enormous disparity in size and importance among the nations of the world. A Country Director responsible for several countries, then, still has desk officers for those countries reporting to him. Nineteen Country Directors are responsible for only one country each, and these, for the most part, are the large nations such as India, Brazil, Japan. Five Country Directors are responsible for two countries each. The largest span belongs to one Country Director in the Bureau of African Affairs who covers 10 geographic entities.

The changeover occurred during the summer of 1966. In the case of the Bureau of Inter-American Affairs, very little change was necessary since the bureau had moved to a flatter structure several years previously to accommodate a "back-to-back" arrangement for State and AID personnel

304

Coordination and Leadership

in the home office. The object was to bring about closer working relationships, a measure of job interchangeability, and physical proximity for improved administration of the Alliance for Progress. Subsequently, an actual merger of State and AID personnel and offices for Latin America took place.

Of the 50 Country Directors, 47 are FSOs and three are FSRs. All 50 are at the top three grades of the FSO-FSR grade structure, and their average age per grade is somewhat lower than the averages for the entire FSO corps (see Chapter 4) :

TABLE 46

Grade and Average Age of Country Directors

Grade	No. of Officers	Average age
1	20	49.5
2	24	45.8
3	6	42.9
Totals	50	Average 46.9

From the high grade level and low average age, it is clear that some care was taken in selecting Country Directors and that the officers are highly regarded. Many of them ultimately will serve as ambassadors. Of the 21 officers serving as Office Directors in 1962, 10 are now ambassadors.

Of the 47 Country Directors who are FSOs, Table 47 shows that 31 entered by the basic examination method, all prior to 1954, and 16 entered laterally. The great majority of the officers have had extensive service.

TABLE 47

Timing and Method of Entry of Country Directors

	Pre-1954	1954-58	1958-62	Total
Examination	31	—	—	31
Lateral	5	9	2	16
Totals	36	9	2	47

The role challenge which has been discussed extensively in this study suddenly became a reality for these men as they assumed the position of Country Director. In the same circular that carried the text of NSAM 341, the functions of the Country Director were described under the heading "Interdepartmental Leadership and Coordination of Country Matters" as follows:

A new position of Country Director will be established in the regional bureaus to serve as the single focus of responsibility for leadership and coordination of departmental and interdepartmental activities concerning his country or countries of assignment. In particular he will:

a. provide continuing departmental and interdepartmental leadership in planning, coordination, and implementation of decisions;

b. raise specific matters for consideration by the IRG, and bring detailed knowledge to IRG discussions when so requested;

c. serve as the base for crisis task force operations as necessary.

The Country Director will be responsible for seeing that the Ambassador's needs are served both within the Department and government-wide. He will ensure that the mission is fully supported in the full range of its requirements: policy, operations and administration.

Each Country Director will organize and develop such contacts, channels and mechanisms as are appropriate to and necessary for full interdepartmental leadership on country matters, and for full support to the Assistant Secretary.

To assist in providing guidance and direction to the Country Director, the Assistant Secretary will have one or more Deputy Assistant Secretaries whose areas of responsibility will be defined by the Assistant Secretary.

Coordination and Leadership

Positions of Office Director and officer-in-charge will be abolished as the transition is made to the establishment of Country Director positions.[7]

Coordination at the Country Director Level

It is too early to attempt any definitive assessment of the Country Director reorganization. As reported earlier (see Chapter 3), the high-level interagency groups created by NSAM 341 (the SIG and the five IRGs), as of this writing, have not been fully brought to life and have made little impact. It is possible, however, to discuss some of the attitudes generated by the reorganization and some of the problems that Country Directors face in moving into a new and somewhat vague situation.

The announcement of the reorganization was not received with noticeable enthusiasm. To be sure, much of this was accounted for by the normal reluctance to undertake major change. In addition, there were many issues, with differing degrees of validity, but all of them real in the sense of being deeply felt.

There were, first of all, some organizational and status issues. A man formerly an office director over a dozen countries who now found himself Country Director for two of those countries could feel that he had been downgraded. The desk officer beneath him for one of the countries could also feel downgraded in the sense of having less freedom of movement; his boss was closer to him and was taking on more of the desk officer functions himself than previously. The role of the Deputy Assistant Secretaries had become ambiguous. The Assistant Secretary now has an enlarged span of control so that a Country Director may feel that he has less access than previously. Because of the

---

[7] U.S. Department of State, Foreign Affairs Manual Circular No. 385, "Direction, Coordination and Supervision of Interdepartmental Activities Overseas," Mar. 4, 1966.

lateral spread, the Country Directors may feel less in touch with each other than the Office Directors had been.

There were also serious reservations regarding the authority given Country Directors. It might sound good to talk about a Country Team concept in Washington, Country Directors feel, but the reality is far from the ideal under the conditions of the reorganization. A comparison of the situation of the Country Director to that of the Ambassador is instructive in this regard. The Country Director has almost all the disadvantages faced by the ambassador, plus a few additional ones, and none of the important advantages. He faces a multi-agency coordination problem with no systematic interagency planning, programming, and budgeting tools. The subculture differences and stereotypes are just as pronounced, if not more so. The Country Director has the same problems of intangibility of goals and low visibility of coordination opportunities. His situation is similar to that of an ambassador in terms of time constraints and lack of staff and management research components.

On the other side, the Country Director has no community and social interaction to work with as a base, as does the ambassador, who has an opportunity to build coordinative enterprise on the commonality of experience of serving together in the same foreign country. And finally, the status and authority of the Country Director are not remotely comparable to those enjoyed by an ambassador.

It is not surprising, then, that some Country Directors soon after the reorganization expressed a desire for a more formal delegation of authority. The NSAM, with a great deal of weight and authority behind it, created the SIG and the IRGs with State Department officers in the potentially powerful roles of executive chairmen. But the creation of the Country Director position was entirely internal to the Department of State. If the Country Director is supposed to play the role outlined in Circular 385, the argument went, why not extend the formal structure to the country level by creating the concept of an ICG (Interdepartmental Country Group), with the Country Director as executive chairman.

In trying to develop "such contacts, channels and mechanisms as are appropriate to and necessary for full interdepartmental leadership on country matters," the Country Directors have encountered a difficult problem—the disparate organizational structure of the Washington agencies. No other agency is organized in as much geographical depth as the State Department, and no other agency has officers at nearly as high a rank at the country level. In one sense, this is an advantage. In an interagency meeting of all persons directly concerned with Country X, the State Department Country Director clearly is the ranking officer. There are also disadvantages. A lower-ranking man from Agency Y may not be able to speak for his agency. The man in Agency Y who *can* speak for the agency is at a higher organizational level such that he would have to relate to, say, six or eight Country Directors. If he is status-conscious, he may not feel that he should talk to anyone below the Assistant Secretary level or at least the Deputy Assistant Secretary level. In any event, he cannot possibly attend the meetings of all the Country Directors operating in his geographic purview.

The Country Directors also have an internal problem The change from the narrowly circumscribed role of the country desk officer to the Country Director responsible for interagency coordination is a quantum jump. What was jumped over is a Country Team concept within the State Department itself. Two major functional bureaus—for Intelligence and Research and for Cultural Affairs—are also

309

organized geographically. Other major functional components—the Bureau of Economic Affairs, the Policy Planning Council, the Office of Political-Military Affairs—may take a deep interest in a particular country from time to time. It would not be unusual for a man from Agency Y to attend a State Department meeting and find five State officers there, each representing a different piece of the organization. He may think the State Department is stacking the deck against him, whereas in fact what he is encountering may very well be a show of weakness rather than strength.

Despite all the problems, it is becoming increasingly clear that something important has happened. One's assessment is necessarily very impressionistic at this stage, but perceptibly a new and positive psychological set seems to be developing. The status problems seem to have been left behind. The Office Director may have been responsible for more countries, but not at the depth and lateral reach of the Country Director.

The country desk officer was the low man; all too often he was in the position of bag-carrier. If things got exciting and hot, they were sure to move swiftly away from him, just as surely, all the uninteresting details would gravitate to him. There was no prod nor mandate for him to take the initiative in establishing a comprehensive country view among the various agencies. His interactions with counterparts in the other agencies were at best sporadic and more often than not of a fire-fighting nature.

The Country Directors still have all of the details of daily business, as well as the new go-ahead for interagency coordination. The impression given is that they are having little difficulty in keeping up with the first and are beginning to make tentative forays into the second. For example,

Coordination and Leadership

the Country Director for Brazil has formed the Brazil Interdepartmental Group, appropriately known as BIG. Ten agencies are represented by the 15 persons who attend the periodic meetings.

More recently there seems to be a mood of realism concerning the issue of formal authority, a recognition that attempting to extend formal authority below the IRG level might quickly reach the point of diminishing returns. There seems to be an understanding that success as a Country Director depends less on formal authority and more on personal leadership ability, the development of close rapport with the Assistant Secretary, development of systematic management tools, and attaining a position in which meaningful issues can be raised to the IRG.

At present, there is a great deal of bridge-building going on. Country Directors who are establishing interagency groups are engaging in community-building, in working toward at least one of the advantages that an ambassador has. None of the groups has reached the policy-making or the problem-solving stage. Yet one can see much potential value in simply getting together to exchange views on Country X. Such increased interaction can build mutual confidence and improve understanding of each agency's particular mission and perspective. The group can begin to form its own culture, and the increasing knowledge of the man from Agency Y may build his stature within the agency so that in time he may be able to speak for his agency.

All of this is a radical departure from the recent past. The challenge is a difficult one. At the least, one suspects, what is currently going on will begin to alter one truism about the FSO career, that officers rarely have an opportunity to develop leadership skills.

The Professional Group
The Elite

Thus far in this chapter we have examined some of the forces and conditions affecting the leadership roles that FSOs are called on to play, abroad and in Washington. For the balance of this chapter, our attention will be directed to the leaders themselves, the elite of the corps.

It is an achievement to pass the basic examinations and gain entrance into the FSO corps. For the universe of officers who have accomplished this, however, eliteness then has something of the quality of ascription about it, rather than achievement. One may feel himself to be a member of an elite simply because he is an FSO, not for anything he has achieved. Within the total group, those who have achieved eliteness can be identified in several ways, by the positions they hold, their rank, the esteem with which they are regarded by their colleagues; all three perspectives overlap to some degree.

In terms of positions, the elite would consist of officers serving as ambassadors, DCMs, and Country Directors, plus a handful of others serving as Assistant Secretaries, Deputy Assistant Secretaries, or in special positions such as Director General, Director of the Foreign Service Institute, and so on.

The point was made in Chapter 4 that the lateral entry programs of the past have provided a source of executive talent to the FSO corps as the need for executive talent has increased over the years. We have already seen that one-third of the officers occupying the new position of Country Director are lateral entrants. Table 48 shows the personnel categories of ambassadors and DCMs, comparing the 1966 composition to that in 1962.

A number of interesting points emerge from the table. In the transition from the Kennedy to the Johnson administration, the number of political appointees serving as

Coordination and Leadership

ambassador has declined from 39 to 29, even though the total number of ambassadorships has risen from 101 to 108.

TABLE 48

Personnel Categories of Ambassadors and DCMs, 1962 and 1966

Personnel category	October 1962					
	Ambassadors		DCMs		Total	
	no.	percent	no.	percent	no.	percent
Examination	38	37.6	36	39.1	74	38.3
Lateral	24	23.8	56	60.9	80	41.5
Reserve	—	—	—	—	—	—
Political	39	38.6	—	—	39	20.2
Totals	101	100	92	100	193	100

Personnel category	October 1966					
	Ambassadors		DCMs		Total	
	no.	percent	no.	percent	no.	percent
Examination	41	38.0	62	62.0	103	49.5
Lateral	38	35.2	34	34.0	72	34.6
Reserve	—	—	4	4.0	4	1.9
Political	29	26.8	—	—	29	14.0
Totals	108	100	100	100	208	100

No FSRs were serving as DCMs in 1962, but by 1966 four had been appointed to that position. Altogether, nearly 85 percent of the officers occupying the top two positions in U.S. Missions abroad in 1966 were FSOs. Of the 175 FSOs, 40 percent are lateral entrants, a decline from 1962 when *more* than half of the FSOs in the top two positions were lateral entrants. This is a reflection of the fact that lateral entrants, as a group, tend to be older than examination entrants, and is one of the reasons, as reported in Chapter 4, that their attrition rate has been much higher over the past four years. The age factor is represented in the distribution of lateral entrants in the two positions over time: their number declined in the DCM position from 56 in 1962 to 34 in 1966, and increased in ambassadorships from 24 to 38.

The Professional Group

The official elite within the Service consists of those officers holding the rank of Career Ambassador and Career Minister. Table 49 shows the numbers and methods of entry of officers in these two ranks in 1962 and 1966.

TABLE 49

Career Ambassadors and Career Ministers, 1962 and 1966, Method of Entry

	July 1962			August 1966		
	CA	CM	Total	CA	CM	Total
Examination	7	38	45	8	36	44
Lateral	0	10	10	0	18	18
Totals	7	48	55	8	54	62

There were no lateral entrants at the rank of Career Ambassador in either year. However, the number of lateral entrants at the Career Minister level has risen from 10 in 1962 to 18 in 1966.

To be eligible for selection as a Career Minister, an officer must have served at least three years at FSO-1, and at least one of those years as Chief of Mission or in a position comparable in responsibility. Of the 54 Career Ministers in 1966, 48 have served as ambassadors, although not all of them having so served prior to selection as a Career Minister. The Department of State regulations state that the rank of Career Minister "will be reserved for those few Foreign Service Officers from class 1 who have consistently demonstrated outstanding ability in discharging the most responsible and difficult duties connected with the conduct of the Nation's foreign affairs, and who are qualified and available for assignments to the most important positions at posts abroad and to key positions in the Department and in other foreign affairs agencies."

The selection process consists of the following steps: (1) in the annual promotion process, one of the Selection Boards proposes a list of officers for promotion to Career Minister;

314

(2) this list is reviewed by a special panel drawn from the Board of the Foreign Service; (3) the full Board approves a list of recommended officers for transmittal to the Secretary of State; and (4) the Secretary makes his choices and transmits the names to the president.

The average age of the 54 Career Ministers is 56. They have served an average of 28 years and 6 months with the Department of State, and have been at the rank of Career Minister an average of 5 years and 10 months. In terms of primary functional experience, the Department of State lists 49 of the Career Ministers in the political field, four in the economic field, and one in administration. The breakdown in terms of primary area experience is:

Western Europe	27
Eastern Europe	1
Near East, South Asia	8
Far East	5
Latin America	10
Africa	3

In both functional and area experience, second and third fields of experience are shown for many of the officers.

Recently there has been a strong tendency to emphasize executive ability in the selection of Career Ministers. The precepts to the 19th Selection Boards (1965) carried a special appendix on Career Minister qualifications which was peppered with references to executive ability.[8] It said that a Career Minister "will have demonstrated unusual leadership and command talent," and "a high degree of executive proficiency." The candidate "would normally have been assigned responsibilities of an executive and policy nature requiring synthesis of the several functional areas";

[8] U.S. Department of State, "Precepts for the Nineteenth Selection Boards," Foreign Affairs Manual Circular 358, Sept. 17, 1965.

he probably would have been assigned to another department or agency "which has major programs or is otherwise heavily involved in the international field." Finally, "He will have demonstrated complete awareness of the scope of the senior positions he has occupied and of the new dimensions of diplomacy in the 1960s in both the substantive and management-administrative fields."

The rank of Career Ambassador is the highest honor available to a member of the FSO corps. The number of Career Ambassadors is limited by law to 12. To be eligible for consideration, an officer must have been in government service at least 15 years, including three years or more at the rank of Career Minister and five years of service as Chief of Mission, or comparable experience. A Career Ambassador Review Board is convened from time to time, chaired by the Deputy Under Secretary for Administration, to propose nominees to the Secretary of State who makes his choices for recommendation to the President.

Table 50 shows the Career Ambassadors on duty in 1966. In order to encompass several transactions that occurred at about the same time in 1966, nine Career Ambassadors are listed instead of eight, the number appearing in the tables in Chapter 4. Raymond Hare announced his retirement, and two Career Ministers, Foy Kohler and Douglas MacArthur II, were promoted to the rank of Career Ambassador. In later actions: Johnson was named Ambassador to Japan; Kohler replaced him as Deputy Under Secretary for Political Affairs; and Thompson replaced Kohler as Ambassador to the Soviet Union. It was Thompson's second appearance in Moscow as Ambassador.[9]

9 In still later actions, over the winter of 1967-68, Kohler and Riddleberger retired. Bohlen replaced Kohler as Deputy Under Secretary for Political Affairs and MacArthur replaced Riddleberger as Ambassador to Austria.

Coordination and Leadership

TABLE 50
Career Ambassadors on Duty, August 1966

Name	Post	Age	Length of service Yrs.	Length of service Mos.	Time in class Yrs.	Time in class Mos.
George V. Allen	Dir., Foreign Service Institute	62	31	0*	6	0
Charles E. Bohlen	Ambassador to France	61	37	1	6	0
W. W. Butterworth	Ambassador to Canada	62	38	1	4	3
Raymond A. Hare	Ass't. Secretary, Near Eastern Affairs	65	39	2	6	0
U. Alexis Johnson	Dep. Under Secretary, Political Affairs	57	30	8	1	11
Foy D. Kohler	Ambassador to USSR	58	34	6	0	0
Douglas MacArthur II	Ass't. Sec. for Congressional Relations	56	30	8	0	0
James Riddleberger	Ambassador to Austria	61	36	7	6	0
Llewellyn Thompson	Ambassador-at-Large	61	37	4	6	0

* Retired November 1960; recalled to duty March 1966.

One of the five basic hypotheses in the Janowitz study of the professional soldier has to do with the distinction between the "professional elite" and the "elite nucleus." The hypothesis, which Janowitz says "is probably applicable to all organizations," is that "prescribed careers performed with high competence lead to entrance into the professional elite," but that entrance into the elite nucleus —the smaller group of "prime movers"—is "assigned to persons with unconventional and adaptive careers."[10] Although the careers of the men in the elite nucleus must comply with conventional forms, these men also have taken risks and were willing to innovate. According to Janowitz, the unconventional career "implies that the officer has undergone experiences which have enabled him to acquire new perspectives, new skills, and a broader outlook than is afforded by a routine career."

[10] Morris Janowitz, *The Professional Soldier* (Glencoe: The Free Press, 1960), pp. 11-12 and Chapter 8, "The Elite Nucleus."

317

The Professional Group

Although the unconventionality is not nearly so pronounced as in the careers of the top military men Janowitz discusses, the experiences of the Career Ambassadors offers some support for the hypothesis. For example, in the adjustment to the radical change from prewar isolationism to postwar involvement in foreign affairs, the men who led the way were the new area specialists, in particular the men who become Russian and Chinese experts even before those two nations became major world powers and major threats to the United States. As discussed in Chapter 4, area specialization was the exception in the prewar Foreign Service when the main area of career by far was Europe. The nine Career Ambassadors include only three—Butterworth, MacArthur, and Riddleberger—who have spent most of their service in Europe, and all three have had extensive European experience in a new field, that of multilateral affairs. There are three Soviet experts, Bohlen, Kohler, and Thompson, two Near Eastern experts, Hare and Allen, and one Far Eastern expert, Johnson.

The Career Ambassadors also have had unconventional experiences in serving in roles of leadership and management in the enlarged foreign affairs establishment generated by that transition from isolationism to involvement. The *sine qua non* of becoming a Career Ambassador in the conventional career is service abroad as a Chief of Mission; all nine Career Ambassadors have had that experience, most of them a number of times. Additionally, they all have had the relatively unusual experience of serving in a variety of leadership roles in Washington, in many cases very early in the postwar era. Butterworth was an Assistant Secretary as early as 1949, and Hare served several times at the Deputy Assistant Secretary level in the late 1940s. In 1960, he was Deputy Under Secretary for Political Affairs, the position occupied by Johnson in 1966. Allen was twice head of the information program, in the late 1940s when it was part of the Department of State and in the late 1950s when it was the U.S. Information Agency. Riddleberger was head of the foreign aid program from 1959 to 1961 when it was known as the International Cooperation Administration. Kohler was at one time chief of the Voice of America.

Another indication of who might comprise the elite nucleus in the Foreign Service can be found in the results of an SDP question that asked respondents to write in the names of three persons whom they regarded as "ideal" FSOs. Altogether, 1,628 nominations were received, mentioning more than 150 names. The 15 officers receiving the most votes accounted for nearly half the total cast.

TABLE 51

15 Top-ranked Officers in SDP Survey

Rank	Name	Votes	Rank	Name	Votes
1	Charles Bohlen*	128	9	Julius Holmes*	30
2	Robert Murphy*	96	10	Livingston Merchant*	28
3	U. Alexis Johnson	83	11	Loy Henderson*	28
4	George Kennan*	74	12	Joseph Palmer	27
5	Foy Kohler*	47	13	Raymond Hare*	26
6	Llewellyn Thompson	46	14	Charles Yost*	25
7	Ellis Briggs*	34	15	Fulton Freeman	19
8	Thomas Mann*	33			

* Now retired.

All of these men have had experiences comparable to those of the Career Ambassadors. In fact, four of the Career Ambassadors are on the list and most of the retired officers had achieved that rank. An interesting point is that of the first six names on the list, four are Soviet experts—Bohlen, Kennan, Kohler, and Thompson. Kennan, of course, is famous for his "Mr. X" article which outlined the postwar containment policy.

Perhaps the most unconventional was Murphy who, as

a troubleshooting envoy during World War II, made his reputation by becoming the Foreign Service's first political-military specialist.[11] He subsequently served as Under Secretary of State for Political Affairs.

Mann, a Latin American specialist, was Under Secretary of State for Economic Affairs when he retired. Merchant served as Under Secretary for Political Affairs and on two occasions as Assistant Secretary for European Affairs. Henderson was Deputy Under Secretary for Administration when he retired. Palmer, formerly Director General of the Foreign Service, became Assistant Secretary of State for African Affairs. Yost made most of his career at the U.S. Mission to the United Nations, and Freeman served as Ambassador to Mexico.

Like the nuclear elite in Janowitz' analysis, most of the 15 top-ranked officers have displayed ability to perform multiple roles, to adapt to new situations in their career experience. Janowitz points to a trend away from the "heroic leader" to the "managerial generalist" concerned with new weapons systems and the development of political skills. Such a shift has not as yet become apparent in the nuclear elite of the Foreign Service. The counterpart to the "heroic leader" in the Foreign Service would be the highly successful diplomat—the policy-maker, negotiator, area specialist, the officer who spends much of his career going from one ambassadorship to another. Very few of the top 15—probably only Palmer and Freeman—have achieved any measure of reputation of being specifically interested in modern management techniques.

[11] The wartime experience is described in Murphy's book, *Diplomat Among Warriors* (New York: Doubleday and Co., 1964).

PART III
CONCLUSION

CHAPTER 9

A MANAGERIAL STRATEGY

FOR THE FUTURE

....

IN INTELLECTUAL and political terms, the Foreign Service Officers of the United States adapted very well to the changed circumstances of American foreign affairs that occurred as a result of World War II. They had little difficulty making the transition from isolationism to internationalism; indeed, in many respects, they led the way.

These same changes, however, have generated other challenges to the FSOs as a professional group, challenges which are confronting many professional groups in a world of rapid change. The FSOs have made significant progress in meeting only one of them—the challenge of egalitarianism. Still an elite of talent, the FSO corps is no longer an elite of fortunate birth and means. It has become an avenue of upward mobility for persons from all regions and levels of American society except for Negroes. This last is explained not by any systematic pattern of discrimination, but by much larger and deeper problems of American society as a whole.

Of two other challenges—the exponential growth of knowledge impinging on the substance of foreign affairs and the problem of managing the variegated and semi-chaotic range of activities in foreign affairs—the first has received inadequate recognition and the second has been recognized but inadequately met. From the Janowitz study, it can be seen that the military has made vastly more prog-

Conclusion

ress in dealing with such challenges than the Foreign Service. There are many reasons for this unequal progress—the differences in the two cultures, the much greater resources at the disposal of the Pentagon, the fact that the military profession is largely technology-based. New technology may be resisted for a time, but it is much more likely that the cost of lagging behind in new technology will be visible for the military than will be the cost of lagging behind new knowledge in the social sciences for the Department of State and the FSO corps.

Insofar as new knowledge has been manifested in new functions, adaptive behavior has varied on the part of the Department of State and the FSO corps. There has been increasing acceptance of the concept of specialization in recent years, and a small number of new functional areas has been adjudged legitimate for the FSO corps—political-military affairs, international organization affairs, some specialized fields in economic affairs. However, the major new functions such as information and development assistance have gone to other agencies, and the FSO corps has resisted legitimizing them in terms of adoption by the professional group. FSOs may serve in these functions from time to time and the new USIA recruits are coming in as FSOs, but FSOs have opposed fully taking over these functions as part of the career system.

Speaking of new knowledge in the sense of social science research, applying the results of research, and building bridges to the academic community, the discussion in Chapter 3 made it clear that the State Department and the FSO corps are lagging seriously.

Given this climate, the challenge of the knowledge explosion for the FSO corps becomes part of the challenge of management. In part, this is true for all professional groups, whether they themselves are creating new knowl-

324

edge which contains the seeds of their own change, or, like the FSO corps, they are confronted with potential and actual new knowledge developed elsewhere. Coping with new knowledge in an applied way for social purposes increasingly requires organization, and organization requires management. Management is needed to find resources to support research, to make decisions so that research will be relevant, to create conditions that will favor wise application of research findings, to coordinate specializations that result from new knowledge, to find talent capable of these tasks, to provide ancillary services. This is seen even in medicine, where one of the familiar solutions to the crisis in the profession is to call for teams of salaried specialists operating in comprehensive health centers to replace solo, fee-for-service practice.[1]

This study has shown that the management challenge was virtually forced on the State Department and the Foreign Service. For 15 years the Department and the Service both acted as if the problem did not exist, and rationalized this attitude in the policy-operations dichotomy. Then the challenge was posed directly and bluntly in the dissolution of the OCB, the Kennedy letter, the Herter Report, NSAM 341, and the Country Director reorganization.

The result is that the Department of State and the profession of diplomacy, as practiced by Americans, face a crisis, the general nature of which has been expressed by Mosher: "The failure of a career system to accommodate to growing knowledge and changing requirements—to redefine its self-image and take steps to give reality to a new one—may lead to a slow and agonizing decline in its control over and its influence upon the arena in which it

[1] See, for example, Selig Greenberg's argument in *The Troubled Calling: Crisis in the Medical Establishment* (New York: Macmillan, 1965).

Conclusion

operates."[2] In specific terms, the crisis appears within the FSO corps as the dilemma: if the FSO corps *does not* change adequately to fulfill the new role, there is fear that the Service will gradually lose its appointed central place in foreign affairs; if it *does* change to fulfill the new role, cherished assumptions and traditions might be endangered and the Service might lose its distinctive character as a career system and elite group.

There are two other possible responses, one denying the validity of the crisis, the other appearing to hold that actions can be taken and events might conspire to make the crisis disappear. The first amounts to a view that the classic practice of diplomacy is still the right answer and that those who pose a management challenge to the FSO corps are simply wrong. For the most part, this sums up the views of some of the elders of the FSO corps cited in Chapter 1. It is a view held by several journalists who have come to the defense of the corps. Stewart Alsop and Nathaniel Mc-Kittrick blame the "administrators" for the troubles of the Service and Clayton Fritchey blames the "politicians."[3]

The other line of argument runs something like this: "The world is not the same as it was ten years ago, the cold war is unfreezing, there are increasing possibilities for a detente with the Soviet Union, the Chinese are less of a threat. The United States has too many people and programs abroad. We are too interventionist and should cut back drastically. Already the aid program is beginning to dwindle." A neo-isolationist version of this viewpoint is expressed in a recent book by Edmund Stillman and Wil-

[2] Frederick C. Mosher, *Democracy and the Public Service* (New York: Oxford University Press, 1968), p. 160.
[3] Stewart Alsop, "Let the Poor Old Foreign Service Alone," *Saturday Evening Post*, Mar. 11, 1967, p. 14; Nathaniel McKittrick, "Diplomatic Logjam: Esprit Without a Corps at the Department of State," *New Republic*, Mar. 27, 1965, pp. 8-11; Clayton Fritchey, "The Politicians Versus the Foreign Service," *Harper's*, Jan. 1967, pp. 90-94.

liam Pfaff.[4] A variant which accepts much of the argument, but not the conclusions, holds that many of the activities of the U.S. government could devolve to private interests or international organizations. Eugene Black, whose interest is in freeing development assistance from political influence to the maximum extent feasible, is an exponent of this view.[5] The logical conclusion is that by the time the FSO corps gears up to manage foreign affairs, there might not be much left to manage.

Much of this line of thought emerges from the changing conditions in the mid-1960s discussed in Chapter 1 in connection with the question of a "fifth phase" of postwar American foreign policy. Obviously it is too early to attempt to assess these changing conditions definitively; they are in flux now and probably will continue so for some time to come, before a clear direction emerges. One could imagine a series of catastrophic events that would polarize the situation toward the one extreme of major war or the other extreme of radical American retrenchment, even so far as to a "Fortress America" concept. Obviously either eventuality would eliminate any problem for the Department of State and the FSO corps of coordinating and managing a variety of complex programs in foreign countries.

In the absence of either eventuality, the changing conditions of the "fifth phase" will in all likelihood make the existing managerial problem more difficult and complex, rather than less so.

[4] Stillman and Pfaff, *Power and Impotence: The Futility of America's Foreign Policy* (New York: Random House, 1966).

[5] Black argued for a "separate status" for economic development as an end in itself, in his book, *The Diplomacy of Development* (Cambridge: Harvard University Press, 1960). In a commencement address at Wellesley College, May 3, 1966, Black made a plea for a cutback of official presence, more activity by corporations, universities, and foundations, and the freeing of the diplomat from duties as a manager and administrator so that he could concentrate on the classic art of diplomacy.

Conclusion

The responsibilities of the United States as a world power will not decrease, but its ability to influence directly the course of events in other countries assuredly *will* decrease. International power will become more diffused, sophistication in modern weaponry will increase, revolutionary conditions will intensify, the development gap will grow, and the problems of development will multiply in complexity. The foreign affairs agencies are finding much greater competition for national resources for their programs than heretofore.

All of these conditions, and others, will heighten rather than lessen the need for much improved coordination and management of the American foreign affairs effort. This position is clearly articulated in the interim report of the 1967 Committee on Career Principles of the American Foreign Service Association, discussed in Chapter 7.

These two points of view could be debated at length. Here they can only be treated summarily. The first—that the managerial crisis is spurious—ignores the clear message coming from the White House on what is expected of the State Department and the FSO corps. It amounts to surrendering to the first horn of the dilemma—the gradual erosion of the central position of the FSO corps. The second position is based on a number of persuasive points, but essentially on the truism that the world is getting to be more complex. The argument can be rested here with the observation that this is not likely to make the foreign affairs of the United States less complex. And it is a persuasive thesis that the complexity of foreign affairs will grow at least in pace with any devolvement of activities to the private sector.

Eugene Black and others are certainly correct when they argue that United Nations development assistance activities should be increased and that there should be much more imagination and innovation in the private sector in regard to overseas development. But this need not and should not occur at the expense of any diminution of U.S. government activities in development assistance.

There does not appear to be any realistic escape from the crisis, a view the leadership of the State Department and majority opinion in the FSO corps seem to share. The full meaning of the crisis is that more clearly than ever before the organizational effectiveness of the Department of State and the viability of the FSO career system are on the line.

This is highlighted in some strong hints that have been thrown out in recent years. Recall for a moment Richard Neustadt's words to the Jackson Subcommittee in 1963, cited in Chapter 3, to the effect that the State Department had not lived up to the new role and should be allowed a reasonable time to do so. In his address to the American Foreign Service Association in 1966, Gen. Taylor said that he saw NSAM 341 as a "tremendous challenge to the Foreign Service and the Department of State," which "should be given a thorough trial." He concluded:

> But it means that State has to perform up to the challenge. You will have to put your best players into the key slots for, in due course, I am sure there will be a review made of what has been accomplished under this system. If, as I hope, performance justifies the concentration of responsibility and authority in State, we are on the right track and a longstanding deficiency in our Federal system has been corrected. It not, the only answer will be to review the decision and find another solution.[6]

In their diagnosis and proposal, discussed in Chapter 7, the six mid-career officers expressed their deep concern "lest

---

[6] Jackson Subcommittee, "The Secretary of State and the Problem of Coordination: New Duties and Procedures of March 4, 1966," p. 23.

the Department of State and the Foreign Service forfeit the opportunities for service implicit in" NSAM 341. Columnist Joseph Kraft is dubious about the possibilities for success: "The point, of course, is that an organizational arrangement is not better than the people in it. Asserting the primacy of the State Department cannot be accomplished by fiat. There must be changes of attitude and of people. And if the changes are not forthcoming, then the coordinating function will slip back to the White House."[7]

One also is reminded of Arthur Schlesinger's story that President Kennedy "used to divert himself with the dream of establishing a secret office of thirty people or so to run foreign policy while maintaining the State Department as a facade in which people might contentedly carry papers from bureau to bureau."[8]

The seriousness of the crisis is perhaps no better illustrated than by the ferment within the FSO ranks. There are powerful forces which mitigate against such a ferment happening—the rigidities of the system, the organizational scatter and transiency of FSOs, the pressures for conformity, the high prestige of the diplomatic profession, the widespread ambivalences and feelings of impotence in respect to the system. All of this makes the ferment truly remarkable and portentous. One suspects that if it is met with only halfway measures, the FSO corps will soon begin to exhibit more visibly the classic signs of the declining professional group, the first of which will be an increasing flight of talent at the junior ranks.

In few quarters does there seem to be any appreciation of the magnitude of the change that has been demanded and what it will take to accomplish it. This point has al-

[7] *Washington Post*, Apr. 12, 1966.
[8] Arthur Schlesinger, Jr., *A Thousand Days: John F. Kennedy in the White House* (Boston: Houghton Mifflin, 1965), p. 433.

ready been discussed in respect to the White House, the Secretary of State, and the elders of the FSO corps. There has been a spate of articles on the troubles of the State Department and the Foreign Service. Although here and there the journalists make excellent points, typically they treat only part of the problem. The general utility of these journalistic observations is suggested by comparing two of the articles' titles: "Let the Poor Old Foreign Service Alone" (Stewart Alsop), and "Let's Shake Up the State Department" (Jack Anderson in *Parade Magazine*, April 2, 1967). Among the useful diagnoses are Joseph Kraft on the pathological aspects of the FSO career system, and Smith Simpson on the managerial void at the top of the State Department.[9] The useful ideas are John Diebold on a positive approach to research and technology, and Anderson and William Attwood on the need for larger appropriations for State.[10]

The major theme in most of the commentary, however, is that there is too much paperwork and too many people. The danger is that this may result in severe pressure on the State Department to treat these symptoms while the causes are largely ignored, a very real danger since treating symptoms generally is much simpler in a bureaucracy than dealing with causes. A purge of the senior ranks in the State Department and other such measures would be severely dysfunctional, in that it would reconfirm all of the pathological aspects of the system instead of confronting them and deal-

[9] Kraft's overstated attack on "intellectual torpor, over-formality, and duplication of effort" as the price to be paid for a career service" appears in the *Washington Post*, Sept. 30, 1966. Smith Simpson's devastating critique, "Who Runs the State Department?" appears in *The Nation*, Mar. 6, 1967.

[10] Diebold, "Computers, Program Management, and Foreign Affairs," *Foreign Affairs*, Oct. 1966, pp. 125-34; William Attwood, "The Labyrinth in Foggy Bottom," *Atlantic Monthly*, Feb. 1967, pp. 45-50.

ing with them in a positive way. Already, the forced 10 percent cut mentioned in Chapter 3 threatens to have this deleterious effect.

Altogether, the analyses throughout this study strongly suggest that a comprehensive managerial strategy will be required to meet the crisis, to change the Foreign Service system so that it will fulfill the requirements of the new diplomacy and to change the Department of State so that it will fulfill its management role in foreign affairs. Without such a strategy, the likelihood is that one or more of the following will occur: (1) symptoms instead of basic problems will be treated, (2) change efforts will become dissipated on details or piecemeal reforms, (3) the belief will be generated that the challenge can be met by a single stroke—such as a reorganization or a programming system, (4) a new study commission will be formed.

From the foregoing chapters the major elements of a managerial strategy can be derived. These will be presented, followed by a discussion of the total strategy, of the more controversial elements, and a concluding prognosis. The major elements are:

1. The *installation of a sustaining manager* at the top echelons of the Department of State, no lower than the third-ranking position.

2. A *redefinition of the profession of diplomacy*, preferably generated within the FSO corps, assigning balanced and major roles to the traditional diplomatic arts, managerial skills, and functional specialties.

3. A *merger of State, USIA, and AID*, not simply to create a triad organization, but with full integration in the geographic areas around the Country Directors.

4. The legitimizing of the major new functions in foreign affairs by *extending the career system* to include professional-level employees of USIA and AID as a major element

in creation of a comprehensive and unified foreign affairs personnel system.

5. Activation of an *integrated foreign affairs planning-programming-budgeting system* with major emphasis and first priority on its use as a management control system at the SIG, IRG, Ambassadorial, and Country Director levels.

6. Creation of a major *research and development* capability, including new technology (i.e., information management system), social science research, and the study of organizational effectiveness (i.e., a sophisticated case study program on crisis management).

7. An *organizational development program* which applies the behavioral sciences to the actual workings of the organization, concentrates on the processes of change and coordination, and proposes system and organizational improvements.

8. Ending the chronic undernourishment of the State Department by *adequate financing* of these measures in a "leadership budget" that would increase the Department's annual appropriation by at least as much as $50 million.

The closest the Department of State has come to a managerial strategy of this kind was the Crockett strategy outlined in Chapter 3. Four of the elements listed above were present in the Crockett program. The additional elements (1, 2, 3, and 8) are designed to overcome the severe handicaps under which the Crockett program labored—the lack of a strong, concerned managerial focal point above the top administrative position of the Department; the lack of understanding and commitment within the FSO corps to the change strategy; the artificial barriers of a multi-agency situation; and seriously inadequate financing.

A great many elements could be added to the eight listed in the managerial strategy above, and many of them would not be minor points (training, recruitment, promotion, and

Conclusion

so on). The problem is to distinguish the fundamental efforts of a managerial strategy, without which the major goals cannot be attained, from the secondary elements which, though not unimportant, are best addressed within the context of a coherent strategy. Without a coherent strategy, change efforts in the secondary areas are likely to be essentially unguided tinkerings; with a strategy, change in the secondary areas will tend to fall much more naturally into place.

Several of the elements of the managerial strategy require some explication in depth at this time, with only brief and subsequent comment for the remaining ones.

The Sustaining Manager

Nothing is clearer about the troubles of the Department of State—and, it might be said, of the FSO corps—than that a major role is missing, that of "sustaining manager."[11] Previously the point was discussed, that no man has ever come into the position of Secretary of State or Under Secretary with a management orientation. Many observers feel that probably the wisest course is to accept the view that neither officer should be expected to play a managerial role, given the other roles they must fulfill and the frequency of foreign policy crises. This was one of the premises on which the Herter Committee based its proposal for an Executive Under Secretary of State as No. 3 man. Nothing has happened since 1962 to indicate that the Committee was wrong.

However, NSAM 341 heightened the image of the Under Secretary for the managerial role by designating him as Executive Chairman of the SIG. Leaving aside the question of the *permanence* of the sustaining manager, which was

11 I am indebted to Charles K. Ferguson of UCLA for the term "sustaining manager," and for some of the ideas in this section.

334

an important consideration in the internal debates of the Herter Committee, the problem comes down to the personalities involved—who the top men are, what kind of experience they have had, how well they understand the managerial problem, and how strongly they are disposed to act. There would be wide consensus in support of Dean Acheson's view that the Secretary of State cannot play the managerial role, but it is certainly conceivable that given the right individuals, a division of labor could be worked out so that the Under Secretary could fulfill the managerial need in an energetic and fulltime way. But it would not work unless he had the full understanding and unflinching support of the Secretary.

Whether the Under Secretary or a new Executive Under Secretary takes the lead, the need is for a man able to develop a managerial strategy such as is outlined here, and able to build support for that strategy. He must possess sufficient status and power to exert a strong influence throughout the foreign affairs community and be able to assemble the relevant people to focus on issues. The important point is that the sustaining manager must come into the organization with change goals and a strategy for attaining them, since it can be anticipated that there will be built-in opposition to some of the needed measures. Moreover, only a firmly-held and comprehensive approach will be able to counter the problem of low visibility of some of the needs, as for example, in the area of research.

The difficulty is that the *cost* of the absence of this role is *not* fully seen by the White House, by the political leadership of the State Department, and quite possibly by most FSOs. The problems—the need for a sustaining manager and the cost of the absence of one—are by no means limited to the Department of State among Federal agencies. But the problems are perhaps more crucial for State since

Conclusion

it has been assigned the catalytic and coordinative role in a multi-agency sector of the federal government. The question might well be, if the State Department cannot manage itself, how can it be expected to manage an interagency complex?

A Redefinition of the Profession

The call for a redefinition of the profession is the only one of the eight elements of the managerial strategy that is somewhat at the hortatory level. Yet it is crucial, and if it does not happen, the FSO corps and Department of State will become even less central to foreign affairs decision-making than now. Also, as we have seen in some detail, the redefining of the profession may already be underway with the corps.

Janowitz depicts three ideal types in the military—the heroic leader, the manager, and the technologist. There is need in the FSO corps for a triumvirate that is at least roughly analogous—the diplomat, the manager, and the specialist. All three are vital, so that measures must be taken to assure that all three are nourished and that there is a viable balance between them. There can be no room for a yes-but syndrome. On the contrary, the need will be to concentrate on weaknesses instead of strength. The strengths currently lie in the diplomatic skills; the major weakness is in managerial skills and outlook. Functional specialization is a long way from full development, yet it is accepted and considerable progress has been made in recent years. There is no single career pattern that will produce high competence in any of the three major areas. Officers may perform in all three at different points in their careers, and may fulfill several of the roles simultaneously.

The managerial challenge is a unique one for the FSO corps. As Mosher has indicated, all professional groups are confronted with a managerial challenge. Yet one suspects that few—not yet at least—are being called on to adopt a managerial concept in a large-scale way as a central element of the substance of the profession. The challenge is a difficult one. Professional groups tend to look on management needs as alien and diversionary, a kind of necessary evil at best.

Mosher points out that "career systems customarily derogate the word and the practice of administration," and that their accommodation to the growing importance of management has been "grudging and slow." He outlines the typical responses:[12]

1. Separation, specialization, and demeaning of "administration," distinct from "substance."

2. Establishing what amounts to a "two-track" channel within the career system, one occupying executive and managerial posts, the others engaged with the substantive work of the system.

3. Bringing in "experts" in managerial fields but in sub-career systems or in the general service, but maintaining direction and control by system members over their activities.

4. Introducing general social and managerial considerations into the system itself—in education, selection, training, assignments, etc.; this seems usually to be a last resort.

All of this has happened or is happening within the FSO corps except the second, and that has been proposed (see Chapter 7). On the last, which is barely beginning, depends the viability of the redefinition of the profession.

Curiously, many of the social scientists who have studied the professions have not encouraged positive, adaptive behavior toward the management problem. They appear, in

[12] Mosher, *Democracy and the Public Service*, pp. 161-62.

Conclusion

fact, to identify with the bias of the professionals. For example, Myron Lieberman discusses the issue as follows:

In industry, government, and to some extent in the professions, those who conduct the research or practice the profession are typically at the mercy of those who work at the task of acquiring power. The gradual but unmistakable trend in all the professions is toward public employment and group practice. As the tendency for the professional worker to become a salaried employee has increased, so also has the tendency for the professions to become dominated by administrators rather than practitioner personnel.[13]

Robert K. Merton speaks of a "rationalized abdication of social responsibility in favor of the administrator" as a result of the "intensified division of labor" that characterizes modern society.[14] Roy Lewis and Angus Meade view the problem as a "dilemma confronting almost every profession . . . whether its members shall concentrate on 'strictly professional' work and lose their power to direct it, or learn administration so as to be able to remain in control of it, thus losing the time to practice it."[15]

Perhaps this stance is not so curious, since the social scientists themselves are professionals. Mosher sheds some light on this thought by recounting that at the University of California the fiery student leader Mario Savio "did not arouse much argument from the professors when he asserted that the job of administration was to keep the sidewalks clean."[16]

[13] Myron Lieberman, *Education as a Profession* (Englewood Cliffs: Prentice-Hall, 1965) , p. 484.

[14] Robert K. Merton, "The Machine, the Worker, and the Engineer," in S. Nosow and W. H. Form, eds., *Man, Work, and Society* (New York: Basic Books, 1962) , pp. 86-87.

[15] Roy Lewis and Angus Meade, *Professional Persons in England* (Cambridge: Harvard University Press, 1953) , p. 7.

[16] Mosher, *Democracy and the Public Service*, p. 161.

338

A Managerial Strategy for the Future

Something is askew here. Instead of reinforcing the view of many professionals that management is an evil force to be contested, precisely the opposite point of view would seem to make more sense. If practitioner personnel are going to "dominate" their professions, they will have to *manage* them. Good management is becoming more and more important in order to multiply the resources of the professions to deal more effectively with larger and more complex problems for social purposes. There is no evidence to support the view that management and professional practice are necessarily mutually exclusive. Moreover, a positive approach to management in professional life can do much to mitigate against "hidden hierarchies" and favor democratic accountability. This sort of approach has important implications for higher education, for the continuing education of professional people, for the viability of the professions in a situation of growing complexity, and for social needs. Instead of finding a whipping boy in the vague appellation "the administrators," the professionals and students of the professions alike might be better advised to give some attention to the difficult question of how managerial talent can be developed with sufficient knowledge of the given profession and yet with a vision that rises above the special interest.

Re-defining a profession is extremely difficult because of the weight of inertia, of tradition, of comfortable association with the known, and fear that one might be lacking in the skills implicit in the new definition. And yet it is crucial that there be genuine involvement and commitment among at least substantial segments of the professional group to the new approach.

Merger of State, AID, and USIA

The proposal to merge State, AID, and USIA is included in the strategy with some reluctance, since there is a tendency to see a major reorganization as a panacea, whereas in fact it usually represents only a beginning toward effective change and can become counterproductive unless associated with other change efforts. The time has probably come in which there are many more reasons in favor of a merger of State, AID, and USIA than against it. In fact, a strong case can now be made that such a merger is indispensable to truly effective change in the foreign affairs community.

One essential condition is that the main feature of the merger be the integration of the geographic units of the three agencies, much as the Latin American components of AID and State have been merged under the Alliance for Progress. This strengthening of the Country Director-IRG geographic line would make the idea of a Country Team approach in Washington viable; in a sense it represents unfinished business left over from the Hoover Commission of 1949 which recommended that geography be the main organizing principle of the Department of State. These three agencies are the principal foreign affairs agencies; this sort of merger would provide a basis for improved coordination of their activities and added weight in coordinating other activities that for a variety of reasons cannot be merged. It would provide true executive content to the Country Director position. These are precisely the advantages that would not accrue to the triumvirate kind of structure proposed by several sources in the 1950s (see Chapter 3), which in actuality would be little different from the present situation.

The information program formerly was located within the State Department, and the foreign aid program has been in and out several times; at present it technically is a part of State. But when located within State, the information and aid programs have remained separate, large, identifiable bureaucracies. Little purpose is served by shifting the organizational location unless there is a genuine merger and reorganization along the geographic dimension. The merger of State and AID personnel in the Latin American bureau under the Alliance for Progress points the way.

There is, of course, a substantial difference between USIA and AID, with respect to the trauma that would attend a merger with State. No merger of this scale could be painless, but the pain would be relatively minor in the case of USIA, which, it can be said, has been preparing itself in a number of ways for just such a merger over about the past 10 years. AID presents a different story. There is a widespread notion that State has a political bias, that AID has an economic bias, and that the two do not mix very well. This is reflected, for example, in President Kennedy's letter to Congress of May 26, 1961, transmitting the bill that created AID: "Economic development assistance can no longer be subordinated to, or viewed simply as a tool for meeting, short-term political objectives." Given the realities of the situation—who has the large appropriations and who has not, and in what direction any merger would occur—the view that economics would lose out to political considerations is naturally held much more strongly by AID officers than by State officers. This is a fascinating subject for further investigation, but it cannot be pursued here; there is room only for blunt opinion. In my opinion, this belief, while not totally devoid of any meaning, is vastly overrated, and worse, is severely dysfunctional. It may have had substance in the early days of foreign aid, but it has little now and would have even less if the other elements of the managerial strategy proposed here were adopted. As discussed several times in this book, the economic function has become extremely important within the FSO corps. A merger would bring the AID economists into State. FSO

341

political officers are rarely Machiavellian types obsessed only with short-term political gain; they are quite capable of balancing political and economic considerations. Moreover, decisions are not made monolithically within State, as if no one were watching; there is often great soul-searching, debate, and the bringing to bear of many points of view. Hardly any important foreign policy decision can be made without deep attention to both political and economic considerations. Keeping the two rigidly separated is a very high price to pay for fear of the possibility that one may systematically dominate the other. Separation creates more problems than it solves. It amounts to ducking the issue rather than confronting it, and reflects a primitive notion of how effective decision-making and collaboration can be achieved in a large organization.

A necessary corollary of the merger would be the break-up of the large functional components already within the State Department, which are themselves organized internally on a geographic basis. The two most prominent ones are the Bureau of Cultural Affairs and the Bureau of Intelligence and Research. Their geographic units should be merged into the geographic bureaus. There would then be a need for much smaller, highly professional, backstopping units for each of the major functions, similar to the units originally envisioned by the Hoover Commission. There would be small, central backstopping units corresponding to the media divisions of USIA, the functional units of AID, and the nongeographic units in the cultural and intelligence areas. Finally, for the sake of visibility and a counterbalancing effect, there is a need for high-level representation for the information and development assistance fields in the Department, just as there is a Deputy Under Secretary for Political Affairs, in an executive team concept.

The other essential condition to the merger would be

the reconstitution of the personnel system which is the next topic to be discussed. This is necessary, among other reasons, to overcome the aura of second-class citizenship and the stereotypes that now exist and which would be worsened if there were to be a merger without a corresponding change in the personnel system; in fact, one of the benefits of the merger would be that it would make even more obvious the need to change the personnel system.

A Foreign Affairs Personnel System

The crucial need in terms of the personnel systems in foreign affairs is to extend the career category (the FSO category) to cover the information and aid functions. This would legitimize the two functions, greatly enrich the career category, do much to solve the problem of executive development, and strengthen the basic position of the three primary foreign affairs agencies (of the State Department if the merger occurs) in dealing with the rest of the foreign affairs community.

This, of course, would mean a large-scale integration, bringing at least 700 USIA officers and probably as many AID officers into FSO status. The persons to be brought in should be those who intend to make a career in foreign affairs, who are performing work at a professional level within the purview of a redefined profession of diplomacy, and who meet certain minimum qualifications. Included from AID would be managerial, administrative, and program personnel at a professional level, as well as specialists in the various technical fields who perform program planning and managerial functions in respect to their technical fields. In other words, technicians per se would not be made FSOs. This is congruent with the trend in AID to obtain technical skills on a contract basis. Therefore, any guess of the number of AID persons to be taken in would be highly tentative, and the exact intake would require a good deal of thought and study. Integration should not, however, be done on a piecemeal basis.

Strong opposition to any such personnel integration is to be expected. Understanding of the basic reasons for the opposition can do much to help ameliorate it to the level where the integration can take place successfully. The denial of professional legitimization of two very large and important functional areas in foreign affairs is a problem that many people have lived with for a long time. It is difficult for them to back away far enough to see how ludicrous the present situation is: a highly-touted career system in which a large proportion of the members, probably more than half, are performing routine and subprofessional jobs, while two large, important, exciting, functional areas are kept at arm's length in second-class status. There is a deep-seated fear on the part of most FSOs of large-scale integration plans born out of the Wriston experience. Many would tend to see integration of AID and USIA officers as just another step in a long-term effort to destroy the FSO corps; they would think further large-scale integrations inevitable.

The analysis of the Wriston program in Chapter 4 is instructive in this regard. To some extent, it reached laterally *within the State Department* to bring into FSO status persons functioning at a professional level. It also reached vertically to integrate persons functioning in subprofessional jobs. The Wriston program found most of its successes in the first case. For example, the Wristonees now serving as executives came mainly from those who were qualified at a professional level before integration. By and large, the failures came because the program reached too deep vertically, and much effort has gone into correcting this overreaching of the program. In other words, the Wriston program dipped down to bring subprofessional jobs

344

into the purview of the professional group, but failed to reach out laterally to the information and aid programs to bring in relevant professional jobs.[17]

The resulting situation is that the wrong kind of integration program has frightened people away from the right kind of integration program.

Legitimizing the aid and information functions would rectify a long-standing wrong. It was not brought out sufficiently in the Hays Bill hearings that many hundreds of dedicated persons in USIA and AID have continued to perform for a long time under conditions of second-class citizenship, including very uncertain tenure.

Righting a wrong, however, is not the major objective of the integration proposal; it is to create conditions that will work toward improved over-all performance in the future. In this regard, integration would do more for the FSO corps than it would for the personnel of USIA and AID. It would open up more responsible, operational jobs for young FSOs, thereby favoring executive development; broadened opportunities would present a more attractive picture for the potential recruit; and conditions for cross-functional collaboration would be improved by cutting away some of the breeding ground for stereotypes.

The fact that Congress created a career personnel category for USIA in 1968 certainly does much to alleviate that agency's personnel problems, but does little to solve the overall problem. For one thing, there appears to be little chance that Congress will ever pass similar legislation for AID so that the situation is still disjointed with two of the three primary foreign affairs agencies having career systems

[17] It should be made clear that the fault, if any, for this failure of the Wriston program should not be attributed to Dr. Wriston and his committee, but to the leadership of the State Department in 1954, which gave the Wriston Committee very limited terms of reference and a short time in which to finish its work.

and the third lacking one. Even were it possible to achieve a career system for AID, the end result would be a kind of *apartheid* structure, an unnecessarily elaborate one which would fall short of the professed ideal of a single Foreign Service of the United States. Integration of the major foreign affairs functions as envisioned here would not be as well served by separate categories as by a single service.

There is a strong tendency (see Chapter 7) for FSOs to come up with good diagnoses of the challenges confronting the corps, but to propose elitist solutions—a two-track system, a three-track system, some form of managerial elite. The difficulty is that these models are based on an essentially negative concept of eliteness in the sense of drawing narrow boundaries around a relatively small group, taking on a defensive attitude, and ascribing eliteness to that group on the basis of function and status. Since one major purpose of change is to improve the possibilities for developing executive talent, a positive approach to eliteness would seem to make more sense. This would imply a relatively open system, with achievement as the basis for eliteness rather than ascription. Since no one has ever demonstrated that there is a single best way to develop executive talent, a broader base that would embrace all the relevant functions would seem to offer the best chance of maximizing opportunities to develop superior talent through continuous sifting and competition. Much is made of competition within the present FSO system; if FSOs are truly an elite, they have little to fear from a broader competitive framework. In contrast, a model based on a negative approach to elitism is a sterile and atavistic response to a modern challenge, one that is almost certainly doomed to failure.

Integration of AID and USIA personnel into the FSO corps should be carried out within the framework of a unified foreign affairs personnel system, such as would have been made possible by the Hays Bill or something very similar. The existence of the Civil Service and Foreign Service systems in the same agencies is a timeworn problem which should be overcome once and for all. Even the category system may be outdated.

Consider, for example, the situation of the British Foreign Service. Following the Plowden Report of 1964 the Foreign Service and Commonwealth Relations Service were merged to create the newly named H.M. Diplomatic Service.[18] In several ways it is in contrast to the American situation: there is no split between domestic and foreign service employees—all are members of the same system; there are no additional foreign services—all functions, including development assistance and information, are performed or managed by members of the Diplomatic Service; and there is a single grade system with such categories as Branch A (equivalent to FSO) and Branch B (equivalent to FSS), abolished although distinctions are maintained internally in terms of entry points, entrance examinations, and promotion streams.[19] If the British, with their conservative and very traditional image, are able to make such changes, one wonders why the experimental and pragmatic Americans are unable to do so.

The abandonment of categories would very likely be regarded by FSOs as a death blow to the elitist concept, as tantamount to the realization of their long-standing fear

[18] For a more complete discussion of the British situation see John E. Harr, "Some Observations on H.M. Diplomatic Service," *Foreign Service Journal*, Aug. 1967, p. 24.

[19] The Diplomatic Service has adopted for internal purposes the Administrative Class and Executive Class categories of the Home Civil Service, but even these may be abolished (for both the Home and Foreign Services) by the recommendations of a new commission (the Fulton Commission) which is studying the Home Service.

347

Conclusion

of simply being taken over by the Civil Service. Yet this does not necessarily follow. One can envision a single foreign affairs personnel system without rigid categories, which would be separate and distinct from the Civil Service system, retaining such important characteristics as rank-in-the-man, higher salary schedule, allowances, selection-out, and others. In a best-man-for-the-job system the FSO-type, with his superior education and qualifications, would do just as well as he does now without benefit of invidious labels. Such an approach would be fully congruent with a concept of elitism by achievement rather than by ascription.

Remaining Elements of the Strategy

The four remaining elements of the managerial strategy need not be explored in depth here, but each is critical to the general success of the change program and to fulfillment of a leadership role in foreign affairs. Without a comprehensive data base and a well-conceived programming system, State has no hope of overcoming the present divisive mechanics of government process to create an integrated, systematic flow of planning, programming, and execution. The knowledge explosion is not only a pressing challenge, but offers a priceless opportunity for leadership as well. A large-scale, effective entry into social science research by the Department of State would place it at the nexus of progressive, innovative thinking in foreign affairs. Because of the magnitude and nature of change that is contemplated in this approach and that is being expected of the State Department and the Foreign Service, an organizational development program becomes a valuable tool in building involvement in and understanding of change, in drawing attention to the processes of change as well as to the substance. Some of the ways that an ACORD program could

348

A Managerial Strategy for the Future

be useful in an over-all strategy for change are described by Chris Argyris at the conclusion of his study.[20]

Finally, it will all cost money, particularly the entry into social science research on a meaningful scale.

Prognosis

The change effort outlined here is a formidable job. Success would require understanding and commitment on the part of the White House, important segments of Congress, the political leadership of the State Department, and the FSO corps. Only a very rash person would be sanguine about the prospects for mounting such a strategy in the first place, and generating and maintaining the kind of commitment necessary to implement it. Yet the challenge is clear and the stakes are high. Without some such fundamental and far-reaching effort, the public will not be as well served as it could be, the FSO corps will become a declining professional group, and the Department of State will come more and more to resemble the Ottoman Empire of the federal government. It may well be that a change strategy of this magnitude would be possible only when a new administration takes power in Washington.

The key need is that of a sustaining manager, and the commitment to a managerial strategy that should go along with creation of that role. For example, the FSO corps appears ready to change, but it cannot do enough by itself. It desperately needs leadership, and it will respond to effective political leadership. The ACORD program has been killed and the programming approach is operating only at a low level in one bureau of the State Department; but there is a legacy of experience in both of these areas,

[20] Chris Argyris, *Some Causes of Organizational Ineffectiveness Within the Department of State,* Occasional Paper No. 2 of the Center for International Systems Research (Washington: Department of State, 1967), pp. 45-52.

349

Conclusion

and both could be regenerated. The merger of the three agencies would require a very strong White House push, and would best occur at the beginning of a new administration. There is support in Congress for an active role by the Department in social science research. Within the context of a managerial strategy and with the support of the FSO corps, something like the Hays Bill would very likely be passed by Congress.

In short, the prognosis could suddenly become reasonably optimistic if two essential conditions are met: recognition at the top of the State Department and in the White House that something more is required than exhortation and issuing directives to bring about effective change, plus the determination to do whatever is required.

APPENDIX I

METHODOLOGICAL APPENDIX

....

THE Survey of the Diplomatic Profession (SDP), used extensively as a data source throughout this study, was designed, pretested, and administered by the author in the spring of 1966, under the guidance of Professor Frederick C. Mosher, Department of Political Science, University of California, Berkeley. This was not an official project of the Department of State, but permission to conduct the survey and help in doing so was sought and obtained.

The purpose of the survey was to learn something about how career Foreign Service Officers currently assess the profession of diplomacy and how they react to changes that have occurred or could occur, affecting the FSO corps.

For reasons of time, distance, and economy, it was necessary to restrict the sample to FSOs serving in Washington; since all FSOs eventually serve in Washington this provides a reasonably representative sample at any given time. The major exception is that the great majority of officers in the junior grades are in training or are serving abroad. For this reason, and also because the nature of many of the questions implies several years of experience in the FSO corps as a minimum, it was decided not to include in the survey officers in the two lowest grades (FSO-7 and FSO-8).

It was also decided to restrict the sample to officers actually serving in funded positions in the Department (and not those in training, or on various forms of leave or spe-

351

cial detail because of the high incidence of turnover in these categories and difficulties of communication).

Questionnaires were sent to 841 FSOs; 588, or 70 percent, returned filled-out, usable questionnaires in time for inclusion in the computer processing of the data (mid-June 1966). Because of the high initial rate of return, no follow-up request was sent out. Informal checking indicated that there was no pattern or bias inherent in those not returned.

In terms of grade level the sample compared to the worldwide FSO population at the same grade levels as follows:

Grade	Sample		June 30, 1966 Worldwide	
	No.	Percent	No.	Percent
Career Ambassador	1	.2	8	.3
Career Minister	11	1.9	55	1.9
FSO-1	67	11.4	276	9.3
FSO-2	106	18.0	404	13.7
FSO-3	136	23.1	660	22.4
FSO-4	121	20.6	629	21.3
FSO-5	71	12.1	461	15.6
FSO-6	75	12.7	457	15.5
Totals	588	100	2,950	100

The 588 returns are equivalent to a 20 percent sample of the total FSO corps at comparable grade levels. The sample was also representative of the total service on another important index, in that one-third of respondents were lateral entrants.

Respondents were invited at several points in the questionnaire to write down any comments that qualified or elaborated their responses, most of which are quite interesting and relevant. They are extensively quoted in several chapters of this study. Parenthetically it might be noted that a relatively small number of respondents commented on the value of the survey itself. These ran about 3-to-1 in favor of the survey, with the favorable comments generally stating that the survey should be of great interest and value. Negative comments generally were based on two points: that the survey took too much time from busy officers or that it was biased, although in no case was the nature of the suspected bias specified.

APPENDIX II

DOCUMENTS

....

Document 1. White House press release containing text of President Kennedy's statement of February 18, 1961, abolishing the Operations Coordinating Board.[1]

White House press release dated February 19, 1961

I am today (February 19) issuing an Executive order abolishing the Operations Coordinating Board. This Board was used in the last administration for work which we now plan to do in other ways. This action is part of our program for strengthening the responsibility of the individual departments.

First, we will center responsibility for much of the Board's work in the Secretary of State. He expects to rely particularly on the Assistant Secretaries in charge of regional bureaus, and they in turn will consult closely with other departments and agencies. This will be our ordinary rule for continuing coordination of our work in relation to a country or area.

Second, insofar as the OCB—as a descendant of the old Psychological Strategy Board—was concerned with the impact of our actions on foreign opinion—our "image" abroad —we expect its work to be done in a number of ways: in my own office, in the State Department, under Mr. [Edward R.] Murrow of USIA (United States Information Agency),

[1] Statement made by the President of the United States, on signing Executive Order 10,920, Feb. 18, 1961, released to the press Feb. 19, 1961, printed in the Department of State Bulletin, Vol. XLIV, No. 1,132 (Mar. 6, 1961), 345.

and by all who are concerned with the spirit and meaning of our actions in foreign policy. We believe that appropriate coordination can be assured here without extensive formal machinery.

Third, insofar as the OCB served as an instrument for insuring action at the President's direction, we plan to continue its work by maintaining direct communication with the responsible agencies, so that everyone will know what I have decided, while I in turn keep fully informed of the actions taken to carry out decisions. We of course expect that the policy of the White House will be the policy of the executive branch as a whole, and we shall take such steps as are needed to insure this result.

I expect that the senior officials who served as formal members of OCB will still keep in close and informal touch with each other on problems of common interest. Mr. Bromley Smith, who has been the Executive Officer of the OCB, will continue to work with my Special Assistant, Mr. McGeorge Bundy, in following up on White House decisions in the area of national security. In these varied ways we intend that the net result shall be a strengthening of the process by which our policies are effectively coordinated and carried out, throughout the executive branch.

Executive Order 10920[2]

Revoking Executive Order No. 10700 of February 25, 1957, as Amended[3]

By virtue of the authority vested in me by the Constitution and statutes, and as President of the United States, it is ordered that Executive Order No. 10700 of February 25, 1957, entitled "Further Providing for the Operations Co-

[2] Fed. Reg. 1,463.
[3] For background see Bulletin of Mar. 25, 1957, p. 204, and Oct. 5, 1959, p. 493.

ordinating Board," as amended, be, and it is hereby, revoked.

The White House,   John F. Kennedy
February 18, 1961.

---

*Document 2. Text of President Kennedy's letter of May 29,
1961, to all U.S. Chiefs of Mission abroad, giving them
responsibility and authority for managing all of the operations of their missions except those of command military
forces.*

C   May 29, 1961

  O

    P

      Y

Dear Mr. Ambassador:

Please accept my best wishes for the successful accomplishment of your mission. As the personal representative of
the President of the United States in   you are part
of a memorable tradition which began with Benjamin
Franklin and Thomas Jefferson, and which has included
many of our most distinguished citizens.

We are living in a critical moment in history. Powerful
destructive forces are challenging the universal values
which, for centuries, have inspired men of good will in all
parts of the world.

If we are to make progress toward a prosperous community of nations in a world of peace, the United States
must exercise the most affirmative and responsible leadership. Beyond our shores, this leadership, in large measure,
must be provided by our ambassadors and their staffs.

I have asked you to represent our Government in
because I am confident that you have the ability, dedication, and experience. The purpose of this letter is to define
guidelines which I hope may be helpful to you.

The practice of modern diplomacy requires a close understanding not only of governments but also of people, their
cultures and institutions. Therefore, I hope that you will
plan your work so that you may have the time to travel
extensively outside the nation's capital. Only in this way
can you develop the close, personal associations that go
beyond official diplomatic circles and maintain a sympathetic and accurate understanding of all segments of the
country.

Moreover, the improved understanding which is so essential to a more peaceful and rational world is a two-way
street. It is our task not only to understand what motivates
others, but to give them a better understanding of what
motivates us.

Many persons in   who have never visited the
United States, receive their principal impressions of our
nation through their contact with Americans who come to
their country either as private citizens or as government
employees.

Therefore, the manner in which you and your staff personally conduct yourselves is of the utmost importance.
This applies to the way in which you carry out your official
duties and to the attitudes you and they bring to day-to-day
contacts and associations.

It is an essential part of your task to create a climate of

dignified, dedicated understanding, cooperation, and service in and around the Embassy.

In regard to your personal authority and responsibility, I shall count on you to oversee and coordinate all the activities of the United States Government in

You are in charge of the entire United States Diplomatic Mission, and I shall expect you to supervise all of its operations. The Mission includes not only the personnel of the Department of State and the Foreign Service, but also the representatives of all other United States agencies which have programs or activities in   . I shall give you full support and backing in carrying out your assignment.

Needless to say, the representatives of other agencies are expected to communicate directly with their offices here in Washington, and in the event of a decision by you in which they do not concur, they may ask to have the decision reviewed by a higher authority in Washington.

However, it is their responsibility to keep you fully informed of their views and activities and to abide by your decisions unless in some particular instance you and they are notified to the contrary.

If in your judgment individual members of the Mission are not functioning effectively, you should take whatever action you feel may be required, reporting the circumstances, of course, to the Department of State.

In case the departure from   of any individual member of the Mission is indicated in your judgment, I shall expect you to make the decision and see that it is carried into effect. Such instances I am confident will be rare.

Now one word about your relations to the military. As you know, the United States Diplomatic Mission includes Service Attaches, Military Assistance Advisory Groups and other Military components attached to the Mission. It does not, however, include United States military forces operating in the field where such forces are under the command of a United States area military commander. The line of authority to these forces runs from me, to the Secretary of Defense, to the Joint Chiefs of Staff in Washington and to the area commander in the field.

Although this means that the chief of the American Diplomatic Mission is not in the line of military command, nevertheless, as Chief of Mission, you should work closely with the appropriate area military commander to assure the full exchange of information. If it is your opinion that activities by the United States military forces may adversely affect our over-all relations with the people or government of   , you should promptly discuss the matter with the military commander and, if necessary, request a decision by higher authority.

I have informed all heads of departments and agencies of the Government of the responsibilities of the chiefs of American Diplomatic Missions for our combined operations abroad, and I have asked them to instruct their representatives in the field accordingly.

As you know, your own lines of communication as Chief of Mission run through the Department of State.

Let me close with an expression of confidence in you personally and the earnest hope that your efforts may help strengthen our relations with both the Government and

the people of   . I am sure that you will make a
major contribution to the cause of world peace and understanding.

Good luck and my warmest regards,

Sincerely,
[Signed]
John F. Kennedy

---

*Document 3. Text of President Johnson's memorandum of
August 25, 1965, to heads of departments and agencies an-
nouncing the introduction of a "planning-programming-
budgeting" system (PPBS).*

The White House
Washington
August 25, 1965

Memorandum to Heads of Departments and Agencies

At the Cabinet meeting today, I announced that we would
begin to introduce a new planning—programming—budgeting system in Government. This will be a large and important job. I want all of you to devote personal attention to it.
The general purpose and outline of the new system are described in the attached statement and charts.

Detailed instructions on this system will be issued by the
Budget Director in a few weeks. In the meantime, the Director and his staff are prepared to discuss with you the general
outlines of what is to be done.

You should begin at once to develop plans for the creation
of your program and planning staffs. I want you to get the
best people possible for these staffs both from within your
organizations and from outside of government.

Appendices

How swiftly, and how smoothly, this new planning, programming and budgeting system begins to work its benefits depends, in substantial measure, on the amount and kind of personal authority and interest you bring to it.

Because of the limited time available, it will be necessary to use an ad hoc arrangement in preparing the national goals and the least costly and most effective means of attaining those goals for the fiscal year 1967 legislative program. For this purpose, it is my desire that you use the Legislative Task Forces that Joe Califano has set up at my direction.

[signed]
Lyndon B. Johnson

Document 4. Text of NSAM 341, as it was released in the State Department's channels as Foreign Affairs Manual Circular No. 385 of March 4, 1966.

FOREIGN AFFAIRS MANUAL CIRCULAR

SUBJECT: Direction, Coordination and Supervision of Interdepartmental Activities Overseas

No. 385
March 4, 1966

1. *Authority and Responsibility of the Secretary of State*

To assist the President in carrying out his responsibilities for the conduct of foreign affairs, he has assigned to the Secretary of State authority and responsibility to the full extent permitted by law for the overall direction, coordination and supervision of interdepartmental activities of the United States Government overseas.

2. *Activities Not Included*

Such activities do not include those of United States military forces operating in the field where such forces are under the command of a United States area military commander and such other military activities as the President elects to conduct through military channels.

3. Definition of "Interdepartmental" Activities

Activities which are internal to the execution and administration of the approved programs of a single department or agency and which are not of such a nature as to affect significantly the overall U.S. overseas program in a country or region are not considered to be interdepartmental matters. If disagreement arises at any echelon over whether a matter is interdepartmental or not in the meaning of this circular the dissenting department or agency may appeal to the next higher authority as provided for in the following paragraph.

4. The Concept of Executive Chairmen

The Secretary of State will discharge his authority and responsibility primarily through the Under Secretary of State and the regional Assistant Secretaries of State, who will be assisted by interdepartmental groups of which they will be executive chairmen, i.e., with full powers of decision on all matters within their purview, unless a member who does not concur requests the referral of a matter to the decision of the next higher authority.

5. The Senior Interdepartmental Group (SIG)

To assist the Secretary of State in discharging his authority and responsibility for interdepartmental matters which cannot be dealt with adequately at lower levels or by present established procedures, including those of the Intelligence Community, the Senior Interdepartmental Group (SIG) is established. The SIG shall consist of the Under Secretary of State, Executive Chairman, the Deputy Secretary of Defense, the Administrator of the

Appendices

Agency for International Development, the Director of the Central Intelligence Agency, the Chairman of the Joint Chiefs of Staff, the Director of the United States Information Agency, and the Special Assistant to the President for National Security Affairs. Representatives of other departments and agencies with responsibility for specific matters to be considered will attend on invitation by the Chairman. Such other departments and agencies may raise matters for consideration of the SIG.

The Chairman of the Senior Interdepartmental Group (SIG) may designate the Under Secretary for Economic Affairs or the Deputy Under Secretary for Political Affairs to chair the SIG in the Chairman's absence.

The SIG will assist the Secretary of State by:

a. ensuring that important foreign policy problems requiring interdepartmental attention receive full, prompt and systematic consideration;

b. dealing promptly with interdepartmental matters referred by the Assistant Secretaries of State or raised by any of its members, or, if such matters require higher level consideration, reporting them promptly to the Secretary of State for appropriate handling;

c. assuring a proper selectivity of the areas and issues to which the United States Government applies its resources;

d. carrying out other duties and responsibilities of the Special Group (counterinsurgency), which has been abolished;

e. conducting periodic surveys and checks to verify the adequacy and effectiveness of interdepartmental overseas programs and activities.

The SIG will encourage interdepartmental action and decision-making at the Assistant Secretary level to the greatest extent possible.

The SIG will meet in the Department of State regularly and specially at the call of the Chairman.

The Chairman will be supported by a full-time staff headed by a Staff Director who will also serve as the Special Deputy Executive Secretary of the Department. Staff personnel will be furnished on the Chairman's request by the departments and agencies represented on the SIG. The Chairman may request departments and agencies to designate a point of contact for the Staff Director on matters affecting their interests.

The Staff Directors of the Interdepartmental Regional Groups will assist the Staff Director of the SIG as he requires by providing staff support on regional matters of interest to the SIG.

6. *The Interdepartmental Regional Group (IRG)*

To assist the Assistant Secretaries, an Interdepartmental Regional Group (IRG) is established for each geographic region corresponding to the jurisdiction of the geographic bureaus in the Department of State. Each IRG shall be composed of the regional Assistant Secretary of State, Executive Chairman, and a designated representative from Defense, AID, CIA, the Organization of the Joint Chiefs of Staff, USIA and the White House or NSC staff. Representatives of other departments and agencies with responsibility for specific matters to be considered will attend on invitation by the Chairman.

The regional Assistant Secretaries, in their capacities as Executive Chairmen of the IRGs, will ensure the adequacy of United States policy for the countries in their region and of the plans, programs, resources and performance for implementing that policy. They will be particularly watchful for indications of developing crises and when such matters require higher level consideration, will recommend appropriate measures to higher authority for dealing with emergent critical situations in their regions.

A regional Assistant Secretary may designate a Deputy Assistant Secretary to chair the IRG in the Chairman's absence. IRG meeting and staff procedures will be patterned on the SIG.

7. *Interdepartmental Leadership and Coordination of Country Matters*

A new position of Country Director will be established in the regional bureaus to serve as the single focus of responsibility for leadership and coordination of departmental and interdepartmental activities concerning his country or countries of assignment. In particular he will:

a. provide continuing departmental and interdepartmental leadership in planning, coordination, and implementation of decisions;

b. raise specific matters for consideration by the IRG, and bring detailed knowledge to IRG discussions when so requested;

c. serve as the base for crisis task force operations as necessary.

The Country Director will be responsible for seeing that the Ambassador's needs are served both within the Department and government-wide. He will ensure that the mission is fully supported in the full range of its requirements: policy, operations and administration.

Each Country Director will organize and develop such contacts, channels and mechanisms as are appropriate to and necessary for full interdepartmental leadership on country matters, and for full support to the Assistant Secretary.

To assist in providing guidance and direction to the Country Director, the Assistant Secretary will have one or more Deputy Assistant Secretaries whose areas of responsibility will be defined by the Assistant Secretary.

Positions of Office Director and officer-in-charge will be abolished as the transition is made to the establishment of Country Director positions.

INTRODUCTION

All of the established professions are experiencing change in one form or another in a world that itself rapidly changing. What is happening to the professions has become a matter of more urgent interest than ever before to scholars, educators, the genral public. One obvious source of information is the opinions of the members of the professional group itself. This questionnaire provides you an opportunity to express your opinions about the diplomatic profession and related matters.

This effort is part of a broader program of research being conducted by Professor Frederick C. Mosher of the Department of Political Science at the University of California, Berkeley. The broad program is concerned with the present character and relationships of higher education, key professional groups, and the public service. Among the sub-projects are surveys of several professional groups.

For reasons of time and distance, this questionnaire has not been sent to every member of the FSO Corps, but only to officers assigned to positions in Washington. You are, of course, under no compulsion whatsoever to complete and return the questionnaire, but we hope very much that you will, since the usefulness of the survey depends on having a high level of response.

Your answers will be confidential. You are not asked to sign your name, and there is no way for anyone to tell which is your questionnaire. For this reason, we hope that you will be completely candid in your responses, which again will make the whole effort con-siderably more useful.

Except for a few factual questions (such as those asking your grade and age), there are no right or wrong answers to the questions. This is an opinion survey, and therefore, there are no answers that have been prejudged as "correct." In other words, this is not a test - it is an attempt to get your frank opinions.

Please answer all questions or as many as you possibly can. The questionnaire should take about an hour or so to complete. Generally speaking, your first impression is the best response.

We hope you find the exercise interesting and thought-provoking. The Department of State has granted permission to conduct this survey and is cooperating in the effort, but does not officially endorse it nor its findings. The results will be made available to the Department and to you, probably in the form of an article prepared for the Foreign Service Journal or the Department of State News Letter. Your cooperation is greatly appreciated.

PLEASE COMPLETE AND RETURN THE QUESTIONNAIRE PROMPTLY!

INSTRUCTIONS

1. Please answer the questions in order - don't skip around. If at all possible, please answer all questions.

2. Most questions can be answered by circling a symbol (a number or a letter) opposite one of the possible responses. If you do not find a response that suits you exactly, circle the one that comes closest to representing your view. For some questions, space is provided for you to write in an answer.

3. Please follow the instructions for each question carefully. If you are asked to "circle one", then circle only one, not two or three reponses. If you have more to say or want to qualify your response to any question, please feel free to write anything you want (referencing the number of the question) on the margin or back cover.

4. After completing the questionnaire, fold it and insert it in the envelope provided which is already addressed to "Study of the Diplomatic Profession", Department of State, Room 943, SA-11, where the results will be processed and forwarded to Professor Mosher. Please do this as soon as possible, but in any event no later than June 6.

5. There may be some questions dealing with material you are not familiar with, through lack of personal experience or other reasons. Please respond to these questions anyway, on the basis of your best impression or intuition on the subject.

I. EDUCATION AND ENTRY

1. When did you enter the Foreign Service Officer Corps?

   CIRCLE ONE: (13)

   before 1954 1
   1954 to 1958 2
   1959 to present 3

2. How did you enter?

   CIRCLE ONE: (14)

   by basic examination x
   by lateral entry . . . . y

3a. In general, what do you think is the main attraction for most young persons who take the Foreign Service examinations each year?

   CIRCLE ONE: (15)

   the image of the FSO Corps as an elite corps of professional diplomats 1

   desire to participate in the making of American foreign policy 2

   desire to live and work in foreign countries 3

   no specific single motivation-- just a vague, general interest. . 4

   not sure 5

   other (write in) _____ 6

   _____

3b. Which of the above comes closest to your reason for taking the basic examination? (If the question is not applicable to you, circle number 7).

   CIRCLE ONE: (16)

   1   2   3   4   5   6

   not applicable 7

4. What is your general impression of the quality of the junior officers who have entered the FSO Corps in recent years?

   CIRCLE ONE: (17)

   poor 1
   average 2
   mixed-some poor, some brilliant. 3
   generally very good 4
   outstanding 5

5. At what point in life did you first develop serious interest in the FSO Corps as a possible career?

   CIRCLE ONE: (18)

   from earliest memory 1

   while in high school 2

   while an undergraduate at college . . 3

   while in graduate school 4

   during military service 5

   during other government employment . . 6

   during employement outside government 7

   don't remember 8

   other (write in) _____ 9

   _____

REMINDER: Please follow instructions carefully.

6. From what source did you develop your initial interest in the FSO Corps as a possible career?

   CIRCLE ONE: (19)

   parent 1

   friend of the family 2

   friend of yours 3

   reading 4

   high school teacher or counselor . . . 5

   college professor or counselor 6

   employer 7

   don't remember 8

   other (write in) _____ 9

---

7. If you ever discussed applying for the FSO Corps with a college professor or counselor, what was his attitude toward the Foreign Service as a career? (If you never had such a discussion, please circle number 1. If you discussed with more than one advisor, answer the question in terms of the general consensus or impression).

   CIRCLE ONE: (20)

   never discussed 1
   very unfavorable 2
   mildly unfavorable 3
   neutral 4
   mildly favorable 5
   very favorable 6
   mixed reactions 7

---

8. What were your major fields of education in college and graduate school?

   CIRCLE ONE IN EACH COLUMN: (21) (22)

	undergraduate major	graduate major
History	x	x
Political Science	y	y
International Relations	0	0
Economics	1	1
Accounting	2	2
Public Administration	3	3
Business Administration	4	4
English	5	5
Language	6	6
Physical Science	7	7
Social Science (Other than those named)	8	8
Humanities (Other than those named)	9	9
Other	A	A
Did not attend	B	B

---

9. How well do you feel your college work prepared you for a career in the Foreign Service?

   CIRCLE ONE: (23)

   did not attend college 1
   inadequately 2
   could have been much better . . . 3
   adequately in some areas, not
   so in others 4
   adequately 5
   very well 6

---

10. If you had a son or a daughter interested in a career in the FSO Corps, how would you react?

    CIRCLE ONE IN EACH COLUMN: (24) (25)

	son	daughter
would oppose it strongly	1	1
would advise against it	2	2
would approve, but not actively encourage	3	3
would encourage	4	4

---

11. If your reaction for either a son or a daughter was positive (either of last two responses above), what would your principal reason or reasons be? Use numbers to indicate the order of importance for your reasons -- "1" for the most important, "2" for the next, and so on - for as many of the five reasons as you would consider of major importance.

    ORDER

    Relatively good remuneration
    and degree of financial security . . ___(26)

    Social status and prestige of the
    diplomatic profession compared to
    alternative occupations . . . . . . ___(27)

    Relatively good opportunity for FSOs
    to make an important contribution to
    the public service . . . . ___(28)

    Relatively good opportunity to con-
    tinue personal intellectual growth
    and development . . . . ___(29)

    Relatively good opportunities to
    enjoy life . . . . ___(30)

---

12. Would you advise a son interested in the FSO Corps to give serious consideration to other opportunities in international relations as well, such as working for the UN or another foreign affairs agency such as AID or USIA?

    (31)

    yes 1
    no 2

- 3 -

II. THE FOREIGN SERVICE AS A CAREER

13. Which functional heading best describes most of the work you have done since entering the FSO Corps?

CIRCLE ONE: (32)

Consular 0
Administrative 1
Political 2
Economic 3
Commercial 4
Labor 5
Program Direction 6
Mixed, in several fields
  about equally 7
Too early in career
  to specify 8
Other (write in) _____ 9

14. If you regard yourself (or are regarded by colleagues) as a functional specialist, which field is your specialty? (If you are not a specialist, circle number 0.)

CIRCLE ONE: (33)

I am not a specialist 0
Consular 1
Administrative 2
Political 3
Economic 4
Commerical 5
Labor 6
Program Direction 7
other (write in) _____ 8

15. In which field would you prefer to spend most of your time in the future?

CIRCLE ONE: (34)

Consular 1
Administrative 2
Political 3
Economic 4
Commercial 5
Labor 6
Program Direction 7
No one field -- would rather
  rotate among several 8
Other (write in) _____ 9

16. If you regard yourself as an area specialist (or are so regarded by colleagues), what is your area? (If you are not an area specialist, circle number 0.)

CIRCLE ONE: (35)

I am not an area specialist 0
Latin America 1
Arabic 2
Other Near East or South Asia 3
Soviet 4
Chinese 5
Japanese 6
Eastern Europe 7
Atlantic Affairs 8
Africa (south of Sahara) 9
Southeast Asia x

If your area specialization is not listed above, or can be stated more specifically, please write it in here: _____ y

(For example, if you are a Turkish specialist, write in "Turkish" in addition to having circled the symbol for "Other Near East and South Asia" in the list above.)

17. Do you believe that the young, entering FSO normally should aspire to becoming an ambassador?

CIRCLE ONE: (36)

yes 1
no 2
not sure 3

18. To what extent do you think it likely that you will become an ambassador?

CIRCLE ONE: (37)

no possibility 1
barely possible 2
possible 3
a good chance 4
very likely 5
I am serving or have already served
  as an ambassador 6

- 4 -

19. In your opinion, **approximately** what percentage of ambassadorships should be held by career officers?

CIRCLE ONE: (38)

    60 per cent 1
    70 per cent 2
    80 per cent 3
    90 per cent 4
    100 per cent 5
    not sure 6

20. Approximately what percentage of DCMs should be career officers?

CIRCLE ONE: (39)

    60 per cent 1
    70 per cent 2
    80 per cent 3
    90 per cent 4
    100 per cent 5
    not sure 6

21. How would you rate the following in terms of importance or usefulness to attaining the top ranks of the Foreign Service and possibly becoming an ambassador? Please evaluate in terms of the real world of what you believe it takes to be a "success," not the ideal of what should be.

CIRCLE ONE RESPONSE IN EACH LINE:

		Possibly Negative	Not Important	Useful	Important	Crucial	
a.	Area specialization	1	2	3	4	5	(40)
b.	Extensive experience in Washington	1	2	3	4	5	(41)
c.	Concentrating on political work	1	2	3	4	5	(42)
d.	An assignment to another foreign affairs agency	1	2	3	4	5	(43)
e.	Several tours in adminis- trative work	1	2	3	4	5	(44)
f.	Senior training	1	2	3	4	5	(45)
g.	Entry at the bottom	1	2	3	4	5	(46)
h.	Managerial experience	1	2	3	4	5	(47)
i.	Weighing each assignment carefully before accepting	1	2	3	4	5	(48)
j.	Extensive pre-service work experience	1	2	3	4	5	(49)
k.	A graduate degree	1	2	3	4	5	(50)
l.	Some experience in all major fields of work of FSO Corps	1	2	3	4	5	(51)
m.	Winning respect of col- leagues in the corps	1	2	3	4	5	(52)
n.	Mastering a foreign language	1	2	3	4	5	(53)
o.	A good basic understanding of economics	1	2	3	4	5	(54)
p.	Having or developing good political connections	1	2	3	4	5	(55)

REMINDER: Did you circle one response in each line?

22. Imagine that you are on home leave and you are introduced to some strangers at a party. They ask what your occupation is. How would you respond?

CIRCLE ONE: (56)

I'm in the Foreign Service 1
I work for the State Department 2
I'm a Foreign Service officer 3
I work for the government 4
I'm in the diplomatic service 5
Other (write in) _____ 6

_____

23. Reflect for a moment about the men presently or recently in the Service who you think most nearly exemplify your conception of the ideal Foreign Service Officer. It is not necessary that you know them personally, only that from what you have heard, read, or seen they represent your notion of the Foreign Service at its best. List the three best officers you can think of in descending order:

a. _____

b. _____

c. _____

---

24. How would you compare the "average" officer in the British Foreign Service with the "average" American FSO?

CIRCLE ONE RESPONSE FOR EACH STATEMENT:

The British officer is generally a more competent representative of his government because he is the product of a longer tradition of diplomatic professionalism.

Agree 1
Disagree . . . 2   (57)
Not Sure . . . 3

The British officer often is more adept at the more traditional diplomatic functions, but he tends to be hidebound by tradition and he has not changed to meet new needs and demands as well as American FSOs have.

Agree 1
Disagree . . . 2   (58)
Not sure . . . 3

The British officer generally comes from a social and educational background which better qualify him for diplomacy than does the social and educational background of the average FSO.

Agree 1
Disagree . . . 2   (59)
Not sure . . . 3

As representatives of their country, American FSOs are as well qualified or better than any diplomats in the world, including the British.

Agree 1
Disagree . . . 2   (60)
Not sure . . . 3

---

25. If you were committed to taking an assignment in another agency and the only question was the choice of the agency, what would your preference be? (In the column headed "First Choice," circle the number which is opposite the agency name of your first choice, and similarly, in the column headed "Second Choice," circle the number which is opposite your second choice agency.)

	FIRST CHOICE (61)	SECOND CHOICE (62)
USIA	1	1
Peace Corps	2	2
CIA	3	3
Commerce	4	4
DOD	5	5
Labor	6	6
ACDA	7	7
AID	8	8
Other (write in):	9	9

- 6 -

26. Imagine the existence of a program in which every year a number of experienced FSOs are given an opportunity to take a year off, something on the order of a sabbatical, but with the understanding that in most cases they would work in some other field in the United States, for personal growth and in order to learn more about some important facet of American society. If such an opportunity were offered to you, what would be your first and second choices among the following experiences:

	FIRST CHOICE (63)	SECOND CHOICE (64)
Working on Capitol Hill, perhaps on a committee staff	1	1
Working in the executive offices of a major industrial firm	2	2
Teaching on a college campus	3	3
Working for a major foundation	4	4
Working on the staff of a mayor or city manager in a medium-sized city	5	5
Free time to travel, think, and write at will	6	6
Undertaking a research project, approved and supported by the Department and a university	7	7
Would rather not take a year off	8	8

27. If for some reason you had not become an FSO, in what other field of endeavor do you think it likely and possible that you might have made a career? You may indicate up to three possible fields by circling the appropriate symbols opposite your fields of choice.

	FIRST POSSIBILITY (68)	SECOND POSSIBILITY (69)	THIRD POSSIBILITY (70)
Civil Service	y	y	y
Military Service	x	x	x
Small Business	1	1	1
Large Business	2	2	2
College Teaching	3	3	3
Public School Teaching	4	4	4
Law	5	5	5
Politics	6	6	6
Science	7	7	7
Engineering	8	8	8
Other (write in):	9	9	9

28. Everyone is concerned about certain things from time to time. Indicate the extent to which the following have concerned you.

CIRCLE ONE RESPONSE IN EACH LINE:

	NEVER	VERY LITTLE	SOMETIMES	FREQUENTLY
a. How well you are accepted and respected by colleagues in FSO Corps.	1	2	3	4 (71)
b. Possible adverse affects of overseas life on one or more members of your family.	1	2	3	4 (72)
c. General condition of the FSO Corps.	1	2	3	4 (73)
d. Possibility of selection-out.	1	2	3	4 (74)
e. How well you are able to live up to demands of your job.	1	2	3	4 (75)
f. How the State Department is managed.	1	2	3	4 (76)
g. How soon you will get promoted	1	2	3	4 (77)
h. Less challenge in your work than you expected or hoped for.	1	2	3	4 (78)
i. Whether or not the FSO Corps is the right career for you.	1	2	3	4 (79)

(Card 2)

29. Turning to the administration and management of the FSO Corps itself, following are listed some of the major functions. In general, how do you evaluate the way each is presently being performed? Circle an evaluation for each of the seven functions. Then, in the box at right, answer the question of whether or not you believe each function must be performed by FSOs, or by groups in which FSOs form a majority, by circling the appropriate symbol.

	DON'T KNOW	DEFINITELY NEEDS IMPROVING	ACCEPTABLY DONE	VERY WELL DONE	MUST BE DONE BY FSOs
a. Recruitment at Junior Officer level	1	2	3	4 (13)	Yes No 1 2 (14)
b. Recruitment-for lateral entry	1	2	3	4 (15)	1 2 (16)
c. Training	1	2	3	4 (17)	1 2 (18)
d. Assignment	1	2	3	4 (19)	1 2 (20)
e. Promotion	1	2	3	4 (21)	1 2 (22)
f. Selection-out	1	2	3	4 (23)	1 2 (24)
g. Inspection	1	2	3	4 (25)	1 2 (26)

REMINDER: Did you respond to both parts of Question 29 - the evaluations and the box at right?

III. PATTERNS OF CHANGE

30. There has been a great deal of discussion about changes in the ways that the United States conducts its foreign affairs in recent decades. How would you evaluate the following changes that have occurred? Make your evaluation in terms of your view of the general value or utility of the change, not in regard to how well it may have been accomplished.

CIRCLE ONE RESPONSE IN EACH LINE:

	BAD	PROBABLY NOT GOOD	ACCEPT-ABLE	GOOD	VERY MUCH NEEDED	
a. Development of new foreign affairs tools and programs.	1	2	3	4	5	(27)
b. Resurgence of summit diplomacy.	1	2	3	4	5	(28)
c. More emphasis on trying to influence events than on observing and reporting.	1	2	3	4	5	(29)
d. Enlargement of FSO Corps to bring in persons skilled in functions other than the traditional diplomacy.	1	2	3	4	5	(30)
e. Emergence of the "Country Team" concept.	1	2	3	4	5	(31)
f. Build-up of doctrine emphasizing managerial role of ambassador over total U.S. Mission as well as his diplomatic role.	1	2	3	4	5	(32)
g. Placing responsibility on State Department for directing overseas operations of all agencies as well as for policy guidance.	1	2	3	4	5	(33)
h. Large-scale involvement of the U.S. in multilateral organizations.	1	2	3	4	5	(34)

31. Which of the following most nearly represents your preference for the future state of the FSO Corps?

CIRCLE ONE: (35)

It should expand to encompass more persons at a professional level who serve abroad in making a career of service in one or more major programs in U.S. foreign affairs. 1

It should stay roughly as it is now in terms of size and functions. 2

It should contract in size to become a smaller and more elite corps of professionals practicing the core skills of diplomacy. 3

It should contract in size but also include more officers at a high professional level in all of the major functions of foreign affairs. 4

Not sure. 5

32. This question asks your opinion in identifying past and future agents of change of the FSO Corps. Under the first heading, "Main Agents of Change in the Past," circle the symbol in the first column opposite the group or body you feel has been the principal source of change, and then circle the symbol in the next column for the next most important source of change in your view.

Repeat the process under the second heading, "Should Be Main Agents of Change," that is, indicating your first and second choices for the groups you feel ought to be the main change agents in the future.

CIRCLE ONE IN EACH VERTICAL COLUMN:

	Main Agents of Change in the Past		Should be Main Agents of Change	
	1st Choice (36)	2nd Choice (37)	1st Choice (38)	2nd Choice (39)
a. The Congress	1	1	1	1
b. Senior policy officials of the Department	2	2	2	2
c. Senior administrative officials of the Department	3	3	3	3
d. Senior career FSOs	4	4	4	4
e. Special study groups such as the Herter Committee and the Wriston Committee	5	5	5	5
f. The White House	6	6	6	6
g. The Bureau of the Budget	7	7	7	7
h. Other (Write in) _____	8	8	8	8
i. None -- don't believe change has or should be great enough to specify an agent of change	9	9	9	9

33. Following are several statements of opinion about the FSO Corps. What is your reaction to each one?

CIRCLE A RESPONSE FOR EACH STATEMENT:

The general public's estimation of the professional diplomatic corps has declined since the end of World War II.
Agree 1
Disagree . . . 2   (40)
Not sure . . . 3

The professional competence of the FSO Corps has been weakened by too much lateral entry.
Agree 1
Disagree . . . 2   (41)
Not sure . . . 3

The real role of the FSO Corps is to develop a managerial class to supervise all programs and functions in U.S. foreign affairs.
Agree 1
Disagree . . . 2   (42)
Not sure . . . 3

The historic functions of diplomacy -- representation, reporting, negotiating -- are as important today if not more important than they ever were before.
Agree 1
Disagree . . . 2   (43)
Not sure . . . 3

By and large, the FSO Corps has resisted bringing into its ranks the men and skills representing the newer functions in U.S. foreign affairs.
Agree 1
Disagree . . . 2   (44)
Not sure . . . 3

The problem of young officers having more talent and intelligence than their jobs generally call for is getting worse, and something should be done about it.
Agree 1
Disagree . . . 2   (45)
Not sure . . . 3

The FSO Corps has steadily increased in competence and is today probably the best diplomatic corps in the world.
Agree 1
Disagree . . . 2   (46)
Not sure . . . 3

34. Here are some more specific changes affecting the FSO Corps that either have taken place or could take place. How do you evaluate them in terms of their effect on the professionalism and competence of the FSO Corps?

CIRCLE ONE RESPONSE IN EACH LINE:

	DON'T KNOW	BAD	PROBABLY NOT GOOD	ACCEPT-ABLE	GOOD	VERY MUCH NEEDED	DOESN'T GO FAR ENOUGH	
a. The Hays Bill.	1	2	3	4	5	6	7	(47)
b. Integration of more than 700 USIA career officers.	1	2	3	4	5	6	7	(48)
c. Increasing use of FSRs to fill special needs.	1	2	3	4	5	6	7	(49)
d. A planning-programming-budgeting system for the foreign affairs community.	1	2	3	4	5	6	7	(50)
e. Greater use of systems and computers.	1	2	3	4	5	6	7	(51)
f. Extending National Policy Paper effort to more countries.	1	2	3	4	5	6	7	(52)
g. More emphasis on training at each career stage.	1	2	3	4	5	6	7	(53)
h. Cutback in the Number of U.S. agencies and their personnel operating abroad.	1	2	3	4	5	6	7	(54)
i. Maintaining a consistent volume of lateral entry every year.	1	2	3	4	5	6	7	(55)
j. Removing some consular and administrative jobs from the FSO Corps to the Staff Corps.	1	2	3	4	5	6	7	(56)

IV. STATE OF THE PROFESSION

35. Professional groups tend to have certain core skills or functions which form the essence of the profession. Please register your impression of what the core skills of the diplomatic profession are by means of rank-ordering the eleven functions listed below. The functions you cite as 1, 2, and 3 for example, will be those you regard as of central importance, while those at the other end of the spectrum (9, 10, 11) you may regard as necessary and important from time to time but as relatively peripheral to the main business of the professional diplomat. Disregard considerations of who performs the functions, when they do it, or how widely the function is practiced. The only criterion is your opinion of the relative extent to which the function is or should be toward the core of the diplomatic profession as you understand it today.

Because rank-ordering is always difficult, you might find it useful to read through the list of functions before attempting to order them, then start at either or both ends of the rank-order and work toward the middle.

RANK ORDER BY CIRCLING ONE SYMBOL IN EACH LINE:

FUNCTIONS	Order of Importance										
	1st (57)	2nd (58)	3rd (59)	4th (60)	5th (61)	6th (62)	7th (63)	8th (64)	9th (65)	10th (66)	11th (67)
a. Explaining U.S. policies whenever possible to American citizens.	x	x	x	x	x	x	x	x	x	x	x
b. Conducting negotiations with representatives of foreign governments.	0	0	0	0	0	0	0	0	0	0	0
c. Developing formal statements of U.S. policy to guide the activities of our missions in specific countries.	1	1	1	1	1	1	1	1	1	1	1
d. Reporting on significant events and trends in the host country.	2	2	2	2	2	2	2	2	2	2	2
e. Protecting the rights and safety of American citizens in foreign countries.	3	3	3	3	3	3	3	3	3	3	3
f. Representing the United States on major ceremonial occasions.	4	4	4	4	4	4	4	4	4	4	4
g. Briefing Congressmen and other visitors on the situation in the host country.	5	5	5	5	5	5	5	5	5	5	5
h. Managing and coordinating a variety of programs designed to advance U. S. interests in the host country.	6	6	6	6	6	6	6	6	6	6	6
i. Influencing citizens of the host country to understand and support U.S. policies.	7	7	7	7	7	7	7	7	7	7	7
j. Persuading citizens of the host country to undertake ways of improving their own society.	8	8	8	8	8	8	8	8	8	8	8
k. Issuing visas to foreign nationals for immigration or travel to the U.S.	9	9	9	9	9	9	9	9	9	9	9

REMINDER: Make sure that you circled one and only one symbol in each of the 11 vertical columns.

- 12 -

36. Every professional group tends to develop its own code of ethics -- its values, ideals, prescribed
behavior. How would you rate the following styles of behavior in terms of their propriety and
importance for the professional diplomat?

CIRCLE ONE RESPONSE IN EACH LINE:

		IRRELEVANT OR UNIMPORTANT TO THE PROFES- SIONAL DIPLOMAT	COMPLETELY OPTIONAL- THIS BEHAVIOR DEPENDS ENTIRELY ON THE SITUATION	USUALLY IMPERATIVE- MOST OFFICERS SHOULD ACT THIS WAY MOST OF THE TIME	IMPERATIVE- AN FSO SHOULD ALWAYS ACT THIS WAY	
a.	Placing the "good of the service" over one's own personal good.	1	2	3	4	(68)
b.	Not being completely frank in negotiations if it helps win one's point.	1	2	3	4	(69)
c.	Readiness to serve anywhere in the world in any job at the discretion of the Secretary of State.	1	2	3	4	(70)
d.	Acting rationally and avoiding any display of emotion.	1	2	3	4	(71)
e.	Taking whatever steps one can to strengthen the pro- fessional group.	1	2	3	4	(72)
f.	Entertaining regularly as part of the job.	1	2	3	4	(73)
g.	Following political deci- sions fully even when one personally disagrees.	1	2	3	4	(74)
h.	Maintaining proper dress and manners.	1	2	3	4	(75)
i.	Advocating positions which may be unpopular but which one feels to be important.	1	2	3	4	(76)
j.	Avoiding the use of politi- cal influence for one's own career.	1	2	3	4	(77)

Are there any elements of behavior not included among the above which you consider of extreme
importance to the professional diplomat? If so, please WRITE IN: _____
_____

- 13 -

37. The environment in which diplomacy is practiced has changed greatly in recent decades. There has been much discussion about whether or not the profession has changed, to what extent it has changed, and how. Following are three viewpoints on the matter. Which corresponds most nearly to your own view of the state of the profession?

CIRCLE ONE: (13)

DIPLOMACY NO LONGER A PROFESSION: It is no longer possible to consider diplomacy a profession in the same sense that law and medicine are professions because the situation has changed so much that one cannot say with any precision what the profession is or does. Instead of "diplomacy" one can only speak of "foreign affairs" which is something much broader and is no more a profession than is the general public service. 1

DIPLOMACY A PROFESSION, BUT BASICALLY CHANGED: Diplomacy is a profession today, but it has changed basically; it has become the "new diplomacy." It is no longer useful to think of foreign affairs as a single professional field. Rather, it is a broad spectrum into which a number of professions, some of the orthodox domestic variety, and other peculiar to foreign affairs, must be fitted and modified. This places a premium on the capacity to coordinate activities. Each foreign affairs profession is part of the profession of the new diplomacy, and the highest form of it is the capability for leadership and direction of the varied fields. 2

DIPLOMACY NOT BASICALLY CHANGED AS A PROFESSION: Diplomacy is a profession today, and it has not changed basically. It is true that there are a great many functions and specialties in foreign affairs today, but diplomacy is not to be confused with these nor with management of the varied functions. Diplomacy involves the conduct of formal relationships among sovereign states and is characterized chiefly by the historic functions of representation, negotiation, and reporting. Some may regard diplomacy as one specialty among many in foreign affairs today, but if so it is first among many and it is the only one which may truly be classed as a profession. 3

OTHER: If none of the above fits nearly enough your point of view, take as much space as you need to write in your own definition and description of the profession of diplomacy as you see it today. Use the back cover if you need more space. 4

REMINDER: Feel free to use this space for any additional comments.

38. In studies of the professions, there have been numerous attempts to isolate the characteristics or criteria of professionalism. Scholars generally agree that there is no perfect set of criteria. One scholar points out that none of the recognized professions completely fulfills all criteria and that no occupation is completely devoid of all criteria. There is thus agreement that one can only speak of a scale of professionalism, of relative rather than absolute differences. There are also obvious differences between professions located entirely in the government service and the so-called "free" professions such as law and medicine.

In this question, you are asked to rate three well-known professions in terms of the extent to which they fulfill the criteria of professionalism listed in the left-hand column.

One is the profession probably best known to most people -- the medical profession. Another is a profession about which you have great deal of knowledge -- diplomacy. The third is a profession with which you are probably more familiar than the average person -- the military profession (the career military officer corps).

For each of the 13 criteria, please rank each of the three professions on a scale of 1 to 5, 1 being the lowest score and 5 the highest. Here is the meaning of the rankings you are asked to use:

          1 . . . . . very nearly or totally devoid of the criterion
          2 . . . . . considerably lacking in the criterion
          3 . . . . . about average -- fulfills the criterion to a moderate extent
          4 . . . . . fulfills the criterion to a considerable extent
          5 . . . . . very nearly or completely fulfills the criterion

CIRCLE A RANKING FOR EACH CRITERION IN ALL THREE COLUMNS:

Criteria	Medical	Diplomatic	Military
a. A self-conscious sense of professionalism -- members feels strongly that they are professional men.	1 2 3 4 5 (14)	1 2 3 4 5 (15)	1 2 3 4 5 (16)
b. Provides a unique, definitive, and essential social service.	1 2 3 4 5 (17)	1 2 3 4 5 (18)	1 2 3 4 5 (19)
c. Has an articulated, professionally-approved code of ethics.	1 2 3 4 5 (20)	1 2 3 4 5 (21)	1 2 3 4 5 (22)
d. A high degree of self-government and internal control within constraints imposed by society.	1 2 3 4 5 (23)	1 2 3 4 5 (24)	1 2 3 4 5 (25)
e. Has a professional association which concerns itself with research into the substance of the profession -- the development of new knowledge.	1 2 3 4 5 (26)	1 2 3 4 5 (27)	1 2 3 4 5 (28)
f. An emphasis on intellectual techniques in performing its service.	1 2 3 4 5 (29)	1 2 3 4 5 (30)	1 2 3 4 5 (31)
g. Entry at a relatively young age based on rigorous selection, and long-term career commitment.	1 2 3 4 5 (32)	1 2 3 4 5 (33)	1 2 3 4 5 (34)
h. A relatively set pattern of preparatory education, largely controlled by the professional group itself.	1 2 3 4 5 (35)	1 2 3 4 5 (36)	1 2 3 4 5 (37)
i. A belief that members should constantly strive to stay abreast of new knowledge relevant to the profession, often involving formal training.	1 2 3 4 5 (38)	1 2 3 4 5 (39)	1 2 3 4 5 (40)
j. A broad range of autonomy for both the individual practitioner and the professional group as a whole.	1 2 3 4 5 (41)	1 2 3 4 5 (42)	1 2 3 4 5 (43)
k. An acceptance by the practitioner of broad personal responsibility for judgement made and acts performed within the scope of professional autonomy.	1 2 3 4 5 (44)	1 2 3 4 5 (45)	1 2 3 4 5 (46)
l. An emphasis on the service to be rendered, rather than the economic gain to the practitioner.	1 2 3 4 5 (47)	1 2 3 4 5 (48)	1 2 3 4 5 (49)
m. Success in resisting the breakdown of professional autonomy as organizational or bureaucratic constraints grow stronger.	1 2 3 4 5 (50)	1 2 3 4 5 (51)	1 2 3 4 5 (52)

V. BACKGROUND INFORMATION

The questionnaire concludes with some brief questions on your personal background. They, of course, are just as confidential as the rest of the questionnaire and cannot be traced back to you.

39. What is your present grade?

CIRCLE ONE: (53)

    Career Ambassador x
    Career Minister 0
    0-1 1
    0-2 2
    0-3 3
    0-4 4
    0-5 5
    0-6 6
    0-7 7
    0-8 8

40. In what year did your last promotion occur? Write in the last two digits of the year (for example, if you were last promoted in 1961, write in "61").

WRITE IN: (54, 55)

_____
(If no promotions yet, write "None")

41. What is your present age to your nearest birthday?

WRITE IN: (56, 57)

_____ years

42. How would you characterize your personal political beliefs?

CIRCLE ONE: (58)

    Conservative 1
    Somewhat conservative 2
    Somewhat liberal 3
    Liberal 4
    Neither liberal nor
      conservative 5

43. What was the highest level of formal education of your parents?

CIRCLE ONE IN EACH COLUMN: (59)   (60)
                             Father   Mother

    8th grade or less 1 1
    Part high school 2 2
    High school graduate 3 3
    Bachelor's degree 4 4
    Graduate or professional
      degree 5 5

44. What was your father's occupation?

CIRCLE ONE: (61)

    Business (small) 1
    Business (large) 2
    Farmer 3
    White collar 4
    Workingman 5
    Professional or managerial 6
    Other 7

45. If your father was a professional man, what was his profession? (If he was not a professional man, circle the x).

CIRCLE ONE: (62)

    Diplomat 1
    Military Officer 2
    Doctor 3
    Lawyer 4
    Clergyman 5
    Missionary 6
    Engineer 7
    College Professor 8
    School Teacher 9
    Other 0
    not a professional man x

46. In what religious faith were you raised?

CIRCLE ONE: (63)

    Protestant 1
    Roman Catholic 2
    Jewish 3
    Other 4
    None 5

47. Up to your graduation from high school, did
    you live abroad for any substantial period
    of time (two years or more)?

    CIRCLE ONE: (64)

        Yes 1
        No 2

---

48. What is your estimate of your family's average
    annual income category during the years you
    were in high school?

    CIRCLE ONE: (65)

        Less than $5,000 1
        $5,000 to $7,499 2
        $7,500 to $9,999 3
        $10,000 to $14,999 4
        $15,000 to $19,999 5
        $20,000 and over 6
        not sure 7

---

49. In regard to your upbringing, which of the
    following statements applies to your back-
    ground?

    CIRCLE ONE: (66)

    a. I lived with both parents through-
       out my school years up to graduation
       from high school 1

    b. For reasons of death or divorce,
       I lived with my mother for a sub-
       stantial period of time up to
       graduation from high school . . .2

    c. For reasons of death or divorce,
       I lived with my father for a
       substantial period of time up to
       graduation from high school . . .3

    d. For reasons of divorce or
       separation, I lived alternately
       with my mother and father for a
       substantial period of time up
       to graduation from high school . .4

    e. None of the above statements
       applies accurately to me 5

50. On a fulltime basis, how much training have
    you had since entering the FSO Corps?

    CIRCLE ONE: (67)

        less than three months 1
        three to six months 2
        six months to a year 3
        one year to 18 months 4
        18 months to two years 5
        more than two years 6

---

51. How do you feel about the length of time you
    spent in training?

    CIRCLE ONE: (68)

        should have had more 1
        should have had less 2
        about right 3

---

52. Which of the following best describes the
    community that you think of as your home town
    during most of your school years--up to high
    school graduation?

    CIRCLE ONE: (69)

        Farm or rural 1

        Suburb in a metropolitan area of

        More than 2 million population . .2

        500,000 to 2 million 3

        100,000 to 500,000 4

        less than 100,000 5

        Central city in a metropolitan area or city of

        more than 2 million population . .6

        500,000 to 2 million 7

        50,000 to 500,000 8

        10,000 to 50,000 9

        less than 10,000 0

        changed too frequently to say
        any one type of community x

NOW THAT YOU HAVE FINSHED THE
SURVEY, PLEASE FOLD IT AND INSERT
IT IN THE ENVELOPE PROVIDED, AND
PUT IT IN THE INTER-OFFICE MAIL.
THANK YOU VERY MUCH.

USE THIS PAGE IF YOU WISH TO MAKE ADDITIONAL COMMENTS.

RETURN TO: STUDY OF THE DIPLOMATIC PROFESSION
               ROOM 943
               SA-11

BIBLIOGRAPHY

······································

PUBLIC DOCUMENTS

Commission on Organization of the Executive Branch of the Government (Hoover Commission). *Foreign Affairs*, Washington: Government Printing Office, 1949.

———. *Task Force Report on Foreign Affairs (Appendix H)*. Washington: Government Printing Office, 1949.

———. *Task Force Report on Overseas Economic Operations*. Washington: Government Printing Office, 1955.

Great Britain. *Report of the Committee on Representational Services Overseas*. Cmnd. 2276. London: Her Majesty's Stationery Office, February 1964.

The White House Conference on International Cooperation. *Report of the Committee on Research on Development of International Institutions*. Washington, Nov. 28-Dec. 1, 1965.

U.S. Bureau of the Budget. "The Organization and Administration of the Department of State," Report Submitted at the Request of the Secretary of State by the Director of the Bureau of the Budget, August 1945.

U.S. Congress. *Legislation on Foreign Relations*. Joint Committee Print of the Senate Committee on Foreign Relations and the House Committee on Foreign Affairs, 89th Cong., 2nd Sess., Jan. 21, 1966.

U.S. Department of State. *This Worked for Me*. . . . 1964.

———. Office of the Deputy Under Secretary for Administration. *A Management Program for the Department of State*, September, 1966.

———. *Department of State Manpower*. Issued annually by the Management Reports Staff.

———. *Improvements in Administration: 1961-64*.

———. *Foreign Affairs Manual Circulars*, 1950-1968.

———. *Toward a Stronger Foreign Service*. Report of the Secretary of State's Public Committee on Personnel, Department of State Publication No. 5,458, June 1954 (The Wriston Report).

U.S. House of Representatives, Subcommittee on International Organization and Movements of the Committee on Foreign Affairs. *Behavioral Sciences and the National Security*. 89th Cong., 1st Sess., December 6, 1965.

———. Committee on Government Operations. *Hearings, Reorganization Plans Nos. 7 and 8*. 83rd Cong., 1st Sess., 1953.

———. Committee on Foreign Affairs. *Reorganization of the Foreign Service*. Report No. 2,508, 79th Cong., 2nd Sess., July 12, 1946.

———. International Operations Subcommittee of the Committee on Government Operations. *Foreign Service and Departmental Per-*

Bibliography

sonnel Practices of the Department of State. 83rd Cong., 1st Sess., 1953.

———. Subcommittee on State Department Organization and Foreign Operations of the Committee on Foreign Affairs. Foreign Service Act Amendments of 1965, 89th Cong., 1st Sess., 1965.

———. Committee on Foreign Affairs. An Analysis of the Personnel Improvement Plan of the Department of State. 82nd Congress, 1st Sess., Committee Print (No. 81,407), 1951.

———. International Operations Subcommittee of the Committee on Government Operations. Administration of National Security. 84th Cong., 1st Sess., 1955.

U.S. Senate, Committee on Government Operations. Organizing for National Security: A Bibliography. 86th Cong., 1st Sess. Washington: Government Printing Office, 1959.

———. Committee on Expenditures in the Executive Departments. Progress on Hoover Commission Recommendations. Senate Report No. 1158, 81st Cong., 1st Sess., Oct. 12, 1949.

———. Special Subcommittee of the Committee on Foreign Relations. Establishment of a Single Foreign Affairs Personnel System and Nominations of USIA Officer as Foreign Service Officers. 89th Cong., 2nd Sess., 1966.

———. Jackson Subcommittee (Subcommittee on National Security Staffing and Operations of the Senate Committee on Government Operations), Reports and Hearings, 1959-1968.

BOOKS

Abrahamson, Mark. The Professional in the Organization. Chicago: Rand McNally, 1967.

Ahmad, Jaleel. The Expert and the Administrator. Pittsburgh: University of Pittsburgh Press, 1959.

Almond, Gabriel. The American People and Foreign Policy. New York: Frederick A. Praeger, 1960.

American Assembly. The Representation of the United States Abroad. New York: Columbia University Press, 1956.

———. The Secretary of State. Englewood Cliffs: Prentice-Hall, 1960.

Argyris, Chris. Some Causes of Organizational Ineffectiveness Within the Department of State. Occasional Paper No. 2 of the Center for International Systems Research. Washington: Department of State, 1967.

Aronson, Sidney H. Status and Kinship in the Higher Civil Service. Cambridge: Harvard University Press, 1964.

Barnes, William, and John Heath Morgan. The Foreign Service of the United States; Origins, Development, and Functions. Washington: Department of State Publication, Government Printing Office, 1961.

Barnett, Vincent M., Jr., ed. The Representation of the United States Abroad. New York: Frederick A. Praeger, 1965.

Beaulac, Willard L. Career Diplomat. New York: Macmillan, 1964.

388

Bibliography

Bendix, Reinhard. *Higher Civil Servants in American Society*. Boulder: University of Colorado Press, 1949.

Bernstein, Marver H. *The Job of the Federal Executive*. Washington: The Brookings Institution, 1958.

Bishop, Donald G. *The Administration of British Foreign Relations*. Syracuse: Syracuse University Press, 1961.

Black, Eugene. *The Diplomacy of Economic Development*. Cambridge: Harvard University Press, 1960.

Boyce, Richard Fyfe. *The Diplomat's Wife*. New York: Harper & Row, 1956.

Briggs, Ellis. *Farewell to Foggy Bottom*. New York: David McKay Company, 1964.

Byrnes, James F. *Speaking Frankly*. New York: Harper and Bros., 1947.

Caplow, Theodore. *The Sociology of Work*, Minneapolis: University of Minnesota Press, 1954.

Cardozo, Michael H. *Diplomats in International Cooperations: Stepchildren of the Foreign Service*. Ithaca: Cornell University Press, 1962.

Carroll, Holbert. *The House of Representatives and Foreign Policy*. Pittsburgh: University of Pittsburgh Press, 1958.

Carr Saunders, A. M., and P. A. Wilson. *The Professions*. Oxford: Clarendon Press, 1953.

Chapman, Brian. *The Profession of Government*. London: George Allen and Unwin, 1959.

Childs, J. Rives. *American Foreign Service*. New York: Henry Holt and Company, 1948.

Claude, Inis. *Swords into Plowshares*. New York: Random House, 1959.

Cleveland, Harlan, and Gerard J. Mangone. *The Art of Overseasmanship*. Syracuse: Syracuse University Press, 1957.

Cleveland, Harlan, Gerard J. Mangone and John Clark Adams. *The Overseas Americans*. New York: McGraw-Hill, 1960.

Crane, Katherine. *Mr. Carr of State: Forty-seven Years in the Department of State*. New York: St. Martin's Press, 1960.

David, Paul T., and Ross Pollock. *Executives for Government, Central Issues of Federal Personnel Administration*. Washington: The Brookings Institution, 1957.

Davies, John Paton, Jr., *Foreign and Other Affairs*. New York: W. W. Norton, 1964.

deCaillières, François. *On the Manner of Negotiating with Princes*. Paris, 1716; trans. by A. F. Whyte. New York: Houghton Mifflin, 1919.

DeConde, Alexander. *The American Secretary of State, An Interpretation*. New York: Frederick A. Praeger, 1962.

Elder, Robert E. *Overseas Representation and Services for Federal Domestic Agencies*. New York: Carnegie Endowment for International Peace, 1965.

————. *The Policy Machine: The Department of State and American Foreign Policy*. Syracuse: Syracuse University Press, 1960.

389

Bibliography

Elliott, William Yandall et al. United States Foreign Policy: Its Organization and Control. New York: Columbia University Press, 1952.

Esman, Milton J. Needed: An Expanded Education and Research Base to Support America's Expanded Commitment Overseas. Pittsburgh: University of Pittsburgh Press, 1961.

Fielder, Frances, and Godfrey Harris. The Quest for Foreign Affairs Officers—Their Recruitment and Selection. New York: Carnegie Endowment for International Peace, 1966.

Friedmann, Georges. The Anatomy of Work. Glencoe: The Free Press, 1961.

Fuller, C. Dale. Training of Specialists in International Relations. Washington: American Council on Education, 1957.

Gibb, Corinne. Hidden Hierarchies: The Professions and Government. New York: Harper & Row, 1966.

Greenberg, Selig. The Troubled Calling: Crisis in the Medical Establishment. New York: Macmillan, 1965.

Gross, Edward. Work and Society. New York: Thomas Y. Crowell, 1958.

Haas, Ernest, and Allen Whiting. Dynamics of International Relations. New York: McGraw-Hill, 1956.

Harr, John E. The Anatomy of the Foreign Service: A Statistical Profile. New York: Carnegie Endowment for International Peace, 1965.

———. The Development of Careers in the Foreign Service. New York: Carnegie Endowment for International Peace, 1965.

Haviland, H. Field, Jr. et al. The Formulation and Administration of United States Foreign Policy. Washington: The Brookings Institution, 1960.

Herz, John. International Politics in the Atomic Age. New York: Columbia University Press, 1962.

Hilsman, Roger. Strategic Intelligence and National Decisions. New York: Free Press of Glencoe, 1956.

Hoffman, Stanley. Contemporary Theory in International Relations. Englewood Cliffs: Prentice-Hall, 1960.

Howe, Fisher. The Computer and Foreign Affairs: Some First Thoughts. Occasional Paper No. 1 of the Center for International Systems Research. Washington: Department of State, 1966.

Hughes, Everett C. Men and Their Work. Glencoe: The Free Press, 1958.

Ilchman, Warren Frederick. Professional Diplomacy in the United States, 1779-1939. Chicago: University of Chicago Press, 1961.

Jackson, Henry M., ed. The National Security Council. New York: Frederick A. Praeger, 1965.

Janowitz, Morris. The Professional Soldier. Glencoe: The Free Press, 1960.

Johnson, E.A.J., ed. The Dimensions of Diplomacy. Baltimore: The Johns Hopkins Press, 1964.

Jones, Arthur G. The Evolution of Personnel Systems for U.S. Foreign Affairs. New York: Carnegie Endowment for International Peace, 1965.

Kaplan, Morton, ed. The Revolution in World Politics. New York: John Wiley and Sons, 1962.

Bibliography

Kaufman, Herbert. *The Forest Ranger: A Study in Administrative Behavior.* Baltimore: The Johns Hopkins Press, 1960.

Kaufmann, William W. *The McNamara Strategy.* New York: Harper & Row, 1964.

Kennan, George F. *American Diplomacy: 1900-1950.* Chicago: University of Chicago Press, 1951.

Kertesz, Stephen D., and M. A. Fitzsimons, eds. *Diplomacy in a Changing World.* Notre Dame: University of Notre Dame Press, 1959.

Kilpatrick, Franklin P., Milton C. Cummings, Jr., and M. Kent Jennings. *The Image of the Federal Service.* Washington: The Brookings Institution, 1964.

Kuhn, Delia and Ferdinand, eds. *Adventures in Public Service.* New York: The Vanguard Press, 1963.

Lerner, Daniel, and Harold Lasswell. *The Policy Sciences.* Palo Alto: Stanford University Press, 1951.

Lewis, Roy, and Angus Meade. *Professional Persons in England.* Cambridge: Harvard University Press, 1953.

Lieberman, Myron. *Education as a Profession.* Englewood Cliffs: Prentice-Hall, 1956.

McCamy, James L. *The Administration of American Foreign Affairs.* New York: Alfred A. Knopf, 1950.

―――. *Conduct of the New Diplomacy.* New York: Harper & Row, 1964.

Macmahon, Arthur W. *Administration in Foreign Affairs.* Tuscaloosa: University of Alabama Press, 1953.

Mann, Dean E. *The Assistant Secretaries.* Washington: The Brookings Institution, 1965.

Masland, John W., and Lawrence J. Radway. *Soldiers and Scholars.* Princeton: Princeton University Press, 1957.

Mosher, Frederick C. *Democracy and the Public Service.* New York: Oxford University Press, 1968.

Murphy, Robert. *Diplomat Among Warriors.* New York: Doubleday, 1964.

Nicolson, Sir Harold. *Diplomacy.* 2nd edn. London: Oxford University Press, 1950.

―――. *The Evolution of Diplomacy.* New York: Collier Books, 1962.

Nosow, S., and W. H. Form, eds. *Man, Work, and Society.* New York: Basic Books, 1962.

Novick, David, ed. *Program Budgeting.* Copyright 1964, 1965 by the RAND Corporation. Washington: Government Printing Office.

Palmer, Norman, and Howard Perkins. *International Relations.* 2nd edn. Boston: Houghton Mifflin, 1957.

Parks, Wallace Judson. *United States Administration of Its International Economic Affairs.* Baltimore: The Johns Hopkins Press, 1951.

Perkins, Dexter. *The American Approach to Foreign Policy.* Cambridge: Harvard University Press, 1952.

Plischke, Elmer. *Conduct of American Diplomacy.* 2nd edn. Princeton: Van Nostrand, 1961.

Price, Don K. *The New Dimension of Diplomacy: The Organization of*

Bibliography

the U.S. Government for Its New Role in World Affairs. New York: Woodrow Wilson Foundation, 1951.

Ransom, Harry Howe. *Central Intelligence and National Security.* Cambridge: Harvard University Press, 1958.

Robinson, James A. *Congress and Foreign Policy-Making: A Study in Legislative Influence and Initiative.* Homewood, Ill.: Dorsey, 1962.

Roetter, Charles. *The Diplomatic Art.* Philadelphia: Macrae Smith Co., 1963.

Rostow, W. W. *View from the Seventh Floor.* New York: Harper & Row, 1964.

Sapin, Burton M. *The Making of United States Foreign Policy.* Washington: The Brookings Institution, 1966.

Satow, Sir Ernest. *A Guide to Diplomatic Practice.* 4th edn., ed. by Sir Neville Bland. London: Longmans, Green, 1957. Earlier edns. 1917, 1922, 1932 (rev. by H. Ritchie).

Sayre, Wallace S., and Clarence E. Thurber. *Training for Specialized Mission Personnel.* Chicago: Public Administration Service, 1952.

Schlesinger, Arthur M., Jr. *A Thousand Days: John F. Kennedy in the White House.* Boston: Houghton Mifflin, 1965.

Simpson, Smith. *The Anatomy of the State Department.* Boston: Houghton Mifflin, 1967.

Snyder, Richard C., H. W. Bruck, and Burton M. Sapin. *Decision-Making as an Approach to the Study of International Politics.* Princeton: Princeton University Press, 1954.

Snyder, Richard C., and Edgar S. Furniss, Jr. *American Foreign Policy: Formulation, Principles, and Programs.* New York: Rinehart and Co., 1954.

Sorenson, Theodore. *Kennedy.* New York: Harper & Row, 1965.

Stein, Harold, ed. *Public Administration and Policy Development: A Case Book.* New York: Harcourt Brace, 1952.

Steiner, Zara S. *Present Problems of the Foreign Service.* Princeton: Princeton University, Center of International Studies, 1961.

————. *The State Department and the Foreign Service: The Wriston Report—Four Years Later.* Princeton: Princeton University, Center of International Studies, 1958.

Stephens, Oren. *Facts to a Candid World; America's Overseas Information Program.* Stanford: Stanford University Press, 1955.

Stillman, Edmund, and William Pfaff. *Power and Impotence: The Futility of America's Foreign Policy.* New York: Random House, 1966.

Strang, Lord. *The Diplomatic Career.* London: The Trinity Press, 1962.

Stuart, Graham H. *American Diplomatic and Consular Practice.* 2nd edn. New York: Appleton-Century-Crofts, 1952.

Taylor, Maxwell D. *Responsibility and Response.* New York: Harper & Row, 1967.

Thayer, Charles W. *Diplomat.* New York: Harper and Bros., 1959.

Thompson, Kenneth W. *American Diplomacy and Emergent Patterns.* New York: New York University Press, 1962.

Thomson, Charles A., and Walter H. C. Laves. *Cultural Relations and U.S. Foreign Policy.* Bloomington: Indiana University Press, 1963.

Bibliography

Vagts, Alfred. *The Military Attaché*. Princeton: Princeton University Press, 1967.

Villard, Henry Serrano. *Affairs at State*. New York: Thomas Y. Crowell, 1965.

Walther, Regis. *Orientations and Behavioral Styles of Foreign Service Officers*. New York: Carnegie Endowment for International Peace, 1965.

Warner, W. Lloyd, Paul P. Van Riper, Norman H. Martin, and Orvis F. Collins. *The American Federal Executive*. New Haven: Yale University Press, 1963.

Weintal, Edward, and Charles Bartlett. *Facing the Brink: An Intimate Study of Crisis Diplomacy*. New York: Charles Scribner's Sons, 1967.

Winfield, Louise. *Living Overseas*. Washington: Public Affairs Press, 1962.

Wright, Quincy. *The Study of International Relations*. New York: Appleton-Century-Crofts, 1955.

Wriston, Henry M. *Diplomacy in a Democracy*. New York: Harper and Bros., 1956.

PERIODICALS AND ARTICLES

Alsop, Stewart. "Let the Poor Old Foreign Service Alone," *Saturday Evening Post*, Mar. 11, 1967.

Attwood, William. "The Labyrinth in Foggy Bottom," *Atlantic Monthly*, Feb. 1967.

Atwater, Elton. "The American Foreign Service Since 1939," *American Journal of International Law*, Vol. 41 (Jan. 1947), pp. 73-102.

Barnett, Vincent M. "Changing Problems of United States Representation Abroad," *Public Administration Review*, Vol. XVII (Winter 1957 #1, 20-30.

Bowles, Chester. "Toward a New Diplomacy," *Foreign Affairs*, Jan. 1962, pp. 244-51.

Briggs, Ellis O. "The Case Against a 'West Point' for Diplomats," *New York Times Magazine*, May 3, 1964, pp. 20ff.

Chapin, Selden. "Training for the Foreign Service," in Joseph E. McLean, *The Public Service and University Education*. Princeton: Princeton University Press, 1949, pp. 104-120.

Daedalus. Special issue devoted to "The Professions," Vol. 92, No. 4, Fall 1963.

Department of State Bulletin, 1950-1968.

Department of State News Letter, 1961-1968.

Diebold, John. "Computers, Program Management, and Foreign Affairs," *Foreign Affairs*, Oct. 1966.

Editorial staff. "Toward a Stronger Foreign Service," *Christian Science Monitor*, Vol. 56 (Jan. 14, 1964), 16.

Fisher, Glen H. "The Foreign Service Officer," *The Annals of the American Academy of Political and Social Science*, Vol. 368 (Nov. 1966).

Foreign Service Journal, 1926-1968.

393

Bibliography

Fritchey, Clayton. "The Politicians Versus the Foreign Service," *Harper's*, Jan. 1967.

Hodge, Robert W., Paul M. Siegel, and Peter H. Rossi. "Occupational Prestige in the United States, 1925-63," *The American Journal of Sociology*, Vol. LXX, No. 3 (Nov. 1964), 286-302.

Kennan, George F. "The Future of Our Professional Diplomacy," *Foreign Affairs*, Vol. 33 (July 1955), 566-86.

McCamy, James L. "Rebuilding the Foreign Service," *Harpers*, Vol. 219, (Nov. 1959), 80-89.

————, and Alessandro Corradini. "The People of the State Department and Foreign Service," *American Political Science Review*, Vol. 48 (Dec. 1954), 1,067-82.

McKittrick, Nathaniel. "Diplomatic Logjam: Esprit without a Corps at the Department of State," *New Republic*, Mar. 27, 1965.

Marrow, Alfred J. "Managerial Revolution in the State Department," *Personnel*, Vol. 43, No. 6 (Nov.-Dec. 1966).

Mosher, Frederick C. "Personnel Management in American Foreign Affairs," *Public Personnel Review*, Vol. 12 (Oct. 1951), 175-86.

————. "Careers and Career Services in the Public Service," *Public Personnel Review*, Jan. 1963, pp. 46-51.

Myers, Dennis P., and Charles F. Ransom. "Reorganization of the State Department," *American Journal of International Law*, Vol. 31 (Oct. 1937), 713-20.

New York Times, 1950-1968.

Nisbet, Robert A. "Project Camelot: An Autopsy," *The Public Interest*, No. 5 (Fall 1966), 45-69.

Reissman, L. "A Study in Role Conceptions in Bureaucracy," *Social Forces*, No. 27 (1949), 305-10.

Rogoff, Natalie. "The Decision to Study Medicine," *The Student Physician*. Cambridge: Harvard University Press, 1957.

Simpson, Smith. "Who Runs the State Department?" *The Nation*, Mar. 6, 1967.

Smith, Mapheus. "An Empirical Scale of Prestige Status of Occupations," *American Sociological Review*, Vol. 8, No. 2 (April 1943), 185-92.

Symington, Stuart. "Let's Have a West Point for Diplomats," *This Week* (August 2, 1959), pp. 8-9.

Washington Post, 1962-1968.

Williams, Murat W. "Life in the Diplomatic Service, 1939-62," *American Oxonian*, July 1962.

Wriston, Henry M. "Thoughts for Tomorrow," *Foreign Affairs*, Vol. 40, No. 3 (April 1962).

————. "Young Men and the Foreign Service," *Foreign Affairs*, Vol. 33 (Oct. 1954), 28-42.

REPORTS

"An Improved Personnel System for Foreign Affairs," A Report to the Secretary of State by the Secretary's Advisory Committee on Personnel (the Rowe Report), August 1950.

Bibliography

The Brookings Institution. *Administration of Foreign Affairs and Overseas Operations.* Report prepared for the Bureau of the Budget. Washington: Government Printing Office, June 1951.

Committee on Foreign Affairs Personnel. *Personnel for the New Diplomacy.* New York: Carnegie Endowment for International Peace, 1962.

Occidental College American Assembly. *The Secretary of State.* July 26-29, 1962.

Stanford Research Institute. *Documents Compiled for the Second Meeting of the Advisory Group to the Secretary of State on Foreign Affairs Planning, Programming, and Budgeting.* September 19, 1966.

Woodrow Wilson Foundation. *United States Foreign Policy: Its Organization and Control.* New York: Columbia University Press, 1952.

UNPUBLISHED MATERIAL

Brandt, Edward R. "Regional Specialization in the Foreign Service." Unpublished Master's Thesis, School of Government, Business, and International Affairs, The George Washington University, 1965.

Harr, John E. "Key Administrative Problems of the United States Information Agency." Unpublished Master's Thesis, Department of Political Science, The University of Chicago, 1961.

McKibbin, C. R. Unpublished tabular material on birthplaces and last places of formal education of Foreign Service Officers. Drake University.

Mosher, Frederick C. *The Professions, Professional Education, and the Public Service.* In preparation, to be published by Chandler Press, San Francisco.

————, and John E. Harr. *Program Budgeting Visits Foreign Affairs.* In preparation, to be published by the Inter-University Case Program, Syracuse University.

National Opinion Research Center. "College Graduates and Foreign Affairs." Survey No. 452, NORC, The University of Chicago, May 1962 (mimeographed).

Warwick, Donald. "An Interdisciplinary Approach to the Study of Comparative Foreign Policy." Paper presented to the Conference on Comparative Foreign Policy, University of Michigan, March 10-11, 1967 (mimeographed).

OTHER SOURCES

U.S. Department of State. Personal Interview with William J. Crockett, Deputy Under Secretary for Administration, Jan. 30, 1967.

————. U.S. Information Agency, Agency for International Development. Personal interviews with selected officers, 1962-67.

U.S. Foreign Service posts abroad. Interviews with selected officers of the Department of State, USIA, AID, Peace Corps, Department of Defense, Department of Agriculture, 1962-66:

1962: *Embassies*—Lagos, Khartoum, Ankara, Beirut, Paris; *Consulates General*—Istanbul; *Consulate*—Ibadan; *Special Missions*—Paris USRO, U.S. Mission to the United Nations, New York.

Bibliography

1963: *Embassies*—Santo Domingo, Caracas, Bogota; *Consulates*—Cali, Medellin.
1964: *Embassies*—Mexico City, Bonn, Vienna, Rome, Cairo, New Delhi, Tel Aviv, Athens; *Consulates General*—Frankfurt, Munich, Genoa, Bombay, Calcutta, Tijuana; *Consulates*—Nogales, Mazatlan, Mexicali, Port Said, Florence; *Special Mission* —Berlin.
1965: *Embassies*—Rome, Bonn.
1966: *Embassies*—London, Paris; *Consulate General*—Frankfurt.

INDEX

Acheson, Dean, 61, 107, 335
ACORD, *see* organizational development
administrative work, 25, 141ff, 159, 160; cutback of jobs, 239-40; dislike of "administrators," 37-38, 261; and lateral entry, 261-62; overseas, 300
Advisory Committee on Government Reorganization, 96
AID, 36, 77, 102-103, 108, 304-305; career service, 78, 345-46; mission chief, 294; merger with State, 332, 339-43; operating style, 298-99; in unified personnel system, 343ff. *See also* development assistance function; foreign aid
Allen, George, 77, 317-19
Alliance for Progress, 26, 305, 340-41
Almond, Gabriel, 19ff, 126
Alsop, Stewart, 266, 326, 331
amalgamation issue, 58, 60; Herter Report, 79; Rowe Report, 62-63; Wriston Report, 70ff
ambassadors, 301, 312; authorities, 293-94, 296-97; and Country Directors, 306; leadership styles, 292-97, 320; as managers, 109, 237; noncareer, 39; status, 206-207; and "success," 210; techniques, 221, 222
American Foreign Service Association, 16, 40, 48, 267, 280, 282, 329; Career Principles Committee, 284-87, 328; and "group of 18," 283-84; on Hays Bill, 90-91; on Rowe Report, 63-64
Anderson, Jack, 331
appraisal system, *see* efficiency reports
area specialization, 59, 163-66
Argyris, Chris, 229-32, 280, 349
Arms Control and Disarmament Agency, 25, 108

assignment practices, 70, 223, 225-27
Assistant Secretaries, 101-102, 109, 114, 312; and Country Directors, 306-308
Attwood, William, 266, 331

Ball, George, 107, 119, 136
"BALPA" exercise, 289
Barrett, Richard W., 116-17, 130
Battle, Lucius D., 280-82, 287
Berger, Samuel, 295
Black, Eugene, 327-29
Board of Examiners, 57, 61
Board of the Foreign Service, 57, 61, 84-85
Bohlen, Charles, 163, 317-19
Bowles, Chester, 41, 107
Brazil Interdepartmental Group, 311
Briggs, Ellis, 36-39, 117, 319
British Foreign Service, 49, 92, 200-201, 347
Brookings Institution, 65-68, 70, 75, 97, 108, 110
Brownson, Congressman Charles, 96
Bundy, McGeorge, 26, 98, 100-101, 355
Bureau of the Budget, 38, 88; and EROP, 118-19; and MUST, 129; 1945 study, 66, 67, 70, 110; opposition to CCPS, 132-33; opposition to Foreign Service Act of 1946, 50-53, 57-58; opposition to "Personnel Improvement Program," 65; and PPBS, 118
bureaucracy, 110, 133, 301-302, 330-31, 340-41
Bureau of Far Eastern Affairs, 302-303
Bureau of Inter-American Affairs, 304-305, 341
Butterworth, W. W., 317-18
Byrnes, James F., 51, 53, 95-96

Index

Index

Index

Index

Index

403

204-209; of functional fields, 141-42; occupational, 200
Stein, Harold, 20n, 47, 50, 52-53, 57-58
stereotypes, 139, 189, 299-300, 308, 345
subcultures, 299-300, 308
substantive-administrative dichotomy, 104, 141, 195, 226, 337
summit diplomacy, 236
"sustaining manager," 332, 334-36, 349. *See also* Executive Under Secretary
Symington, Sen. Stuart, 81-82

"T-group" method, 130-32
Taylor, Gen. Maxwell, 26; and NSAM, 341, 122-23, 329
Thayer, Charles, 38
Thompson, Llewellyn, 316-19
tour of duty policy, 161-62, 165
"track" system, 277-79, 337, 346
training, 38-39, 56, 70, 223, 224, 240
Truman, President Harry S, 21, 53

Under Secretary of State, 107, 334-35
unified Foreign Service system, 58-59, 66, 68, 332-33, 343-48
United Nations, 17, 20, 320, 328-29
U.S. Embassies, 29, 109, 292, 298
U.S. Forest Service, 94, 224

USIA, 24, 36, 66, 68, 77, 84, 292, 324, 354; career service, 74-75, 78, 92n, 287, 345-46; integration list, 86, 88, 239, 260, 271, 282; junior officers, 190-91; merger with State, 332, 339-43; overseas operations, 297-98; public affairs officer, 294-95; in unified personnel system, 343ff. *See also* information program
USIS, *see* USIA

Vietnam war, 33, 91-92, 134, 288
Villard, Henry S., 36-38, 48-49

Walker, Lannon, 284
Walther, Regis, 189ff, 268
Walton, Richard, 300-301
White House, 97, 98, 100-101, 331, 335, 349, 350; as change agent, 242; challenge to State, 328; and FSO promotions, 227
White House Personnel Task Force of 1954, 67-68, 70
Whitney, John Hay, 77
Williams, Murat W., 18
Wilson, Woodrow, 17
Wriston Committee, 25, 68ff, 128, 142-44, 147, 149, 344-45
Wriston, Henry M., 25, 31, 69
"Wristonization," 25, 73, 143, 285

Yost, Charles, 319-20
Young, Philip, 67-68